D0867754

Ethics of the Business System

MARSHALL MISSNER

University of Wisconsin, Oshkosh

Copyright © 1980 by Alfred Publishing Co., Inc.
15335 Morrison Street, Sherman Oaks, CA 91403

Printed and bound in the United States of America

Library of Congress Cataloging in Publication Data

Ethics of the business system.

Includes index.
1. Business ethics—Addresses, essays, lectures.
I. Missner, Marshall, 1942-
HF5387.B87   174'4   79-22806
ISBN 0-88284-100-9

Cover Design: William Conte

CONTENTS

PREFACE

When I first became interested in ethical discussions of the business system, I assumed there existed a well-developed literature in this area. Much to my chagrin, I discovered my assumption was incorrect. Although there were numerous interesting philosophical discussions of medical ethics, environmental problems, sexual morality, violence, and punishment, serious philosophical works concerning ethical issues in business and economics were rare.

It is true that in the past few years, the topic of justice has been the focus of an intense debate of certain interest to anyone concerned with the ethical foundations of our business system. But justice is not the only relevant issue that needs to be examined. Questions about competition, advertising, and the desire for profit are also of fundamental importance and should be addressed by those who wish to reach a conclusion about the ethics of our business system as a whole.

This collection of articles is designed to examine these issues from differing viewpoints. Each section contains works that are favorable to the business system as well as works that are critical. There are also instances in which the writer of a particular article specifically discusses another article included in this collection: Robert Schmitt's article in the section on profits is examined by the paper of Thomas Torrance; F.A. von Hayek's views on justice are criticized in the selections by John Rawls and Robert Nozick; and John Kenneth Galbraith's theory about generating wants is discussed in the subsequent article by Hayek. These contrasting and conflicting views provide a lively, provocative debate. It should also be noted that the articles in each section are arranged roughly in order of increasing philosophical sophistication and rigor.

I have used these works in a class that I teach about the ethics of the business system and have found them to be the source of many a stimulating discussion. I believe that this collection would also be valuable as part of a course in ethics, introduction to philosophy, business ethics, or any course that examines basic aspects of our society.

I wish to thank the students in my "Business and Ethics" classes, who have given me as much as I hope I have given them. I would also like to thank Max Oelschlaeger at North Texas State University for his careful reading of the manuscript and thoughtful suggestions for improvement. Alice Rhyner of the University of Wisconsin-Oshkosh library saved me a great deal of time with her skill at finding hard-to-find sources. Sally Wilke's typing was of great help, and, finally, Nathalie Moore was invaluable in preparing the manuscript.

1.

Introduction

In the 1970s there have been almost daily reports of unethical business practices: illicit contributions to political campaigns, misrepresentation, bribery, fraudulent advertising, price fixing, collusion, and on and on. The quantity of reported examples of illegal behavior by businessmen has sparked an interest in the topic of business and ethics. Now the number of news articles about unethical practices is almost being equaled by the number of discussions of business ethics. These discussions cover a wide range of topics—from practical concerns about how to formulate a code of responsible business behavior to general questions about whether the system itself is ethical.

Because there is such a diversity of business issues being discussed, it would be difficult to collect a coherent group of articles dealing with all the topics generally included under the title "Business and Ethics." For that reason the following articles will deal specifically only with questions that are relevant to morally evaluating the system as a whole. There are good reasons for believing that an examination of these general questions could have great significance in finding answers to other questions of business and ethics. However, before presenting these reasons, it would be useful to say something about the subject matter of ethics, the field in which moral evaluations are studied, and also to mention some of the basic moral questions that have been raised about the American business system.

One way to get an understanding of the problems studied in ethics is to contrast it with a closely related subject, *prudence.* A person concerned with prudence would be interested in what sorts of actions are beneficial or harmful to the people who perform them. For example, consider the well-known aphorism, "Honesty is the best policy." This is an example of prudence, for what this is really saying is that if one wants to advance one's own interests, it is a good idea to be honest. The kind of reasoning behind this advice is familiar. A person who loses his reputation for honesty cannot be trusted and will not be able to enlist anyone else's help in accomplishing any task. To get what one desires in life one often needs the help of others, and this is why one should try to build a reputation of honesty. The best way to have this reputation is to tell the truth.

While this advice may sound familiar, it should be noted that the reasoning behind it deals only with what policy would advance a person's own interests. A very different approach would be taken by someone interested in ethics. In that field the question is not, What will I get if I am honest? but rather, Are honest actions right or wrong, good or bad? It is not unusual for a person to know that lying in a situation would be in his own interest and still wonder if it would be the right thing to do. The advice of prudence is to lie if it will be beneficial to one's own life. But the advice of ethics is to consider not just what is beneficial to oneself, but what is right and what is wrong.

To further illustrate the difference between ethics and prudence, consider a prudential accountant. He might investigate how to fill out an employer's income-tax form so that the employer pays the smallest possible amount, for then the accountant undoubtedly will benefit himself. He might even explore legal and illegal ways to fill out the tax form while weighing the risks of getting caught. Each one of this accountant's actions would be directed toward the goal of benefiting himself. The ethical accountant in the next office, however, would take a different approach. He would fill out his employer's tax form in a way that he thinks is right—not just right for him or right for his employer, but simply right. He might also try to find ways to pay the smallest possible tax, but he would not explore illegal methods for doing so, even if the risk of getting caught were negligible. The prudential accountant asks himself, How can I fill out the tax form in a way that would benefit me? The ethical accountant asks a different question: How can I fill out the tax form in a way that would be right and proper?

Even though these two accountants would take different approaches, they ultimately might perform the same actions. The prudential accountant might conclude that it would be in his own best interest to be completely honest and to follow the letter and the spirit of the tax laws. The risks of getting caught might be too high, or this accountant might be afraid of developing a habit of cutting corners, which he thinks might get him into trouble in the long run. But while he might thus decide to be law-abiding and not to cheat in any way, his reasons for doing so would be clearly different from the reasons the ethical accountant would have for his actions. Thus, even though these two approaches might have the same conclusion, the reasons behind them would be dissimilar.

Consider another case. A prudential salesman, in developing his presentation, will ask himself: How can I best present this product? What sorts of things can I say that will make it attractive? Can I tell any lies about it and get away with it? Will it be to my advantage to use a hard-sell approach and pressure some milquetoast types into buying it? The ethical salesman, however, would ask different questions. He might ask: How can I present this product fairly? What is the truth about it? In what ways is this product really better than what the competitors are offering? What can I do to respect the feelings of my customers? Again, even though the questions are different, both salesmen may come to similar answers and make similar presentations. Different approaches can lead to the same action, but they might also lead to divergent actions.

The ethical accountant and the ethical salesman ask themselves, How can I do what is right? This raises a problem that has puzzled thinkers for centuries: What does one do to determine what is right? There is, unfortunately, no universally agreed-upon answer to this question. Even so, there is no doubt that someone concerned with ethics would not simply try to figure out what actions would be in his own best interests.

The ethical approach is clearly different from the prudential one in determining what actions one should perform, and this distinction has an obvious application to behavior in business. Another kind of concern about business, however, falls only within the ethical realm and is not a question of prudence at all. In ethics, one not only investigates whether actions are right or wrong; one also discusses the moral value of things, such as governments or economic systems. Prudence, being a study of individual actions in a given context, does not deal with moral values. The prudential man asks how he can act to benefit himself in a particular situation. He might also ask how he could change the situation to his own advantage, but questions about what situations are good or bad in general are questions of ethics, not prudence. Thus, the prudential accountant would still be dealing with prudential questions when he weighs which version of a tax bill under consideration by the legislature would be the most favorable to his employer. However, once the accountant begins to think about the general question of whether a tax law is good, fair, or right, and not just good for him or for his employer, he has left the realm of prudence and is now concerned with ethics.

Similarly, the prudential salesman might be concerned with creating a situation in which he can best prosper. But once he begins to consider what situation would be best not only for him but for the customers and other salesmen as well, he has become someone who is interested in ethics. Ethics is, therefore, not only distinguished from prudence by the different approach it adopts to the question What should I do? but by its concern with questions in which the questioner's self-interest may not even be considered.*

Prudence is not the only field that should be distinguished from ethics. Another important area is a field called *practical concerns.* One interested in this field would try to find the best means for achieving some desired goal. The goal can be one that is desired for ethical or for prudential reasons. For example, even if the prudential accountant decides that a certain tax law would be the most beneficial for him and his employer, he still has the practical concern of how to get this law passed. This practical concern would require figuring out which legislators should be lobbied and which should be pressured. It would also deal with building up public support for the favored tax bill. Clearly, how to achieve a goal desired for prudential reasons is a different question from deciding what really would be in one's self-interest.

In the next office, the ethical salesman might come to the conclusion that it would be a good idea if customers had a chance to sit quietly somewhere and decide if they really want to buy a certain product. This would be desirable, the ethical salesman believes, because it would enable people to make rational judgments and it would encourage salesmen to make more persuasive and reasoned presentations. The practical concern then is to develop some means for achieving this end. This might involve passing certain legislation and setting up some administrative agencies. It might also involve convincing other businesses and salesmen. The practical concerns in this case are extremely important and probably would provide a significant challenge to anyone interested in dealing with them. How-

---

* It should be noted that there is a theory called *egoism,* which denies, in effect, that there is any difference between ethics and prudence. According to this theory the right thing to do is always to advance one's own interests. The reason this view has not been mentioned is that the theory of ethical egoism does not provide any way to discuss questions about the ethics of the business system as a whole.

ever, they are different from ethical investigations, which usually are concerned with desirable goals rather than with efficient means.

These distinctions between ethics, prudence, and practical concerns are rough-and-ready; however, it is useful to keep them in mind. Each of these three kinds of concerns has been included under the rubric of "Business and Ethics," but in this collection, matters of prudence and of practical concern will generally be avoided, and the focus will be on matters of ethics.

For one interested in ethical discussions related to business, there is available a huge literature about relevant right or wrong actions. Many people have discussed such topics as telling the truth and keeping promises—two actions that are clearly pertinent to business behavior. However, there is nothing solely relevant to business in these discussions, since telling the truth and keeping promises are actions that occur in many other areas of life as well.

The literature that is specifically about business ethics is much smaller. Many writers interested in ethical matters have said very little about business, and not many writers interested in business have been interested in ethics. Still, while the literature in this field does not compare in size to ethical discussions of other topics, there do exist some significant and lively discussions concerning ethics and business. These discussions have focused on four, not necessarily distinct, aspects of the business system:

1. Profit. The view that all businessmen are greedy to the point of rapaciousness is not as universally held as it used to be. Some economists now even think that businessmen do not really desire to continually get bigger and bigger profits, but rather, that there is a certain level of profit that would be found satisfactory by most of them. In any case, it is generally agreed that the desire to gain profit is an essential element of our business system. This desire is not only the goal of all businessmen; consumers also are interested in getting the best deal they can, an interest usually considered to be just another aspect of the desire for profit. What has provoked discussion is the moral evaluation of this desire for profit. Is this desire bad because it is just a form of greed? Does this desire lead to beneficial results for everyone in the economic system? Is this desire simply a fact of human nature and so present in everyone no matter what kind of system they live under?

2. Competition. The pursuit of profit in our system takes place in a competitive context. Intense competition exists in all aspects of the business system. Even in cases such as the automobile industry, in which a few companies dominate the market, there are still strong

competitive pressures. Even in the ranks of large and monopolistic corporations, executives attempt to advance in competition with others. Furthermore, even on the consumer side, individuals compete to buy sale items that are in short supply. There are very few places, if any, in our economic system where one can avoid competition. This fact has been the source of several ethical questions: Does competition lead people to develop the characteristics of aggressiveness and hostility? Does the continual competition influence people to cheat and to break the law? Does competition provide any beneficial results that could not be derived without it? Is competition too harmful to those who lose?

3. Justice. Our economic system can be viewed as a mechanism for distributing goods and services. The portion of the total any individual receives is the result of many factors. If the person has a basic need that he cannot provide for, he may get welfare. If the person has some ability that is greatly desired by others, he will probably be rewarded. If the person has wealthy parents, he can expect to get a nice slice of the economic pie. The fact that the system does not distribute goods and services according to just one criterion makes it harder to develop moral evaluations. Nevertheless, a number of questions have been examined: Do individuals have an equal opportunity to gain the big rewards? Do those who receive large amounts of goods and services do anything to deserve them? Can a system that ignores equal opportunity and does not reward those who are deserving be defended on other grounds?

4. Generating Wants—Advertising. A great deal of time and effort is spent on designing advertisements. Furthermore, everyone in our system is constantly exposed to advertising. Although some believe that constant advertising has little effect on people, most think that advertising is generally effective and that it plays an extremely important role in the functioning of the economic system. Advertising is the means used to inform consumers of the products available, and so it is necessary for generating sales and profits. But exactly what does advertising do? Does it simply inform people of what is available, or does it create needs that otherwise would not have existed? If it does create needs, is there any reason why this is a bad thing to do? Does it just present information, or is it essentially deceitful?

The questions raised in these four topics form the core of most ethical discussions of the American business system. These questions are not only of concern to people who are in what is called the "business world"; they also are of interest to, and discussed by, everyone else. No one can exist in our society without contact with advertisements. Everyone in one way or another is subject to the pervasive economic competition. It is difficult to exist in America and not to desire more than one has or not to spend time trying to get more, either by finding better investments or bargains. Very few people can read about high-salaried athletes without wondering if they should get so much. Interest in these ethical questions is not confined to people in business occupations, because, in a sense, everyone in America is part of the business system.

Although there is interest in these questions of ethics and also a good deal of discussion of them, most people only have vague feelings about these subjects or else subscribe to poorly supported arguments. Critiques and defenses of the American business system abound in these days of doubt and uncertainty, but many of them are either incantations about the "free-enterprise system," or ritual proclamations of "exploitation." The great interest in these questions is not matched by a great number of discussions about them distinguished by insight and intellectual rigor. For that reason it would probably be of benefit to people to become acquainted with views that have been developed by thinkers capable of penetrating and subtle arguments in support of their conclusions.

These discussions are also important for another reason: they can provide a basis for deciding other issues included in the field of business and ethics. For example, recently the issue of business's social responsibility has generated much interest. This issue concerns the question: Should businessmen decrease their profits by spending money on socially desirable projects? Should a business support a cultural event even if there is no reason to expect that this support will lead indirectly to increased profits? Should a company make special efforts to cut down on its pollution of a river even if these efforts are not required by law or by the need to keep up with the competition? Should a business take the initiative in hiring the hard-core unemployed even if this will be costly to the firm in the long run?

These are the questions that come up in discussions about the social responsibility of business. Many of the answers that have been proposed, however, do not deal with ethical issues. Some of the answers concern practical matters such as whether business is an effective means for achieving these socially desirable goals. Other discussions could be called prudential, for they argue that since the public expects businesses to perform socially responsible actions, businesses will not survive unless they do so. Nevertheless, many discussions on the issue of social responsibility are of an ethical nature. As a matter of justice, should a business that makes a great profit contribute some of that profit back to the public? Is the social benefit of a system based on individual profit so great that one would not want to disturb the pursuit of profit for any reason? These are the kinds of ethical questions that arise in discussions of business's social responsibility; and in order to formulate clear and coherent responses to them, it is necessary to investigate the problems concerning the ethical aspects of profits and the justice of the American business system.

One final reason why these ethical issues are important is that they can provide the foundation for developing moral principles relevant to particular business decisions. Many moral principles that apply to business are clearly covered by the laws of the land. For example, principles such as "do not offer bribes" and "do not cheat on income-tax returns" are subscribed to by most people, and even those unconcerned with moral issues know that violating these principles can lead to legal punishment. However, in many instances businessmen make decisions to which no laws are applicable. Suppose a businessman is designing an advertising campaign. He might wonder whether he should just inform the public of an available product, or whether it would be proper to attempt to get the public to desire this *type* of product. A supervisor might be concerned with whether it would be more beneficial to his subordinates, and not just more efficient, if he tried to create competition among them instead of trying to foster cooperation. An executive might wonder if it would benefit a community more to contribute to the restoration of the local opera house rather than to use the money to expand a factory. These problems do not involve any legal issues, and, for each of them, one's views about the ethical nature of profits or competition or advertising would be important in reaching a decision.

Ethical questions about the business system are thus relevant to forming particular business decisions and to deciding matters of business policy (such as whether business has a social responsibility). They are even of concern to those who do not have business occupations. However, like many other important and interesting questions, there is no clear agreement about what the answers are. One finds well-thought-out arguments that defend our business system as well as perceptive arguments that criticize it. The readings in this collection have been chosen to reflect this diversity of opinion.

Furthermore, discussion of these topics is not confined to any one discipline. One reason for this is that intelligent discussion in this area requires knowledge of the work done in the branch of philosophy called ethics, as well as an acquaintance with the fields of business and economics. For some, perhaps revealing, reason, few people have expertise in all these fields. Thus, the writers in this book represent a number of different disciplines: philosophy, economics, business, and sociology. The variety of opinions and the diversity of perspectives result in a provocative clash of ideas, as well as in insights that may lead to answers to the many questions concerning the ethics of the American business system.

2.

Profit

The pursuit of profit makes many people uneasy. Something seems to be wrong with it. Even people who are deeply involved in business are affected by this negative attitude; bank presidents and corporation executives write numerous articles in business periodicals to show that *profit* is not a dirty six-letter word. These articles commonly assert that if people would only understand the role of profits in our economic system and why they are necessary for the welfare of us all the belief that a nice person is not profit minded would disappear.

It is easy to understand why those involved with the pursuit of profit fervently hope understanding will lead to acceptance. Many business people think defending the idea of profit is imperative; if the public ever really becomes convinced that profits are not a good thing, they believe, steps will be taken that will not permit the pursuit to continue. If this happens, the consequences to business people, and to everyone else, will be enormous.

But should the pursuit of profit be allowed to go on? This question does not have a simple answer, for it involves several issues that first must be examined: What does "profit" mean? Who is involved in the pursuit of it? How does it function in the economic system? These questions must be given at least a cursory examination before the ethical problems connected with profits can be usefully discussed.

The concept of profit is often related to the desire people have for money and material goods. In our society, at least, it is apparent that almost everyone likes money and the material things it can buy. There might be a few individuals who believe that any contact with dollar bills, silver coins, or checkbooks is debilitating and dehumanizing; but these few certainly are very hard to find. Again, there are those who think that most of the material goods that currently abound in America—the cars, the refrigerators, the snowmobiles—are really a curse and a misfortune. It is very hard, however, to find someone who does not own or use something of this sort. Our life is so interwoven with these objects that it is not easy to imagine what it would be like without them.

However, the concept of profit does not simply concern a desire for money or for manufactured goods. This is part of the concept but not all of it. There could be a society that uses money and that makes things but that also is different from ours in its interest in profits. The desire for profit is not just the desire to have money and material goods; rather, it is the desire to have more and more of them. If a small businessman is making $15,000 a year, what he desires is to make $20,000; and if he has $20,000, he wants still more. The millionaire who is worth several million dollars desires to be worth several million more. Corporations that determine their profits in terms of billions of dollars attempt to increase their profits to even higher levels.

That businesses and business people are concerned with the pursuit of profit is something that is readily acknowledged, but it is important to realize that it is not just bank presidents, corporation executives, and owners of small restaurants who are interested in having more. In our system everyone is, and this includes college students, retired workers, homemakers, and even those who are unemployed. Of course, the manner in which "nonbusiness" people carry out their desire for more takes a different form from the way people directly involved in business pursue profits. Businessmen gain their profit, for the most part, by selling something. The others pursue their desire for more by the way they buy things and, more specifically, by the way they try to find what they want at the cheapest price.

For example, a person interested in buying a television set usually has a fair idea of what he wants. He might be willing to pay, say, $200 for the kind of set he desires, but what he really would like, if he could get it, is to find a sale so that he would pay even less. The homemaker also tries to find ways to spend less than he would be willing to pay for grocery items. By spending less for some items, the consumer has more to spend for other things, and so the search for sales is really a desire to get more for one's money.

Looking for bargains is not something that is confined just to coupon clippers and those willing to drive all over town in order to pay a penny less for a gallon of gas. Almost everyone in our system is looking for a better deal. Of course, the effort that people put into this search varies, and there are a few who are not interested in this kind of thing at all. But the strong desire to get more can be observed at any corner on which there are two gasoline stations that offer similar service and gasoline that is believed to be of similar quality. The one with a cheaper price will get the majority of customers. In fact, this aspect of consumer profit, if it can be called that, is so ingrained in all of us that it would seem irrational for someone to go to the more expensive station while admitting that there is no difference between them.

Another group interested in profit consists of people who work for salaries. People in this group express their desire for profit in various ways. If they happen to be in a field in which there is a great desire to obtain their services, they can shop around to find the employer who is willing to pay the highest salary. Again, a person in this situation is considered irrational if, in choosing between two equal jobs, he takes the one that pays the lower salary. Would it not seem strange if a plumber said that he could work for Company A for $15,000 per year or Company B for $20,000 and that he decided to work for A even though there was no real difference between them? Imagine the following conversation:

"Wasn't there something about A that appealed to you?"

"No."

"But didn't you have negative feelings about B for some reason?"

"No."

"And you realized that A would pay you less than B?"

"Yes, I realized that."

"And you still took the job with Company A?"

"Yes, that's right."

One can easily understand the questioner's growing befuddlement, for it does seem completely irrational for this plumber to have taken the job with Company A under these circumstances.

Not everyone who works for a salary is in the fortunate situation of the plumber who has more than one employer bidding for his services. Quite a few people work at jobs for which there are many others who could do the work just as well. But even in these cases the workers will try to get higher salaries, usually through group action. The function of unions is to achieve exactly this purpose, for they are organizations formed in order to get higher wages for their members. It is difficult to imagine a union reaching the decision not to demand higher wages from management. This might happen if a company were in a particularly distressed state and the union was convinced that the higher wages would definitely bankrupt the firm. However, suppose a company has a sound financial condition. It is not easy to think of a union leader then saying, "We have decided that we are getting enough. We will not ask for a raise even though we know the company could easily afford to give it to us."

In general it is a feature of our business and economic system that everyone in it desires in one way or another to gain more. How much effort will be expended in order to get more varies from individual to individual, but there is no doubt that this desire is very common, though not necessarily universal.

It should be mentioned that defining profit as the desire to gain more is not the same definition of profit that is given in many works about business and economics. In many cases the concept of profit is used to apply only to those who invest their money, accepting certain risks, with the hope of gaining interest on their investment. According to this definition of profit, only those who own their own businesses or invest in firms are pursuing profit. This is a much narrower concept of profit than has been developed above; for according to this more limited definition, consumers, laborers, and those who work for salaries are not really involved with the desire for profit.

There are two reasons why it will be useful to think of profit in the broader sense of desiring to have more. First, this is the sense in which it is used in the articles that follow. All of the writers in this section are concerned with the ethical aspects of a system in which the pursuit of profit is a fundamental principle, and, for the most part, it is the broader sense of profit that they have in mind when they present their arguments. The conclusions that these writers reach are supposed to apply to everyone who takes part in the economic system and not just to those who earn their income by investing rather than by salaries.

Another reason why it is advantageous to view profit in the broader sense is that by doing so, one dispels the notion that those who earn their income from investments have different attitudes, desires, and expectations from those who work for salaries. The difference between these two ways of earning money is often thought to be based on different attitudes toward risk. A person who works for a salary usually signs a contract that specifies exactly what must be done in order to receive a certain amount of money. If the worker fulfills his part, he has every reason to expect to get paid. The investor does not have the security of a contract. He takes a risk, for he has no assurance that he will get any interest on his investment, and he might even lose the original sum. But he is willing to take this risk because the return he receives on his investment might be a very large amount.

Although this difference does exist to some extent, in several important ways the salaried worker is similar to the investor. The investor tries to choose an investment that he hopes will gain him the greatest possible return. If there is a choice between investing in a restaurant or in a hardware store, and if they are equally risky but the hardware store is more likely to yield a bigger profit, the investor will choose the hardware store. Similarly, one who wants to be paid by salary is going to choose the job, all other things being equal, that pays the highest amount.

Even the feature of risk, which is clearly part of the investor's lot, has its analogous aspect in the situations of many salaried workers. One who signs a contract with a company for a certain salary agrees to do a certain kind and amount of work in return. Suppose a plumber, again, agrees to do a plumbing job for a building company. He puts in the pipes and the sinks, faithfully fulfilling his part of the contract. Now the time comes for him to receive the amount of money he was promised. But suppose he finds that the company has gone bankrupt, or, even worse, suppose he discovers that the company is run by scheming rascals who refuse to pay him and challenge him to sue. In either case the plumber might be able to get the money that is due him, but it also could happen that he only will get part of it or that he will have to absorb a complete loss. Thus, even those who work for a salary are taking a risk (known by anyone who has tried to cash a paycheck that bounces) that the employer will remain solvent and will faithfully fulfill his part of the deal.

It is true that one can agree to work for the United States government or General Motors, two examples of organizations that most likely will not go broke and will probably not renege on a contract. The risk one runs in these two cases is minimal, but it also should be kept in mind that in many investments the risk is also minimal. One can buy government bonds or federally insured certificates of deposit and also be taking very minimal risks. Even so, it is still admittedly the case that investors incur greater risks than salaried workers, but the difference is one of degree and not of kind.

The conclusion is that investors, wage earners, and consumers (a similar argument could be made concerning them) are all involved in the pursuit of profit in the broad sense. Almost all of these individuals desire to get more, and they attempt to satisfy this desire by making choices that involve different degrees of risk. Some individuals are willing to take great risks; others are not. Some are willing to make great efforts to satisfy the desire for more; others take a more leisurely approach. But in any case, nearly everyone has this desire to some extent, and it is a very common motive for action.

Since the desire for profit is ubiquitous, it is likely that it has an important economic function. It is no coincidence, and not just an historical accident, that the desire for more is widespread. Even a superficial glance at our economic system will show that profits play an essential role and that the system could not function without them. The system is supposed to provide people with those material things and services that they want to have, and profits are a necessary element in accomplishing this objective. To illustrate this point, consider the desire people have for sofas. They are thought by many to be a very nice thing to have in one's home, and many people are willing to spend money to buy them. People who invest their money in companies that build sofas will find that they are making a nice profit. Those who invest in companies that make items that people do not want will discover to their chagrin that they are becoming bankrupt. Profits are a signal to an investor that he is involved in providing something that people want.

The desire for more is also involved in another aspect of the system: the way consumers go about satisfying their desires. If a sofa of moderate quality is selling for $200, many consumers would like to find a sofa of the same quality for $180. Or, they hope to be able to purchase a sofa of more than moderate quality for their $200. They want a sofa, and they are willing to pay $200, but they also want something more. Realizing this, if a company can figure out a way to either lower its price or improve the quality for the same price, it will have an advantage over the other firms making sofas. When consumers find out about the bargain, the company that made the improvement will find its profits going up, and the competitors will find that their creditors are not happy. The desire for profit is not only a signal that shows investors what people want; it is also involved in improving the quality of the desired products and in lowering their cost.

The profit motive also has an important effect in influencing people to learn the kinds of skills that are needed in the society and then in encouraging people to move to the areas in which these skills will be the most appreciated. When a service is required, those that can provide it will be able to get a higher salary (to consider salaries again) than if they learned a skill already being practiced by a good number of others. At this time, people who have ability and experience in computer programming can earn a good wage, but as more people go into this field, the salaries will go down (at least, in relation to others). This will be a signal that the need for computer programmers is not as great as it once was and that those interested in high salaries should try another field.

All of these examples illustrating the role the desire for profit plays in our system have been somewhat artificial in that many complicating factors have been left out. The effect of government regulations, advertising, monopolies, labor unions, and other factors that have an obvious effect on what people want and what prices they pay have not been considered. Even so, it is apparent that the desire for more is important in our system; if this desire were to disappear, enormous difficulties and changes would ensue. Suppose, for example, that consumers remain as they are, but they stop being interested in getting more for their money when they shop for sofas. Suppose that investors also change in the one respect that they no longer look for investments that yield the highest return. The consequences of these changes would be dramatic. First of all, the quality of merchandise would start to deteriorate because there would no longer be any reason for companies to try to produce good quality at low prices. A good, fairly cheap sofa would sell as well as a poor, expensive one. Also, since investors no longer worry about profits, they would just as soon invest in a company that returns an extra 5 percent as an extra 25 percent. This would be another inducement for companies to be unconcerned about their products and their sales. The most efficient companies would no longer prosper, and the quality and supplies of goods and services would soon become shoddy and sparse. Eliminating the desire for profit, then, without making any other changes, would turn our economic system into something we would not recognize.

It is a necessary element of the system that everyone in it desires to gain more, and this desire is the engine that keeps the mechanism going. These are just factual assertions, but they raise an ethical question that is easy to ask but very hard to know how to answer: Is the desire for profit, and the system of which it is a part, good or bad?

This question is difficult to know how to approach, but perhaps as a starting point, it will be helpful to consider the problem of how one judges the moral value of a whole economic system. If a reasonable way can be found for making this kind of judgment, there will be at least some grounds for saying that the desire for profits is good or bad. If it can be shown that the desire for profits leads to an economic system that is bad, there will be a strong reason for having a negative view of the desire. Conversely, if the system is good, one has solid ground for applauding the desire for profit. The way one judges the system, however, is a complex matter; it is discussed not only in the four articles directly concerning profits that follow, but it also comes up in almost every one of the articles of the other sections.

One standard that has been considered relevant for making this general kind of moral judgment of the economic system is productivity. An economic system should provide for the material needs of the people in it, and this often amounts to whether it produces enough food and shelter for its participants. Any system that can do this would seem to have at least met the minimal standards that should apply to any economic system. There might be exceptions, however, because a system not doing well on the standard of productivity might still be judged as good because of the extremely limited resources available to it. How well a system uses those resources is another standard that should be used in making an overall judgment. The standard that is being referred to at this point is efficiency. There are other standards that are used in judging economic systems, such as fairness and equity, but since they will be examined in later sections of this book, the focus for the moment will be on productivity and efficiency.

Consider first the standard of productivity. Most economists, and others too, have believed that our system would be graded quite well on this standard. For the most part people do have enough to eat—in many cases, too much—and most people do have adequate shelter. Furthermore, the system not only provides these minimum necessities, it also provides many people with a wide range of luxuries. This is not to deny that there is poverty amid the affluence, but the point is that there is enough being produced to satisfy everyone's basic needs even if this output is not distributed in a way that would do so.

It is more difficult to make a judgment of the economy's efficiency. For a long time resources were plentiful, and it really did not matter very much if the economy was efficient. But now, as energy supplies tighten, the efficiency of the system will be tested to a much greater degree, and one will be able to make a more reasonable assessment. It can be said, though, that since the economy does well in productivity, it must be doing at least tolerably well in efficiency. If it were not, it would not even maintain its great output.

These are two reasons for saying that the system as a whole and the desire for profit, which is an integral part of it, are good. However, this is not the end of the story, for there are other aspects of the desire for profit to consider. These other aspects are more controversial, and some thinkers have concluded not only that they should be put on the negative side of the balance but that they are significant enough to outweigh the positive good attributed to productivity and efficiency.

One of these controversial considerations is the effect of the desire for profit on people's characters. The desire for profit is the desire for more; and if one continually wants more, no matter how much one has, the result seems to be the development of greed. This is one of the major criticisms of the profit motive. The desire for profit has been considered as just another way of describing the vice of greed—one of the seven deadly sins. A greedy person is one who is never satisfied, who wants more and more, who will not accept any limit to this desire, and who will sacrifice other aspects of life to feed the fire of his avarice. Critics have portrayed those who desire profit in an identical way. The critics have claimed that there is really no distinction between wanting profit and being greedy; and so if one believes that the latter is a bad trait, either in itself or because of the misery it causes, one is bound to think that the former is also bad. The selection by Durkheim presents this view in an extremely forceful manner, and even though it was written in France in the nineteenth century, the same criticism of the desire for profits is expressed by many contemporary American critics. Very few of the contemporaries, however, have made the case as well as Durkheim did.

Another possible negative aspect concerning people's characters that many have connected with the desire for profit is the trait of taking advantage of others. Someone who is interested in getting more will seek ways to get it; what this often means is that he will find something that people want, figure out a way to provide it, and then make people pay dearly for it. Of course, if one makes people pay too dearly, the customers might go to the competition, and so what would really be desirable is a situation in which there are no other competitors to go to. Then it really becomes possible to make a killing. This happens when one company comes out with a new product that is not being sold by anyone else, or when a country discovers that they possess a needed natural resource. It also happens when individuals find themselves the only buyer interested in a house that someone else must sell. These are the kinds of situations that everyone in our economic system would like to be in, and it has struck some critics that these are all situations of taking advantage of people. Due to foresight or fortune one has the opportunity to set the price in a way that is disconcerting to those who have to pay it, but pay it they must. Is this really what the profit motive leads to, and is this kind of behavior an aspect of the trait of taking advantage of others?

This issue is examined (along with other criticisms of the desire for profits) in the selection by Acton. He believes that the critics' view of profits is incorrect, and he tries to show that, when considered properly, the desire for profits does not lead to the immoral action of taking advantage of another's necessity. His arguments form an interesting contrast to Durkheim's harsh criticisms.

Ethical arguments about profits have not only been concerned with the character traits that develop as a result of people's desire for more. The debate about profits has also focused on the question of whether this desire is a part of human nature. It is very important to notice, however, that this second controversy is not about whether the desire for profits is good or bad; rather, it is about whether a moral judgment can be made at all about the profit motive. Thus, those who believe that this desire is part of human nature are not saying that the desire is therefore a good one. And those who deny that it is part of human nature are not committed to thinking that the desire is therefore a bad one.

What this debate is really about is responsibility. It is a universally held view in ethics that only those aspects of human life that are under people's control can be judged as good or bad. To say that something happened to someone that he could not help is to absolve the person of responsibility for any bad consequences that might result. No one can be blamed or praised for having been born male or female, or for having been born to rich or poor parents. These are things that just happen. In the same way, it makes no sense to praise someone for having been born intelligent, or to criticize another for being naturally stupid. Once it is admitted that a certain trait is innate, no one becomes responsible for having it, and the trait is then no longer subject to ethical examination.

This is just the point that is being made by those who try to argue that the desire for more is part of human nature. What these people are saying is that all human beings are born with this desire. There is nothing that can be done about it for that is just the way we are. And if this is true, it makes no sense to condemn the desire, or to condemn a system that is based on it. Condemnation is just as silly as criticizing people for having been born with two arms and then morally disapproving of those who make shirts with two sleeves. As long as we have arms, we might as well have sleeves; and as long as we desire more, we might as well take advantage of it.

Those who are on the other side of this debate argue that the desire for more is not an innate feature of human beings; therefore, it is something that we are responsible for and can be morally evaluated. The judgment might not be that this desire is bad, even though most people on this side of the issue have that view. The main point is, however, that the desire is subject to moral examination. If the desire is beneficial, those who encourage it to grow and develop should be praised. But if it is harmful, those same people should be criticized and influenced to stop what they are doing.

Whether the desire for profit is innate would seem to be the kind of straightforward factual question that is not in the province of philosophy; but as the two articles on this issue by Schmitt and Torrance point out, there are a number of conceptual issues that are intricately involved. These issues pertain to the question of how one identifies a motive and how one knows when an action is done from a particular motive. These are issues that have been carefully examined by a number of philosophers in recent years, and Schmitt and Torrance rely on this research to aid them in working out their views on whether the desire for profits is innate.

H. B. ACTON

The Profit Motive

THE IMMODERACY OF PROFIT

In this chapter we shall discuss the moral objection to the competitive market economy that, in depending upon the so-called profit motive, it encourages avarice and selfishness. This charge is complex, and we shall have to consider in turn various features of it.

One of the earliest criticisms of the market economy was put forward by Aristotle. He argued that when goods are produced for sale at a profit their use in satisfying needs is easily lost sight of and is replaced by the desire to accumulate as much money as possible. His idea was that whereas there is a limit or term to the satisfaction of needs, money can be accumulated ad infinitum. Hence the man who enters industry or trade in order to make money is led on by a desire that is by its very nature insatiable. The trader or money-maker introduces something inordinate and unnatural into society, and diverts attention from the satisfaction of satiable needs to the insatiable search for a limitless fortune.

It should be pointed out that any force this argument has applies not only to competitive markets but to any economy in which money is used. It is money values that can be conceived as being added to indefinitely, and these could be the gross national product of a

Source: *The Morals of Markets.* Copyright © 1971 by Longman Group, London, England. Reprinted by permission of the publisher.

socialist economy as well as the profits made in a competitive market economy. The contrast is really between the series of natural numbers on the one hand and satisfactions to which no numerical values in the sense of prices can be given on the other. The fact is that numbers can incite men to useless or harmful activity in any society that has a superstitious reverence for them. Profits themselves, of course, tend to be limited by competition between firms in a competitive market economy, so that any desire for the infinite is kept in check by the leveling processes of the market, so long as entry into it is free. In any case, perhaps Keynes was right when he said that "it is better that a man should tyrannise over his bank balance than over his fellow men."[1]

THE "MAMMON GOSPEL"

Thomas Carlyle's *Past and Present* (1843) contains much of the rhetoric that has since been used in moral criticisms of the competitive market economy. Certain phrases in it, such as "cash nexus"[2] and "captains of industry" have continued in use. Carlyle's device of contrasting the socially and ecclesiastically controlled medieval economic arrangements with the individualism of nineteenth-century capitalism has been copied since, notably by R.H. Tawney in *Religion and the Rise of Capitalism* (1926). Ruskin was influenced by it when he wrote his moral condemnation of the market economy in *Unto This Last* (1860). Friedrich Engels reviewed *Past and Present* when it first came out, and incorporated something of what he had learnt from it in an essay, *Outlines of a Critique of Political Economy* (1844), from which much of the Marxist doctrine takes its origin. A paragraph from *Past and Present* (quoted by Engels in his review of it) may serve as our starting point:

> True, it must be owned, we for the present, with our Mammon-Gospel, have come to strange conclusions. We call it a Society; and go about professing the totalest separation, isolation. Our life is not a mutual helpfulness; but rather, cloaked under due laws-of-war, named "fair competition" and so forth, it is a mutual hostility. We have profoundly forgotten everywhere that *Cash-payment* is not the sole relation of human beings; we think nothing doubting, that *it* absolves and liquidates all engagements of man. "My starving workers?" answers the rich Mill-owner: "Did I not hire them fairly in the market? Did I not pay them, to the last sixpence, the sum covenanted for? What have I to do with them more?"—Verily Mammon-worship is a melancholy creed. When Cain for his own behoof had killed Abel, and was questioned, "Where is thy

brother?" he too made answer, "Am I my brother's keeper?" Did I not pay my brother *his* wages, the thing he had merited from me?[3]

In setting out, in chapter one of *Religion and the Rise of Capitalism,* the historical theme he proposes to investigate, Tawney contrasts "the conception of society as a community of unequal classes with varying functions, organized for a common end", with "that which regards itself as a mechanism adjusting itself through the play of economic motives to the supply of economic needs"; he also contrasts "the idea that a man must not take advantage of his neighbour's necessity" with "the doctrine that 'man's self-love is God's providence,' " and "the view of economic activity which regarded it as one among other kinds of moral conduct" with "the view of it as dependent upon impersonal and almost automatic forces."[4]

Both Carlyle and Tawney, it will be noticed, identify the market economy with society as a whole. They both consider that the market economy comprises or permeates the whole of society, and that in so doing it destroys relationships between people other than those contracted for economic purposes. Furthermore they assert that the society that has thus become identical with a market is one in which self-seeking, callousness, and even downright maleficience are regarded as justified. But if, as I have indicated, the competitive market is only a part of any society in which it exists, then these criticisms are unacceptable. What would have to be shown is first, that where there is a market economy, it must permeate, and hence presumably corrupt, everything else in the society that harbors it. But second, even more fundamental than this is the claim that within the market itself men are necessarily dominated by avarice, lack of concern for others, and wish to harm them. Of course, if it is never right to look after one's own interests in competition with others, then the market economy must be fundamentally bad, since, as we have already indicated, all those participating in it are trying to do as well for themselves as they can.

This criticism must apply, not only to producing and merchanting firms, but to the ultimate consumers as well, for these aim to secure a consumer's surplus, that is, to make as large as possible the difference between what they pay in the market and what they would pay if they had to.[5] Thus we should not speak of profits as if they were, morally speaking, different from the advantages which all those who participate in the market economy hope to gain for themselves by selling, buying, or working for a wage. The ultimate consumer is not generally as good at obtaining the advantages open to him as firms are good at making profits, for the purchasing of consumer goods is a less organized profession than it was in the days when most house-wives specialized in it. But consumers' associations can bring expertise into the buying of consumer goods just as trade unions can advise and help men to make advantageous wage bargains. Profits, if they are honestly come by, indicate no more avarice than do wages and the purchases of shrewd and cautious buyers.

It might be objected that this only goes to show that in a com-petitive market economy all the participants, and not only those who set out to make profits, are engaged in self-interested activities which should be morally condemned. If the market were the whole of society this might be so, but the market is in practice an element in a society that extends far beyond it. Hence those who engage in market activities do so with aims that are related to the other aspects of the society in which they live. All men belong to a family, many of them have a religion, some of them have a care for social and philanthropic causes, an interest in art and science, a concern for their country. The interests they pursue in the market, therefore, are not merely private and personal, but are imbued with ambitions and predilections to which monetary success is often subordinate. Most men's market dealings are linked with their desire to provide for their families, but they may also be concerned to promote con-cerns connected with churches, clubs, voluntary societies, and other groups to which they give their loyalty. Firms themselves are influ-enced by the outlooks of their directors and managers, and purchases by individuals manifest "profiles" which vary from one to another. It is true that some people are so taken with the market that they want money for its own sake, and there are others who chiefly want to outdo other people. But they are hardly typical. What should be emphasized is that whatever their nonmarket aims, motives, and ideals, they will not promote them by buying too dear or selling too cheap in market terms.

Tawney, in the passage I referred to above, writes as if the principle that a man should not take advantage of his neighbor's necessity is opposed to the market system. To establish and exploit, say, a monopoly of food during a famine would undoubtedly be immoral, but such monopolies, I suggest, go against the market system, and cannot be taken as typical unless it is the case that competitive markets *must* tend to develop into monopolies. Sickness and poverty among those who cannot help themselves may have to be dealt with outside the market mechanism,[6] which may, as Lord Robbins emphasized, have to be suspended in times of scarcity imposed, for example, by the siege conditions of war.[7] But this is not to say that in the course of market activities people are taking unfair or otherwise reprehensible advantage of one another. The market, as a method of recording consumer preferences and allocating resources, can respond to any distribution or redistribution of income. In one sense, indeed, people *are* taking advantage of one another, and it is a very good thing that they do so. For in competitive markets people who need goods and services receive them from people who see advantage to themselves in providing them. To take advantage of people's necessities in this way is not morally reprehensible unless it is always wrong to require payment for goods provided or for services rendered. The better one meets the needs of others, the more profitable market activity becomes. This brings us to a crucial aspect of the morality of markets.

ECONOMIC HARMONIES AND THE "INVISIBLE HAND"

"Taking advantage of one's neighbor's necessity," we have seen, can mean two things. It can mean the exploitation by the strong of the weak or helpless by creating a monopoly and taking advantage of it; and it can mean the supplying for pay of goods and services that our neighbor wishes to buy. No one is going to defend exploitation by monopoly, but it should not be confused with responding to demand, and the question is whether the latter, which is the market method of helping one another, is to be morally condemned as well. Put in its very simplest terms, the question is: "Is it always wrong to require payment for providing help?" The answer is undoubtedly no, and it is instructive to consider why.

Let us suppose a society in which there is division of labor and a belief among all its members that it is wrong to require payment for anything. In this society the man who grows potatoes wants to give them to those who need them, and the man who makes shoes wants to do the same. How do the potatoes and the shoes get to those who want them? Presumably these people go around and take some. But where do the potato growers and shoemakers go for spades and leather? Has some kind man realized that these implements and materials will be needed, and has he produced them for the potato grower and the shoemaker? He would have to find out what sort they required, but what would happen if they did not like them? After all, there is something indelicate about criticizing gifts. Nor can gifts be demanded either, and yet the potato grower may need the spade when his friend is making one for some other friend who is breaking the ground for a much needed house.

Such considerations make it clear that a society with division of labor and limited resources cannot rely upon gifts to get its products distributed. Benevolence is good, but it is business that is needed, and business means mutual agreements, times of delivery, specifications and quantities, contracts, exchange, and sales. These agreements and deals take place in order that people's needs shall be satisfied. But the satisfactions are reciprocal. Each producer needs the products of some or all the other producers, and some or all of them need what he produces. In producing for sale what he is good at producing, each producer supplies the others with what they want. The buyer, unlike a recipient of gifts, can require the producer to make what is wanted. The producer or seller, unlike a bestower of gifts, is led to supply the types and quantities needed at times when they are of use.

This, I suggest, is what ought to be meant by the system of economic harmony. It is not that each individual seeks his own interest and that some "invisible hand," to use Adam Smith's famous expression, sees to it that this results in benefits for all. For such a hand might lose its cunning or become paralyzed. It is rather that the very structure or system of free exchange in a society with division of labor and limited resources is one in which what each party produces is for some others to have in return for what the producer would like to have from them. Benefiting oneself by providing what others need is the raison d'être of the whole affair. It is not that the good of others is a contingent by-product of selfishness, but that each party can only benefit himself by benefiting others. He may from time to time benefit others without benefiting himself, by making gifts, or what comes to the same thing in a market, by selling below what he knows to be the market price. But persistently to do this would be to opt out of the system, the very functioning of which requires service to be by exchange rather than by gift. If there is to be business, it had better be business.

In *The Wealth of Nations*[8] Adam Smith seems to be recommending the method of exchange on the ground that it is better for an able-bodied man who wants what others have to offer something in exchange for it rather than "by every servile and fawning attention to obtain their good will." He also suggests in the same passage that the methods of the beggar are not likely to be consistently successful, human selfishness being what it is, that they would lead to a great waste of time, and that they neither do nor can "provide him with them ['the necessaries of life'] as he has occasion for them." The last two seem to me to be the really compelling reasons, as they would still apply, as I have suggested above, even if human beings were primarily and fundamentally altruistic. For the system to work, even altruistic prople have to look to their own benefit. Does this mean that they have to make themselves selfish? Not at all. What it means is that, whatever their outlook or their temperament, they must try to look after themselves while they play their part in the competitive market system. If they are honest and honorable men the part they play will be in keeping with their character. If they are not, they may still be kept in line by fear of the law or their knowledge that others will not do business with them if they are suspected of double-dealing. If they are misanthropic, they may try to forget that they cannot benefit themselves without providing other people with things they want to have. But if they provide what others do not want they will find themselves out of business.

The system was described very well in the eighteenth century by Le Mercier de la Rivière when he wrote:

> It is of the essence of [this] order that the particular interest of each individual can never be separated from the common interest of all; we find a very convincing proof of this in the complete freedom which ought to obtain in trade, if property is not to be damaged. The personal interest which this great freedom encourages, strongly and continually urges every individual to improve, to multiply the things that he wishes to sell; in this way to enlarge the mass of enjoyments which he can provide for other men, in order to enlarge by this means, the enjoyments that other men can provide for him in exchange. Thus *the world goes by itself* (va du lui-même); the desire for enjoyment and the freedom to enjoy, never ceasing to induce the multiplication of products and the growth of industry, impress on the whole of the society a motion which becomes a perpetual tendency towards its best possible condition.[9]

We may no longer share the eighteenth-century writer's optimistic belief that all this will lead to "the best possible condition," nor have we yet considered the relation of the analysis to freedom. But the central position, it seems to me, is correct, that is, the claim that in competitive markets individuals, whether firms or persons, provide for others in working for themselves. We might equally well say that in working for others they work for themselves. Hence, someone who was averse to helping other people would, once he understood the logic of the system, be rather disconcerted if he had to play a part in it. For business success depends on supplying people with what they want, and hence involves helping them.

It may still be objected that there is something paradoxical about the morality of urging people to act selfishly in order to promote the common good, for, it may be said, while someone is deliberately pursuing the common good he cannot be acting selfishly, and while he is acting selfishly he cannot be deliberately promoting the common good. Is there any real difference, it may be asked, between advising people to look after themselves on the one hand, and asking them to look after themselves in order to promote the common good on the other? Will not this be taken, and rightly so, as an invitation not to bother about other people? Historians of the subject say that Adam Smith was influenced by Mandeville's paradox that private vices are public virtues when he argued that an "invisible hand" secured a result, viz. the interest of the society, that the individual had not intended. The word *intend* was not very fortunately chosen by Smith, for we can hardly intend something as remote as the interest of the society, we can only aim at it or try to bring it about. What we intend are things much closer to us than the interest of the society. When we intend to do something it is something we think we know quite well how to do. Again, when Smith says "It is not from the benevolence of the butcher, the brewer, or the baker that we expect our dinner, but from their regard to their own interest,"[10] he is right but a little misleading, for in a competitive market economy these people do try to give their customers what they want. They must try to do this if they are to sell their goods. The word *benevolence* suggests gratuitous or unremunerated help, and certainly butchers do not give their meat away. But remunerated help is help nevertheless, and the point of trading in a market is that the help that men can afford one another is extended over a wide area and rendered more efficient by the device of free exchange. Giving help and receiving it are united in one process. Not only is self-help rewarded, but misanthropy is rendered difficult by being made to result in self-injury.

THE MARKET AND ITS LIMITS

From time to time ministers of religion assert that religion ought not to be confined to church and to private life and call for the application of Christian principles of conduct to economic affairs. More generally, critics of the market economy often say that moral principles should be applied throughout society and not only in the nonmarket sections of it. This is Tawney's view when, in the passage quoted above, he contrasts the "view of economic activity which regarded it as one among other kinds of moral conduct" with "the view of it as dependent upon impersonal and almost automatic forces." The suggestion is that there is an impersonal system going on like clockwork—and we have recall Le Mercier de la Rivière's world that "goes on its own"—with no kind of moral conduct in it, and a world quite distinct from the economic world, in which moral conduct does occur.

But if Tawney's words mean what they say, then they certainly say one thing that is wrong, for it is obvious that moral conduct, in the sense of conduct that is morally right or wrong and is in general subject to moral standards, does take place in the market as it is and does not need to be imported into it. For in the market people can be just or unjust, honest or dishonest, reliable or unreliable, and these are moral characteristics. They can also be cautious or rash, and these may be regarded as moral characteristics too, although some might say that they belong to the sphere of prudence and its opposite rather than to morality. Whether or not we say that prudence belongs to the moral sphere, there is not necessarily anything *wrong* in it, and hence there is nothing necessarily wrong in the looking after one's interests that the market calls for. The suggestion, therefore, that people must be immoral or amoral in their market activities is quite unfounded, for, even if prudence is not to count among moral virtues, honesty undoubtedly must. If it is argued that it is not genuine honesty because it is enforced by legal or professional sanctions, the answer is that genuine honesty is no more removed from the world of business because there are penalties for cheating, than genuine love is removed from the nonbusiness world because there are penalties for assault.

On examination, therefore, we find that there is absolutely nothing in the complaint that markets are by their very nature immoral or amoral,* although many of those who participate in them cheat or would cheat if they dared. All that remains to charge the market with on this score, therefore, is that in it the Christian virtues of humility, charity, and self-sacrifice are not displayed, or are displayed markedly less than in the political management of the economy.

But how could humility, charity, and self-sacrifice be shown in the market? If we ask how they could be exercised by business firms, the absurdity of the question becomes apparent. A firm can give away money that might otherwise have been distributed as profits, but it must be in a financial position to do this if it is not to fall into financial difficulties. The very idea of a firm showing humility or sacrificing itself is absurd, and the idea of these virtues being exercised by individual participants in the market is hardly less so. If

---

* Some are, of course, such as markets in men, love, scandal.

a man constantly deferred to others and could not bring himself to accept an order if someone else would thereby fail to get it, he could not long survive in business. We shall have more to say about this when we discuss the morality of competition, but it should be pretty clear already that no one who does not try to make a profit, or, what is the same thing, to avoid a loss, can effectively take part in market activities. Nor can he long remain in a position to make gifts to good causes or be taxed for any means whatever.

But this does not mean that even the Christian virtues must be absent from the business world altogether. Between the members of a firm or between its employees there is plenty of scope for humility and charity, and perhaps even for self-sacrifice as well. For example, a man might allow a friend to be promoted to a position which he would have liked to occupy himself. But this, although it happened in the business world, would not in itself be a market activity. There just would be no sense in a firm's allowing another firm to take its business from it. I hardly think, either, that we should regard it as humility or self-sacrifice if an employee took no steps to prevent his employer from underpaying him, unless his employer were a friend or a charity which the employee hoped to help thereby. Furthermore, those expending funds for good causes have a duty to make their expenditures as economically effective as possible.

In *Unto This Last* (1860), Ruskin says that it is the duty of a soldier to die rather than to leave his post in battle, of a physician to die rather than to leave his post in a plague, of a pastor to die rather than to teach falsehood, of a lawyer to die rather than to countenance injustice. Then Ruskin asks: "The merchant—what is *his* due occasion of death?" His answer is that the merchant's function is to provide for society and that he must therefore face death or damage "rather than fail in any engagement, or consent to any deterioration, adulteration, or unjust exorbitant price of that which he provides." Furthermore, the merchant must so conduct his business as to promote the welfare of his employees: "And so it becomes his duty, not only to be always considering how to produce what he sells in the purest and cheapest forms, but how to make the various employments involved in the production, or the transference of it, most beneficial to the men employed."

The comparison of the merchant and the industrialist with the soldier was repeated by Tawney in *The Acquisitive Society:*

> The idea that there is some mysterious difference between making munitions of war and firing them, between building schools and teaching in them when built, between providing food and providing health, which makes it at once

inevitable and laudable that the former should be carried on with a single eye to pecuniary gain, while the latter are conducted by professional men, who expect to be paid for their services, but who neither watch for windfalls nor raise their fees merely because there are more sick to be cured, more children to be taught, or more enemies to be resisted, is an illusion only less astonishing than that the leaders of industry should welcome the insult as an honour and wear their humiliation as a kind of halo. The work of making boots or building a house is in itself no more degrading than that of curing the sick or teaching the ignorant. It is as necessary and therefore as honourable. It should be at least equally bound by rules which have as their object to maintain the standards of professional service. It should be at least equally free from the vulgar subordination of moral standards to financial interests.[11]

This passage occurs in the course of a section headed: "Industry as a Profession." Like Ruskin, Tawney contrasts businessmen, whose aim is to make profits, with professional men who do not "watch for windfalls." Industry, he says, is organized for the protection of rights, "mainly rights to pecuniary gain," a profession "for the performance of *duties*," the measure of their success being "the service which they perform, not the gains which they amass."[12] Thus, the suggestion is that if professional men acted on commercial principles, doctors would raise their fees during epidemics, teachers would demand more pay when the numbers of their pupils increased, and soldiers would do the same in time of war. The argument based on this suggestion is that since doctors, teachers, and soldiers would regard it as wrong to do these things, businessmen should behave more like professional men and look to other things besides pecuniary gain. Curing the sick, it is said, counts most for the doctor, getting children to think and to exercise skills counts most for the teacher, defending the country counts most for the soldier. By analogy, therefore, supplying the needs of his customers should count most for the businessman who should not, therefore, have "a single eye to pecuniary gain." We must now proceed to examine the analogy and the argument.

BUSINESS AND THE PROFESSIONS

There are so many different factors involved in these comparisons that it is very difficult to disentangle the essential from the irrelevant. Professions, for example, are very much concerned with their members' rights, and trades and industries and firms have to recognize all sorts of duties to suppliers, customers, and employees. This was so in 1921, when Tawney was writing, as well as today, and hardly seems to present a fruitful topic for examination. As the businessman is compared with a number of different professions, perhaps it will be best if we first consider his side of the comparison.

Does the businessman have "a single eye for pecuniary gain"? From what we have said about the competitive-enterprise system this is true, insofar as the businessman is in business to avoid losses or to make a profit. If he gives anything away, this, unless it is a part of his marketing activity, is outside his business dealings, the very point of which is that he gets what he can by supplying goods and services that are in demand. What he can get is determined by what the buyers can and will pay and by the quality of his goods by comparison with that of the goods offered by other suppliers. He is required to be honest, to keep his promises about dates of delivery, to refrain from misdescribing his goods. He is not called upon to die for his customers, although keeping his promises to them may require him to work very hard on their behalf as well as on his own— and in a competitive system, in doing the latter he will be doing the former as well.* A lazy distributor of insulin or of "heart machines" is not only unbusinesslike but also insensitive or callous.

Now let us suppose that there is a shortage, not of his contriving, of the goods that a merchant supplies. This will bring the price up, but it may not bring more profit to the merchant, for the volume of his sales may diminish. If there were a very serious shortage and the price went high, the poorer customers might have to buy less or nothing at all. If, however, the suppliers did not put up the price, the goods would be bought up by the earliest buyers, probably those who first realized that there was a shortage. If in such conditions there was only one supplier, he might be able to make very high profits, especially if there were no substitutes for the products he sells. The profits of each would be limited if there were competition between the sellers. If the shortage were a general shortage of food it would be considered wrong to allow the demand to push the prices up to such an extent that the poorer people were brought to starvation or near to it, and in such circumstances a publicly controlled system of rationing would be introduced. A new law, penalties for

---

* In an overstretched economy suffering from wage inflation, he will not be able to *keep* his promises about deliveries, and if he does not *make* the promises he will not get the orders. This is one way in which inflation corrodes basic morality. To compare the selfishness of businessmen with the public spirit of professional men in such circumstances is fatuous, but it is only fair to mention that Tawney had in mind quite a different set of economic conditions in a non-inflationary economy.

breach of it, the registration of individuals, the issue of ration books would then become necessary.

We may now examine the contrasting cases cited by Tawney. The doctors he had in mind are supposed to be working privately for fees. What happens when there is an epidemic? Tawney assumes that they would not think it right to put up their fees. But they would then have to see more patients and would in consequence receive *more* in fees, even though the fees had not been raised. But perhaps the epidemic is so great that not all patients can be treated by the existing body of doctors. Then each doctor would be expected to treat those who needed treatment most, as far as he could find this out. It is important to notice that he can judge the varying needs of his patients much more easily than a shopkeeper could judge the varying needs of his customers, for the doctor examines the patient, even goes into his home, whereas the shopkeeper, unless he serves a village, does not know much about the personal circumstances of his customers. Hence a doctor can act as his own rationing authority and, indeed, might be *better* at it than any Ministry of Health. Treating patients is a very different sort of service from selling goods, and the differences between what is reasonable from shopkeepers and merchants in times of famine and what is reasonable from doctors in times of epidemics depend on this distinction. Perhaps a reason why traders are criticized in times of famine more than doctors are in times of epidemic is that the former can often get food for themselves whereas doctors run the same risks of disease as everyone else, if not more.

We need not consider the case of doctors employed by a national health service, as the comparisons we need may be examined by relation to teachers and soldiers, the other cases mentioned by Ruskin and Tawney. According to Tawney, then, teachers would not consider it right to demand salary increases in return for teaching more children. But if this meant that they would have to work much harder, it would not be wrong of them to make such a demand, and the increased salary may be essential to attract more people into teaching and away from other employments. The difference between teachers and traders is largely due to differences in what they do. Teachers have continuous personal relationships with considerable numbers of children, and are bound to them by likes (and dislikes) and by their understanding of their characters and personalities. They are expected to give encouragement and to have sympathy and loyalty. These are not qualities much required in the processes of marketing, and businessmen exercise them, if at all, in their relation to colleagues within the firm. What is necessarily central in the activity of teaching is peripheral in the activity of trading. Hence it is inappropriate that the professional attitudes of teachers should find their way into industry and commerce, even though in business certain teaching functions are necessary here and there. It is worth noticing, too, that whereas a teacher's pupils are, so to say, his final products, the businessman's subordinates are links in a chain of production and distribution.

The comparison with soldiers raises some points of interest. It would be disgraceful for soldiers to demand more pay in time of war with the threat of not fighting at all unless the increase was granted. Yet the trader will not forgo a rise of price in times of scarcity. But for the trader's action in not raising prices to have any point he would have to ration his supplies, and his customers might not like that at all—he needs the authority of the state to do such things. The soldier is part of the state's authority, and if he refuses to fight he mutinies, and if he does so successfully, he seizes authority from its former holders. Why should not the merchant risk his life for something or other as the soldier risks his life for his country? Under a system of division of labor the merchant's circumstances do not generally require this. His function is to take another sort of risk, that of financing a transaction before its total costs are known and before the demand from customers is known either. The soldier is housed and fed and clothed by the state, while the entrepreneur takes the responsibility for these things himself and faces economic uncertainties. Here again, therefore, the idea of transferring the responsibilities of a soldier to the man of business is seen to rest on similarities too slight to produce any conviction, once the negative analogies are brought to light.

It is absurd, then, to criticize the man of business for not exhibiting the devotion of a hard-working doctor, the sympathy of a schoolteacher, or the self-sacrifice of a soldier. His circumstances do not normally call for these virtues, but for foresight, honesty, reliability in keeping promises, and a readiness to accept the consequences of the risks he has to take.

IS PRIVATE TRADING WICKED?

It may be argued that we have still failed to identify the central moral defect of profit making, which is to be found in the very process of bargaining itself. There is, it may be said, something essentially ignoble in the higgling of the market. Traders are engaged in wicked work. We are not surprised to find such an attitude in the writings of Plato and of other upholders of an aristocratic form of society, for trading has always been looked down upon by the nobility, who use traders and sometimes have pillaged them. But why should this aristocratic attitude survive into present-day society? Can any convincing reasons be put forward in support of it?

The best attempt to do this that I know of was that of J.A. Hobson. One of Hobson's earliest books was his *John Ruskin* (1898), in which he expounded and upheld Ruskin's economic theories. In his later writings Hobson applied Ruskin's ideas about noneconomic goods to the social problems of the 1920s and 1930s, and endeavored to show that dealings in markets are essentially bad. In *Wealth and Life* Hobson wrote:

Save in the rare cases when both parties are equally strong in finance, knowledge and organization, business bargains distribute the gain unequally and proportionately to an economic force which, in its final issue, means the power "to starve the other out."[13]

In the same passage he also wrote:

By their very nature the bargaining processes inhibit the consideration of the good of others, and concentrate the mind and will of each party upon the bargaining for his own immediate and material gains. . . . this constant drive of selfish interest involves a hardening of the moral arteries.[14]

And in a lecture entitled *The Moral Challenge to the Economic System,* given to the Ethical Union in 1933, he said:

Sometimes the market is favourable to the sellers, sometimes to the buyers. What does that mean? It means that a superior bargaining power belongs to one side or the other, and that the price will be determined by this superiority of power, distributing the gain not with equity but force.[15]

Let us first consider the claim that in market dealings it is "force" or "power" that prevails over "equity." Does force or power prevail in practice? Certainly not in the sense in which it would prevail if, instead of there being an exchange or sale, the stronger party had taken from the weaker party what he wanted from him. Markets can only operate when force of this sort (what Bastiat called "spoliation") has been eliminated. Competitive markets require law and peace and order if they are to work at all. Thus, "power" and "force" must mean something else, "the power to starve the other out" mentioned by Hobson in *Wealth and Life.* But no such power is exercised when the prices of cabbages, meat, bread, and other foods are settled in ordinary markets. Of course, the producers and owners of these things need not sell them and could, if they could concert to stop all rival suppliers, hold them back until their customers got really hungry. But the producers and merchants are in business to sell, and if one firm tried to make its customers feel the pinch of hunger, other firms would sell to them. In a competitive market a price, so to say, *emerges,* by reference to the demand and to the available supply. If someone cannot pay the market price, then he has to go without, and hence the very poor cannot satisfy their needs as well as the rich can satisfy theirs and may have to be given additional money. Force is present in that if the very poor tried to *take* what they could not *buy,* they would face arrest and punishment. But if very many were in this position, the price would have to come down, otherwise the goods would not be sold. It should not be forgotten that not only do consumers wish (or need) to have, but that producers and merchants want to sell. Furthermore, employers may have fixed capital investment at stake, whereas their employees can walk out and leave them with the consequences.

Force or power are much more apparent, I suggest, when there is *no* market, as when governments in time of war barter large quantities of goods or contract bulk sales and purchases with governments of other countries. In such circumstances there cannot be a market and, as experience showed in the last war, the parties finally settle because they have to.* Even so, it is not necessarily the *stronger* that gets his way. For the weaker party can bargain from its very weakness, arguing, sometimes successfully, that the stronger power has more to lose in the event of the weaker power's collapsing. So-called oriental bargaining, again, is either a form of amusement, or else possible only because one or both of the parties is ignorant of the state of the market. In developed competitive markets there is very little bargaining because there is no need for it among those who understand the supply situation.

---

* At that time the Russians searched through Western trade journals to find the highest prices quoted in them for the commodities they wished to sell.

I suggest, therefore, that Hobson's account of bargaining in a market is more like bargaining in the absence of markets. It is indeed, more like politics than trade, and one must conclude that, in spite of his discoveries about the effects of oversaving, he did not really know what goes on in markets.[16]

Another element in Hobson's indictment of the market is that the price is not determined by equity. By this he means that the market price is not a just price. The passage we have quoted from his Ethical Union lecture suggests that Hobson thought that a price would be just, or at any rate less unjust, when there is no large discrepancy in bargaining power between buyers and sellers. It is certainly an appealing picture of economic justice that Hobson sets before us, in which no one is under pressure from anyone else and everyone exerts the same economic influence as all the others. In order that such a situation could exist, it would be necessary for no one to be so poor that he paid prices that he regretted having to pay. In such a situation, sellers too would not be forced to receive less than their goods had cost them. There would be no shortages, no commercial miscalculations, no governmental muddles, no obstinate or arbitrary men making use of an advantageous position. That is, in order that just prices could be established, supplies would have to be ample and yet not constitute a glut, and a population of reasonable, moderate men, free from inordinate desires, would have to be in possession of incomes that made them invulnerable to economic pressures. This may be an ideal situation; it is neither a real nor a likely one. The prices established in a competitive market have the function of getting goods and services from suppliers to consumers in the conditions that prevail. With increasing prosperity these prices might get established with less urgent pressures on the parties involved and so approach nearer to Hobson's conception of justice. But to complain that they are not just in this sense is to refer to an unavoidable consequence of the world's scarcities and man's imperfection.

In a part of his Ethical Union lecture which I have not quoted, Hobson shows that a major injustice in the settling of market prices which he has in mind, is the price paid for labor. The "vital resources" of employers, he argues, are larger than those of their employees, so that employees are forced by their employers to accept lower wages than they would do if they had no fear of losing their jobs. Hence, it is wage bargaining in a competitive market which he considers to lead to particularly unjust results.

Hobson was writing at a time when there was much unemployment and when, therefore, employees were at a disadvantage because the employer could generally find someone else to do the job if the employee were disposed to press his demands. But the position now is very different. When there is less unemployment and when most employees are ready (or are persuaded) to strike when their unions require them to do so, the bargaining advantage is on the side of the wage earners. According to Hobson's view of justice, therefore, at a time of full or overfull employment it would be employers who are unjustly treated, and justice can only be made possible when employment is less than full, and in consequence employers have a prospect of resisting some of the claims the unions make upon them. His notion of a just wage, therefore, comes very close to that of a wage established in a competitive market between parties who have alternative bargains open to them; in this case, between employees who can offer their services elsewhere and employers who can hold their employees to their agreements without thereby risking a strike. It is interesting to note that Professor Michael Fogarty, in his defense of the scholastic theory of the just wage, assumes a fairly freely working labor market in which monopolistic and monopsonistic positions are not exploited.[17]

Another difference between Hobson's day and ours is that unemployment benefits are now less adequate, and receiving them is not regarded as a stigma. To this extent, the employee is under less pressure in making his wage bargain and is therefore less forced than in the past. His choice is not now between accepting the employer's terms or starving and becoming an object of contempt. It is rather between working for a higher remuneration or striking and receiving strike pay himself and state assistance for his family. He might even find another job while the strike is on. Leaving moral considerations out of account, a man might opt for leisure and lower remuneration rather than for work with higher remuneration. Insofar as fear of unemployment is fear of idleness or of loss of dignity, it presupposes the value and dignity of work and of providing for oneself and one's family. If voluntary unemployment and idleness ceased altogether to be regarded as disgraceful, and if it were legally possible and sufficiently well provided for, wage bargaining would be of interest only to the more energetic, ambitious, and conscientious members of the community. Trade unions, therefore, have a material interest in the dignity of labor, and stand to lose their functions if it is belittled or denied.

NOTES

1. J. M. Keynes, *The General Theory of Employment* (London: Macmillan, 1960), p. 374.
2. Carlyle wrote of "Cash payment the sole nexus" in *Chartism* (1839). *Critical and Miscellaneous Essays* 5 (London: Chapman and Hall, 1896), p. 383.
3. Thomas Carlyle, *Past and Present* (London: Chapman and Hall, 1843), pp. 198-99.
4. R. H. Tawney, *Religion and the Rise of Capitalism* (1926; reprint ed., London: Pelican Books, 1940), p. 29. On p. 71 Tawney writes that in medieval times "the problem of moralising economic life was faced and not abandoned."
5. Alfred Marshall, *Principles of Economics*, 9th ed., Bk. 3, ch. 6 (London: Pelican Books, 1961). For subsequent discussion of the ideal see E.J. Mishan, "Realism and Relevance in Consumer's Surplus," *Welfare Economics: Five Introductory Essays* (New York: Random House, 1964), pp. 184-198. The great subtlety of the metaphysics of the theory is unnecessary for the point that the purchaser aims to do as well as he can for himself and is thus in the same moral boat as the profit seeker.
6. The advantages claimed for the reversed income tax by Professor Milton Friedman is that it would redistribute income outside the market. *Capitalism and Freedom* (Chicago: University of Chicago Press, 1962).
7. Lionel Robbins, *The Economic Problem in Peace and War* (London: Macmillan, 1947).
8. Adam Smith, *Wealth of Nations*, ed. E. Canaan, Bk. 1, ch. 2, 5th edition (New York: Modern Library, 1937).
9. Le Mercier de la Rivière, *L'Ordre Naturel et Essentiel des Sociétés Politiques* (London: J. Nourse, 1767), vol. 2, p. 444. The passage occurs in a chapter describing the benefits of commerce.
10. Smith, *The Wealth of Nations*, p. 14.
11. R. H. Tawney, *The Acquisitive Society* (London: Bell, 1921), Fontana edition (London: Collins, 1961), pp. 91-2.
12. Ibid., p. 89.
13. J. A. Hobson, *Wealth and Life* (London: Macmillan, 1929), pp. 211-12.
14. Ibid., p. 213.
15. J. A. Hobson, *The Moral Challenge to the Economic System* (London: The Ethical Union, 1933), p. 15.
16. His interesting *Confessions of an Economic Heretic* (London: Allen & Unwin, 1939) bears this out. Hobson lived in the world of books and journalism and was sheltered by a private income. He complains that no university department of economics in the country ever *asked* him to take a job with them, but he does not say that he ever *applied* for one.
17. Michael Fogarty, *The Just Wage* (London: G. Chapman, 1961), esp. pp. 12 and 264-65.

EMILE DURKHEIM

Anomic Suicide

If anomy* never appeared except ... in intermittent spurts and acute crisis, it might cause the social-suicide rate to vary from time to time, but it would not be a regular, constant factor. In one sphere of social life, however—the sphere of trade and industry—it is actually in a chronic state.

For a whole century, economic progress has mainly consisted in freeing industrial relations from all regulation. Until very recently, it was the function of a whole system of moral forces to exert this discipline. First, the influence of religion was felt alike by workers and masters, the poor and the rich. It consoled the former and taught them contentment with their lot by informing them of the providential nature of the social order, that the share of each class was assigned by God himself, and by holding out the hope for just compensation in a world to come in return for the inequalities of this world. It governed the latter, recalling that wordly interests are not man's entire lot, that they must be subordinate to other and higher interests, and that they should therefore not be pursued without rule or measure. Temporal power, in turn, restrained the scope of economic functions by its supremacy over them and by the relatively subordinate role it assigned them. Finally, within the business world proper, the occupational groups—by regulating salaries, the price of products, and production itself—indirectly fixed the average level of income on which needs are partially based by the very force of circumstances. However, we do not mean to propose this organization as a model. Clearly it would be inadequate to existing societies without great changes. What we stress is its existence, the fact of its useful influence, and that nothing today has come to take its place.

Actually, religion has lost most of its power. And government, instead of regulating economic life, has become its tool and servant.

* According to Durkheim, anomy is a state in which the social norms that are necessary for regulating human life are either completely lacking or, if present, ineffective. This social state, Durkheim believes, is a major cause of suicide—ED.

The most opposite schools, orthodox economists and extreme socialists, unite to reduce government to the role of a more or less passive intermediary among the various social functions. The former wish to make it simply the guardian of individual contracts; the latter leave it the task of doing the collective bookkeeping, that is, of recording the demands of consumers, transmitting them to producers, inventorying the total revenue, and distributing it according to a fixed formula. But both refuse it any power to subordinate other social organs to itself and to make them converge toward one dominant aim. On both sides nations are declared to have the single or chief purpose of achieving industrial prosperity; such is the implication of the dogma of economic materialism, the basis of both apparently opposed systems. And as these theories merely express the state of opinion, industry, instead of being still regarded as a means to an end transcending itself, has become the supreme end of individuals and societies alike. Thereupon the appetites thus excited have become freed of any limiting authority. By sanctifying them, so to speak, this apotheosis of well-being has placed them above all human law. Their restraint seems like a sort of sacrilege. For this reason, even the purely utilitarian regulation of them exercised by the industrial world itself through the medium of occupational groups has been unable to persist. Ultimately, this liberation of desires has been made worse by the very development of industry and the almost infinite extension of the market. So long as the producer could gain his profits only in his immediate neighborhood, the restricted amount of possible gain could not much overexcite ambition. Now that he may assume to have almost the entire world as his customer, how could passions accept their former confinement in the face of such limitless prospects?

Such is the source of the excitement predominating in this part of society, and which has thence extended to the other parts. There, the state of crisis and anomy is constant and, so to speak, normal. From top to bottom of the ladder, greed is aroused without knowing where to find ultimate foothold. Nothing can calm it, since its goal is far beyond all it can attain. Reality seems valueless by comparison with the dreams of fevered imaginations; reality is therefore abandoned, but so too is possibility abandoned when it in turn becomes reality. A thirst arises for novelities, unfamiliar pleasures, nameless sensations, all of which lose their savor once known. Henceforth one has no strength to endure the least reverse. The whole fever subsides and the sterility of all the tumult is apparent, and it is seen that all these new sensations in their infinite quantity cannot form a solid foundation of happiness to support one during days of trial. The wise man, knowing how to enjoy achieved results without having constantly to replace them with others, finds in them an attachment to life in the hour of difficulty. But the man who has always pinned all his hopes on the future and lived with his eyes fixed upon it, has nothing in the past as a comfort against the present's afflictions, for the past was nothing to him but a series of hastily experienced stages. What blinded him to himself was his expectation always to find further on the happiness he had so far missed. Now he is stopped in his tracks; from now on nothing remains behind or ahead of him to fix his gaze upon. Weariness alone, moreover, is enough to bring disillusionment, for he cannot in the end escape the futility of an endless pursuit.

We may even wonder if this moral state is not principally what makes economic catastrophes of our day so fertile in suicides. In societies where a man is subjected to a healthy discipline, he submits more readily to the blows of chance. The necessary effort for sustaining a little more discomfort costs him relatively little, since he is used to discomfort and constraint. But when every constraint is hateful in itself, how can closer constraint not seem intolerable? There is no tendency to resignation in the feverish impatience of men's lives. When there is no other aim but to outstrip constantly the point arrived at, how painful to be thrown back! Now this very lack of organization characterizing our economic condition throws the door wide to every sort of adventure. Since imagination is hungry for novelty, and ungoverned, it gropes at random. Setbacks necessarily increase with risks and thus crises multiply, just when they are becoming more destructive.

Yet these dispositions are so inbred that society has grown to accept them and is accustomed to think them normal. It is everlastingly repeated that it is man's nature to be eternally dissatisfied, constantly to advance, without relief or rest, toward an indefinite goal. The longing for infinity is daily represented as a mark of moral distinction, whereas it can only appear within unregulated consciences which elevate to a rule the lack of rule from which they suffer. The doctrine of the most ruthless and swift progress has become an article of faith. But other theories appear parallel with those praising the advantages of instability, which, generalizing the situation that gives them birth, declare life evil, claim that it is richer in grief than in pleasure and that it attracts men only by false claims. Since this disorder is greatest in the economic world, it has most victims there.

Industrial and commercial functions are really among the occupations which furnish the greatest number of suicides (see Table 1, p. 43). Almost on a level with the liberal professions, they sometimes

TABLE 1—Suicides per Million Persons of Different Occupations

	Trade	Transpor- tation	Industry	Agricul- ture	Liberal * Professions
France (1878-87) †	440	....	340	240	300
Switzerland (1876)	664	1,514	577	304	558
Italy (1866-76)	277	152.6	80.4	26.7	618 ‡
Prussia (1883-90)	754	....	456	315	832
Bavaria (1884-91)	465	....	369	153	454
Belgium (1886-90)	421	....	160	160	100
Württemberg (1873-78)	273	....	190	206	......
Saxony (1878)		341.59 §		71.17	......

　* When statistics distinguish several different sorts of liberal occupations, we show as a specimen the one in which the suicide rate is highest.
　† From 1826 to 1880 economic functions seem less affected (see *Compte-rendu* of 1880), but were occupational statistics very accurate?
　‡ This figure is reached only by men of letters.
　§ Figure represents Trade, Transportation, and Industry combined for Saxony.

surpass them; they are especially more afflicted than agriculture, where the old regulative forces still make their appearance felt most and where the fever of business has least penetrated. Here is best recalled what was once the general constitution of the economic order. And the divergence would be yet greater if, among the suicides of industry, employers were distinguished from workmen, for the former are probably most stricken by the state of anomy. The enormous rate of those with independent means (720 per million) sufficiently shows that the possessors of most comfort suffer most. Everything that enforces subordination attenuates the effects of this state. At least the horizon of the lower classes is limited by those above them, and for this same reason their desires are more modest. Those who have only empty space above them are almost inevitably lost in it, if no force restrains them.

　Anomy, therefore, is a regular and specific factor in suicide in our modern societies, one of the springs from which the annual contingent feeds. So we have here a new type to distinguish from the others. It differs from them in its dependence, not on the way in which individuals are attached to society, but on how it regulates them. Egoistic suicide results from man's no longer finding a basis for existence in life; altruistic suicide, because this basis for existence appears to man situated beyond life itself. The third sort of suicide, the existence of which has just been shown, results from man's activities lacking regulation and his consequent sufferings. By virtue of its origin we shall assign this last variety the name of *anomic suicide.*

Certainly, this and egoistic suicide have kindred ties. Both spring from society's insufficient presence in individuals. But the sphere of its absence is not the same in both cases. In egoistic suicide it is deficient in truly collective activity, thus depriving the latter of object and meaning. In anomic suicide, society's influence is lacking in the basically individual passions, thus leaving them without a checkrein. In spite of their relationship, therefore, the two types are independent of each other. We may offer society everything social in us, and still be unable to control our desires; one may live in an anomic state without being egoistic, and vice versa. These two sorts of suicide therefore do not draw their chief recruits from the same social environments; one has its principal field among intellectual careers, the world of thought—the other, the industrial or commercial world.

ROBERT SCHMITT

The Desire for Private Gain

Capitalism has been attacked and defended on purely economic, as well as political, and on psychological grounds. Marx attacked capitalism for its economic performance, predicting that monopolistic practices would stifle competition, that the gap between the rich and the poor would continue to grow larger and larger, and that, finally, the system would break down completely under the strain of progressively worse and more frequent crises. The first of these predictions is widely recognized as valid. The second and third are more controversial. But they retain sufficient force for defenders of capitalism to have put more stress on the political and psychological justifications of the system. Thus they claim that political freedom, for example, can exist only under capitalism.[1] As Woodrow Wilson said: "If America is not to have free enterprise, then she can have freedom of no sort whatsoever."[2] And in terms of the psychological

Source: *Inquiry,* Vol. 16, 1973. Reprinted with permission of Universitetsforlaget, Oslo, Norway.

line of defense it is claimed that the desire for private gain is a fundamental human trait which, more than others, spurs men to activity. Capitalism, more than any other form of social and economic organization, gives free rein to this desire. It is, for this reason, peculiarly well adapted to human nature. Whatever capitalism's shortcomings, alternative systems stifle human initiative and thus are even less productive.

This paper will deal with the psychological defense of capitalism. From the very beginning, the theory of capitalism was closely linked to claims about human nature. Adam Smith stressed human "self-love" as a central motive for human actions.[3] Mill makes the link between the desire for private gain and the economy a matter of definition. He defines political economy as dealing with the "social phenomena in which the immediately determining causes are the desire for wealth."[4] In our century, since the spectacular, if temporary, collapse of the capitalist economy in the late twenties, and the close link of major industries to German National Socialism, as well as to repressive régimes all around the world, both the economic and the political defense of capitalism have been less persuasive. Current writers are, for instance, ready to admit that capitalist systems have tended to stifle free competition by means of monopolistic practices, that they have forced millions to work under extremely undesirable conditions, that they have not dealt adequately with problems of poverty. The performance of capitalism is not unambiguously successful.[5] Nor has it escaped notice that great wealth and right-wing sentiments often go together. Much weight is therefore placed by defenders of capitalism on claims about human nature. According to Frank Knight:

> ... there is in some effective sense a real positive connection between the productive contribution made by any productive agent and the remuneration which its "owner" can secure for its use. Hence this remuneration (a distributive share) and the wish to make it as large as possible, constitute the chief reliance of society for an incentive to place the agency into use. ... The strongest argument in favor of such a system as ours is the contention that this direct selfish motive is the only dependable method for guaranteeing that productive forces will be organized and worked efficiently.[6]

Whatever the shortcomings of capitalism, it is so peculiarly adapted to human nature that it will, more than any other system, induce people to make the most efficient use of the productive resources of their nation. For this reason, the performance of a capitalist economy can be expected to be better than that of alternative systems.

This passage claims explicitly that people, on the whole, strive for private gain—as much of it as they can get—and concludes from this that capitalism is the proper form of social and economic organization. But this conclusion follows only if we accept a further, implicit claim, namely that the desire for private gain is not a consequence of the capitalist social and economic arrangements but, instead, motivates the actions of all mankind. The defense of capitalism would be totally implausible without this second, implicit assumption.

In this paper I want to accept the first, explicit claim about the pervasive behavior in our society, but reject the implicit one about the universality of this behavior. As a consequence, I shall also reject the attendant defense of capitalism.

Let us, first, be clear about what is not at issue.

There has been a good deal of discussion, in recent years, of the connections between motives and causes. It has alternately been asserted and denied that motives are causes. This controversy is not relevant here.* The claim made by Knight is an empirical one about the pervasiveness of a particular motive, not a conceptual one about all motives. Nor is Knight, presumably, making any ethical claims about the ethical justifications of a perfectly (or imperfectly) competitive market or about the goodness of competing. The defense rests on one normative assumption, namely that an efficient use of resources is preferable to an inefficient one. That, too, is not an ethical claim but an economic one. It is, moreover, not a controversial assumption.** For the rest, the argument deals with relations of ends and means: If efficient use of resources is sought, then an economy that appeals to the desire for private gain will come closer to achieving the desired end.

This argument rests on the assumption that the springs of behavior

---

* The psychological defense of capitalism seems to include the claim that the desire for private gain is a necessary condition for a large class of human actions. If one could show that motives are not causes, this would serve to invalidate the psychological defense unless the notion of causation used were to exclude the notion of causes as necessary conditions. The relevance of the question whether motives are causes thus depends entirely on what sense one gives to the concept of cause.

** The concept of efficiency has a technical use in economics. It is doubtful, however, that it can be defined, in this technical use, without drawing on the apparatus of the capitalist economic model. To use the term *efficient* in this technical sense in the defense of capitalism would clearly beg the question at issue. The sense in which *efficient* is used in this defense must, therefore, be an informal nontechnical one in which the assumption is, indeed, noncontroversial, if only because it is rather vague.

of men under capitalism are no different from what motivates behavior in differently organized societies. As an empirical claim, this
is hard to refute.[7] But if we consider the concept of motive with
some care, we can see that the behavior of men under capitalism is
not caused by the desire for private gain but is, instead, a consequence
of living in a capitalist society.

In the course of this paper, I shall argue . . . that we talk about a
person's motives when we need to make clear the links between his
actions and the circumstances under which they occur. This is the
primary use of talk about motives. Secondarily, we talk about motives
as the sort of links that we find frequently between certain kinds of
actions and the range of situations in which these actions normally
occur. A particular motive is identified by citing, on the one hand,
the action which it motivates and, on the other hand, other actions
which we expect from a person susceptible to this particular motivation. Thus individual motives like "ambition" or "desire for private
gain" name lists of actions that flow from having these particular
motives. We can explain what it is, say, to desire private gain by
listing what a person with that motive will do.

After having clarified some important features of talk about
motives, I will proceed . . . to apply the results of this discussion to
a specific motive, the desire for private gain. The demonstration that
desiring private gain is not a universal human desire but is, on the
contrary, just the sort of thing that people will do in a capitalist
society, will follow. In fact, we call a society "capitalist" because in
it one will do the sorts of things by reference to which we identify
peoples' motives as the desire for private gain.

There are some obvious questions to be raised about the alleged
pervasiveness of the desire for private gain. Economists talk about it
a great deal. But when philosophers discuss motives, they mention it
extremely rarely and then only with some doubt as to its existence.
Professor Anscombe refers to the "desire of gain" as an instance of
a popular conception that lacks clarity.[8] We may well ask whether
this desire for private gain exists as a distinct motive.

If we decide that such a motive does exist, we need to ask further
how it should be described. Economists use a variety of related but
not identical expressions. Adam Smith speaks of "self-love," Mill of
"desire of wealth." Others speak of a motive for "profit maximiza-
tion" or a "private profit motive." What are the essential features
of this alleged motive and how does it differ from motives more
familiar to us?

Finally, there seems considerable implausibility to claiming that
the desire for private gain, however it is to be specified in detail, is

the all-pervasive motive that economists claim it is. People act from all kinds of motives: ambition, love, resentment, greed, or generosity, etc. There is no particular reason to assume that the specific class of actions that economists are primarily concerned with, namely competing in the market for goods and services, should by and large have only one motive and thus be strikingly different from all other classes of human actions. The economists' claim for the universality of the profit motive seems particularly implausible in the light of the fact that no sharp distinction can be drawn between a man's actions in the marketplace and those outside of it. It is not easy to find examples of behavior that are not "market behavior."

These are empirical questions, of course, but we will not be able to answer them unless we have a fairly clear idea of how one identifies motives, how one distinguishes one motive from another, and how one tells when one has anything approaching a complete characterization of a motive.

Philosophers have in recent years spent a good deal of energy on a variety of controversies respecting motives. They have argued whether motives are causes or not, whether all actions have motives or only some, and whether motives are inner, mental goings on or whether to speak about motives is to make predictions about future behavior. But none of these controversies, including the last which addresses itself to the question What is a motive? has ever faced the question of identity criteria for motives. Philosophers participating in these controversies begin their papers with a few examples of motives and argue about them. The concept of a motive is generally specified by ostension and not by philosophical analysis. That this is a serious oversight is nowhere more obvious than in the context of the present controversy. A reasonable understanding of the identity criteria for motives shows up the psychological defense of capitalism as a sham. Without such criteria it has seemed to be, at least, plausible.

Philosophers have given a surprisingly varied list of examples of motives:

Character traits as, e.g., ambition, diligence, greed
Long-lasting emotions like resentment
Moods like depression
Inclinations like "an interest in symbolic logic"
Feelings like feeling threatened
Mental acts like making a decision
Mental states like intending
Capacities like stupidity
Physical feelings like sexual desire

Convictions like patriotism
Attitudes like optimism
Needs like being hungry or thirsty
Habits like being punctual

There are several questions concerning identity criteria to be raised about these instances of motives. First, What determines whether a phenomenon shows up in one's list of motives or not? I.e., what are the criteria for being a motive rather than something else? Second, given that we have decided that a given phenomenon does belong on our list of motives, what serves to distinguish it from other items on that same list? This question has two subparts: How do we decide that two motive descriptions are not descriptions of the same motive? How do we decide that two motive descriptions are descriptions of the same motive?

WHAT DISTINGUISHES MOTIVES FROM OTHER PHENOMENA?

The list of motives includes a wide variety of mental or physical phenomena. While all of them may function as motives at one time or another, not every emotion, feeling, mood, capacity, or sensation is a motive. Talk about motives fits into a very specific context, namely the context of explaining why someone acted or refrained from acting in specific ways. But we say many other things about people besides trying to explain their actions. We describe, criticize, exhort, flatter, etc. In all those cases we may speak about emotions, capacities, etc., but we are not always speaking about motives. Any of the items on the list may be called a "motive" when we try to explain an action. But any of them can function in contexts where no action is involved. Not all the feelings I have at any moment, or sensations, or capacities, have a bearing on what I am doing. They do not function as motives at that time.

Some states of persons function as motives in contexts where they affect action. We refer to motives, therefore, to explain actions. But not all explanations of actions are motive explanations. "I killed him because he killed my brother"[9] is a perfectly good explanation but does not involve, nor does it require, mentioning a motive. But in many situations we do not feel that an action has been explained adequately if we only know the surrounding circumstances. "I killed him because he asked me for money" is not a transparent explanation. If someone asks you for money, you might give a number of responses that would be more readily intelligible. Any attempt to make that action more intelligible might very well begin with more details about the situation in which I act. ("He was blackmailing me.") One might specify in more detail the character of the other person or the history of our relation. If, after a more complete account of the situation, it still remains unclear why I acted, I may then begin to talk about my motives. Motive explanations serve a very specific function: they bridge the gap between action descriptions and descriptions of the environment in which the action takes place. Where the relation between the two is not intelligible, talk about motives will often help. "He had asked me for money so many times before. When he asked me again, I flew into a blind rage."

The function of motive explanations, in turn, throws light on the nature of motives. The fact that "I killed him because he killed my brother" is an adequate explanation does not prove, as Anscombe thinks, that there are no motives for the action. The explanation, to be sure, is adequate for us. It might not be for a visitor from a tribe that does not know about revenge. To him we might have to speak about motives. Motives provide the link between the agent's environment and his actions. Given a certain situation, a person may act or he may not act. If he does act he may act in different ways. Whether he acts at all and what he does depends on how he perceives the situation, on his beliefs about the situation as well as on his beliefs about what it is good to do in given situations. His actions are further determined by his needs, by any number of attitudes, by his abilities, his short-term and long-term emotions. All of these go to make up the rather heterogeneous list of phenomena that philosophers provide as examples of motives, because all of them function in similar ways in establishing the connection between a situation and the action a person takes in that situation.

The common feature of all the phenomena that may function as motives is not easy to specify. The temptation to call them "inner" states or events must be resisted. For such a designation seems to suggest that we know our motives by introspection and I shall argue that that is not true. What I shall have to say about motives implies that it is a mistake to differentiate motives from actions as what is "inner" from what is "outer" or public. To draw the distinction between motive and action in that way is not so much false as misleading. Philosophers who have drawn the distinction in that way have done so because they did not reflect sufficiently upon the wide variety of phenomena that function as motives. It will therefore be more useful to mark off the sorts of phenomena that can function as motives by saying that no phenomenon that can be ascribed to a dead body or to a person in a coma for a long time can function as a motive. Such a person has no capabilities, no moods or emotions. His needs and attitudes have disappeared.

With this beginning for a criterion for motives in hand we may now go on to the second question.

WHAT SERVES TO DISTINGUISH ONE MOTIVE FROM ANOTHER?

That question has two parts, namely what the meaning is of "same" and of "different" when we speak about individual motives. We know what is meant by "same" as applied to motives if we have some idea of how we identify any particular motive. That question, in turn, subdivides into how we identify our own motives and how we identify those of others.

There is a controversy concerning what sorts of data we use to identify our own motives. On the one hand, some philosophers believe that I introspect to determine what my motive is in any given case. On the other hand, other philosophers want to deny that introspection plays any role in the identification of my own motives. They claim that I identify my motives by my actions actually performed and by my propensities to act in certain ways. A look at the list of the sorts of phenomena that philosophers cite as examples of motives shows that this is a pointless controversy. For, on the one hand, I do know by introspection, by direct acquaintance with myself, that I am hungry and what I am hungry for. I know in similar ways what I believe, what I intend to do. Insofar as desires, beliefs, and intentions are among the phenomena that may function as motives, it seems clearly true that some of them are known to me by introspection. It is equally clear, if we go back to our list, that not all of the phenomena that sometimes function as motives are known to me in that way. I may know by introspection that I am angry now, but my character trait, irascibility, is not known by introspection. To say that someone is irascible is to say that he is often and suddenly angered. One can know that about me only by observing the frequency of my anger and its suddenness. The same is true of capacities. I don't know introspectively that I am intelligent. Neither do I know my attitudes, like optimism, in that way. It is clear that some of the phenomena that may function as motives may be known introspectively and others not.

These observations settle the controversies between those philosophers who claim that I know all my motives exclusively by introspection and those who deny that introspection enters into knowledge of my motives at all. But they do not settle the really interesting question, namely whether I ever know *completely* by introspection what motivated an action of mine.

Some of the phenomena that may function as motives are completely identifiable by introspection. I identify a sudden craving for black bread and cheese by having the craving and in no other way. I do not need to wait until I go into the kitchen to find out what I am hungering for. In fact, I may decide to resist the craving so that it does not motivate any action. I can still identify the feeling however. But the *motive* is not identified by identifying the craving for bread and cheese. It is analytic that identifying a motive is identifying something about me that is connected to an action. To ascribe a motive to someone is not merely saving something about his "inner" states; it implies that he performed an action. Thus identifying a motive involves reference to an action produced by that motive. A motive is therefore not completely identified by introspection, because you also need to identify the action motivated.* This fact has escaped notice because motives are most frequently discussed in the context of the explanation of actions, where the action motivated is given to begin with. In such contexts it often seems to philosophers that one can talk about motives without mentioning actions explicitly.[10]

References to actions may be more or less specific. At one end of the spectrum is the reference to an action, any action whatsoever. At the other extreme is the reference to a certain action, performed by a certain agent at a certain place and time, with the smallest time span compatible with anything being called an action. Pulling the trigger takes less time than shooting the gun, beginning to squeeze the trigger takes less time than either. "Beginning to squeeze the trigger" is thus a relatively more specific action description.

In order to identify any state of the agent as a motive it does not suffice to refer to any action whatsoever; the reference must be to the action brought about by the motive. "He acted from ambition" is incomplete. The motive is completely identified only by "in x-ing he acted from ambition," where any number of plausible candidates can be substituted by "in x-ing," but "in surrendering all chances for satisfying his ambition" cannot. If we identify an actual motive ascribed to an actual person, we need to refer to the actual action thought to be produced by that motive. Talk about motives occurs primarily in explaining actions, specifically by establishing the link

---

* Having a certain feeling is partial evidence for ascribing a certain motive to oneself. The absence of that feeling, however, is very weak evidence for denying that one has that certain motive.

between a given action and the surrounding conditions. Parasitic on this sort of talk about motives are situations where we speculate whether someone had the requisite motive to perform an action (for instance, if we do not know whether he did perform the action in question) or where we praise or condemn certain classes of motives (as when we disapprove of being competitive) or say what sorts of motives, generally, move certain sorts of people to do certain sorts of things. In these and similar contexts, we talk about motives as the sort of thing that explains many instances of actions in the most common circumstances. Thus a secondary use of "motive" consists of talking about what is frequently true of agents when they perform certain familiar kinds of actions. It is in this secondary sense that I shall say, below, that motives are identified by lists of actions.

It would be a mistake to argue that motives are completely identifiable without reference to actions motivated and that reference to actions is only needed in order to provide evidence for ascribing a motive to a person. With the same feeling, a considerable range of actions may occur. If I suddenly crave black bread and cheese, but find none in the kitchen, I may go back to my study disappointed or I may decide to make do with white bread. I may go down to the neighbors to borrow some black bread, or rush to the store, or begin baking bread. If we claimed that "craving for black bread and cheese" is a complete description of a motive, then we could hardly count "eating white bread and cheese" as unambiguous evidence for ascribing that motive to the agent. What we must do, instead, is to say that the desire for black bread and cheese is such that the substitution of white for black bread is acceptable. That tells us something about the motive. A desire that allows substitutions in the goods satisfying it is different from one that allows no substitutions. Some desires are more specific than others. A desire that can be deferred is different from one that I must satisfy at all costs. Some desires are more urgent than others, some stronger than others. We completely identify motives in these respects only by citing the actions the motives bring about.

The same point can be made about intentions. I can identify intentions introspectively. As motives, I can fully identify them only by speaking also of the actions that I perform in acting on the intentions. For then I must say something as to the specificity of the action intended and how firm my intention is, in the face of difficulties. The same holds for beliefs. I know in many cases what I believe. How firmly I hold a belief and what I regard as instances of the belief, both of which are important when beliefs motivate actions, can be stated only by talking about the actions motivated.

The cases discussed are the most favorable to the view that we know our motives by introspection alone, because they are all cases where the corresponding facts about persons are so identifiable. In many cases inner phenomena are not at all or only very imperfectly identifiable by introspection. In those cases, it is much more obviously true that to identify a motive is to identify the action motivated. Playing slot machines, I begin to feel greedy. But my feelings are not specifically feelings of greed, they are feelings of excitement, of deprivation and need which, in different circumstances, I would identify rather differently. The introspectible data in a case like that are not even adequate for identifying the feeling; even for that I need to talk about what I am doing. In order to identify a corresponding motive, talking about actions is even more indispensable. This is more unambiguously the case with those so-called inner phenomena, like character traits, that are not at all identifiable by reference to introspection.

I have, so far, been speaking about identifying my own motives. It turns out that that involves identifying the actions motivated. Since I do not know anyone else's inner states introspectively, identifying the motives of others also requires identifying the actions motivated.[11]

But to identify the action motivated is not to identify the motive completely. One and the same action may spring from a variety of motives. It is that fact that makes motive explanations interesting. How do we differentiate motives if they eventuate in one and the same action? I attack a fellow philosopher intemperately at a public meeting. I defend my action on the grounds that I was motivated by a desire for truth. His views were totally false and needed to be criticized. Others think that I acted from desire to impress my audience, that I was motivated by ambition. One and the same action may be motivated by different motives. How is the difference between them drawn? It is clear, in the light of what has been said, that introspection may enter into the attempt to be clear about my motives but will not suffice to settle the question whether the desire for truth or ambition was behind my attack. For even if there are specifically ambitious feelings and even if, at the time I attacked the man's speech, I experienced some of these feelings, that does not suffice to establish that I did in fact act from ambition. I may well have been motivated by the desire for truth, all the while experiencing some twinges of ambition. Whether that is true is to be decided by looking at lists of actions. There are lists of actions for ambitious persons in particular situations. An ambitious academic does different things from the ambitious politician. There are for any given list, alternative lists. These are lists of what a person, differently motivated, would be expected to do in the same situations. There are complementary lists of situations in which, say, the ambitious man acts and the lover of truth abstains, and those situations in which the lover of truth speaks out but the ambitious keeps his counsel. All of these lists are incomplete. The accusation that I acted from ambition when I publicly attacked a fellow philosopher comes to saying that I can be expected to seek public victories of similar sorts, even in cases where there is no conceivable question of injury being done to the truth. The accusation also implies that I can be expected to be less outspoken in the defense of truth if to do so would interfere with the realization of my ambitions. The ambitious person can be expected to treat those above him in rank and status with deference and be disinterested in persons that cannot help to advance him. We can expect him to continue striving to enhance his prestige or power beyond points where other men would be content with their achievement. He will do work that is intrinsically repugnant to him if it promises to advance his ambitions. For the same reasons he will conquer fear, dislike for persons, fatigue. Love and friendship will weigh less heavily in his deliberations than satisfying his ambition. Here are fairly definite areas on the lists of actions, and situations, in which I can be expected to act, that constitute what we mean by "being ambitious." But to call someone "ambitious" is not to offer to predict all his actions in any conceivable situation. This is so for a number of reasons. Different persons are ambitious to different degrees. One man will ruthlessly sacrifice personal ties to his ambition; another may at a certain point give up his projects for the sake of seeing more of his family. People are, in the second place, ambitious in different ways. Thus the lists that identify their particular form of ambition are slightly different. One man may have his competitor murdered in order to run the rackets single-handedly. Another may try to achieve the same end by political manipulation and legal maneuvering. No list, finally, enables us to answer extravagant questions like "Would he murder his children if that would enable him to become President?" Nor can we tell, even of persons whose motives we understand fairly accurately, how they will react in great crises, in the face of death. To that extent our lists are incomplete and one's sense of what it means for a person to be ambitious remains indefinite.

Motives are, therefore, only in subsidiary ways identifiable by introspection, if at all. To describe a motive is to describe lists of actions that a person so motivated performs in a series of situations and a list of situations in which a person so motivated is liable to act.

To say, however, that the lists are incomplete is merely to recognize that the vocabulary we use to identify and discuss motives is beset by vagueness. There are many controversies about a person's motives that cannot be settled.

The preceding argument may, nonetheless, leave one wanting to say something like this: "But surely motives are something different from actions or lists of actions. They are not what a person does, but what occasions his doing what he does." The foregoing account does not deny this; in fact it insists on it. I have been talking exclusively about how we identify motives from other states of persons or how we differentiate one motive from another. I have been talking about how we explain actions, if they are not transparent, simply by reference to the surrounding conditions and how we explain what we are saying about a person when we explain his action by talking about his motives. There is a good sense in which I have not said what motives *are*. In the background of the entire argument is the belief that we do not know what motives are, we only know what they do. To know what motives in general and specific motives are we need to know a great deal more physiology that we do now. What moves one to act is a certain configuration of the body which, at present, we know nothing about. But this does not prevent us from distinguishing and identifying motives by means of incomplete lists of actions. Motives are for us a *je ne sais quoi* which we identify obliquely by talking primarily about actions and, in some cases, also about inner states of which we are aware introspectively.

If motives are identified by lists of actions and differentiated from other motives by contrasting lists of actions, there is no better way of answering the questions whether there is a motive properly called "desire for private gains" and what it is, than by listing the requisite actions and contrasting that list with an alternative one. My listing is obviously partial. A much more extensive listing, even of a very incomplete list, is possible. There are different lists for different persons since they are liable to be in different situations. I will suggest some members of the list for academics motivated by the desire for private gain and some of the alternatives:

- a. A person may write a book because a publisher offers to pay him for writing it. He may, alternatively, write one because he wants to, even if he cannot get money for it.
- b. A person may choose his job according to where he gets the highest pay, or he may, alternatively, be oblivious to the pay differentials between different jobs.

c. A man may take administrative work if it pays extra or, alterna-tively, set more time aside for philosophical reflection even if that means less income.

d. A person may seek the job that carries more prestige (e.g., teaching graduate students), or, alternatively, he may seek to do what he feels he is most competent to do.*

e. A person may strive primarily for the respect and recognition of his fellow academics, or he may, alternatively, seek to win the regard of those he teaches.

The list can be extended on and on.** Actions (*a*), (*b*), and (*c*) exemplify a person's using his intellectual interest and expertise as a means toward increasing his income. The alternative actions would be those of people not primarily interested in a higher income. Actions (*d*) and (*e*) illustrate operation in the academic market where people compete with each other. They find their justification not in their sense of their own competence but in performing activities that are highly regarded in the marketplace. The alternative actions are those chosen by a person who judges his own actions and does not judge them by what is currently in demand in the academic market.

For different occupations corresponding lists are easily con-structed. People choose whether to work or not to work, what to work at and where, by reference to monetary considerations. They judge the quality of work and the standards by which quality is to be judged by reference to what is well liked, i.e., is most saleable in the relevant market. By extending the list which I began, and con-structing other ones, anyone can convince himself that there is in fact a desire for private gain and what it is like. The power of this motive is so obvious that philosophers' doubts about it may well make one wonder what philosophers think they are doing.

---

* Teaching graduate rather than undergraduate students does not automatically produce higher income. But it carries more prestige and thus improves the per-son's position in the marketplace. He is in a better position to bargain and improves his chances to increase his earnings. Thus seeking a job with more prestige is a clear member of the list specifying the desire for private gain.

** For instance:

A person will teach what he can get paid to teach. Alternatively, he may refuse to teach anything but what he is competent and/or interested in teaching.

A man may teach although he does not like it and does not find it fulfilling because he gets paid for it, or he may refuse to undertake any work that does not fulfill him.

But is the desire for private gain a separate motive, say, from ambition or the desire to succeed in one's lifework? Given any particular action that can plausibly be said to be an instance of seeking private gain, which thus fits into the list of actions that we would expect someone who is seeking private gain to perform, is there an alternative list in which that same action would also belong, which might be the list for being ambitious, seeking power, or seeking fulfillment in one's chosen profession? Due to the incompleteness of lists, this question is difficult to answer. Insofar as the question does have an answer, we must give a negative one. Whether the desire for private gain is distinct from ambition or seeking fulfillment in one's work is not a question that one can discuss in abstraction from social and historical facts. We must specify the social arrangements under which those people are living into whose motives we are inquiring. In a capitalist society, I shall argue, the desire for private gain is, in fact, what ambition or seeking fulfillment in one's work come to.***

Is the desire for private gain as prevalent as economists claim? Since the question is indefinite, it need not detain us long. The following argument . . . will show that a capitalist society is characterized by the importance of this desire. This is not to say that all the actions or even most of the actions that I perform between getting up in the morning and going to bed at night are direct attempts to satisfy my desire for private gain. But it is to say that a large number of impor-

---

A student will accept the authority of professors he does not respect instead of recognizing as authority only those he does respect.

Teachers will be very critical of their colleagues who do not, by publishing (or in other ways) add to the prestige of their departments, or they may respect others for being what and who they are.

In placing graduate students, a department may be primarily interested in placing people in jobs where they will do the department credit, or they may be primarily interested in the well-being of the students placed.

A person may treat college administrators and trustees with more deference than his students, or he may treat people with the deference that he thinks a particular person deserves regardless of rank in the college hierarchy.

A person will submit his work, and thus himself, to the judgment of his professional colleagues, most of whom he does not know, or he will submit his work to the judgment of those whom he knows and respects.

A person will publish articles because he needs to get security and a raise in pay, or he may publish articles when and if he thinks others will profit from reading what he has to say.

*** The same answer holds for questions concerning the relation of the desire for private gain to the desire for truth, the desire for knowledge, and the desire to be of service to society, and whatever are the motives, more commonly cited, as moving people to become academics.

tant choices, particularly those connected with one's work, are determined by the desire for private gain.

In a capitalist society, goods and services as well as the means for producing goods and for providing services are owned by individual persons. Distribution of goods and services and productive capacities takes place in the market where individuals buy and sell. In its ideal state the market is perfectly competitive and in equilibrium. If it is perfectly competitive no individual buyer's or seller's activity in the market affects prices. If it is in equilibrium demand equals supply and prices are stable. In practice, equilibrium is the rare exception. Too many forces, like a change in supply due to good crops or natural disaster, and changes in demand due to fluctuations in size of population, errors on the part of entrepreneurs, miscalculations due to limited access to information, constantly keep prices fluctuating. Perfect competition is not attainable due to the large variety of goods and services, due to economies of scale, due to the economic advantages accruing from successful restraints of free competition. Under perfect competition, no individual has a sufficient slice of the relevant market to affect prices. Hence no one's actions in a market directly affect the conditions under which another person must operate in that market. In an imperfectly competitive market, on the other hand, or one that is not in equilibrium, the actions of one participant may affect the conditions under which others must operate. In that case, participants are in competition with one another. At any moment the actions of another may worsen my situation. As a consequence, economic security is at a premium in a capitalist society. The participants in the market not only try to buy cheap and sell dear; they must also constantly be on the lookout to consolidate their position in the market and to ward off potential threats to their position.

In a capitalist society, all goods and services are distributed by means of the market mechanism. This means that people will change jobs, change occupations, will leave their homes and move, if such a change will improve their earnings or their prospects for future earnings. Employers will replace employees, if that reduces their wage bill. Manufacturers decide what they will produce, not by what people need, but by what will be most profitable to produce. Whether one sells one's labor and gets wages for that, or owns machines and buys labor to produce goods and services, one's decisions are always guided by the consideration of increasing one's earnings. In short, one pursues private gain. The various ways in which a wage earner or an employer seeks to maintain or improve his position in the market constitute the list of actions to which we refer to explain what it means to seek private gain for people in these positions. Thus to say that a society is capitalist is to say that peoples' behavior conforms to the lists that define the desire for private gain. Seeking private gain, as defined by lists of behavior, is to operate in a market.

On the other hand, the sorts of things that people do from the desire for private gain can, in the vast majority of cases, only be done in a market economy. In a society where feudal or kinship relations determine the relations of worker to his work, he is not free to seek higher pay in different employment. Where people are tied to a particular plot of land by custom or by law, they cannot move at all. One can discharge a worker in a capitalist society to replace him by a machine but one cannot discharge a serf. Under a guild system, custom and law determine one's occupation and what one produces. One cannot switch products to follow the vagaries of supply and demand. The same is obviously true with reference to the more specific lists, cited earlier, that circumscribe the desire for private gain as evinced in the academic world. Where scholarship is one of the functions of a monastic institution, the individual scholar cannot act as an entrepreneur as he can, and must, when he operates in the academic marketplace. He is tied to his order. He is bound by rules to its discipline and the guidance of his superiors. At other times scholarship and learning were signs of good breeding, adopted by the aristocracy to distinguish itself from the commercial middle classes to whom it had lost its political power. In such a setting, where the point of being learned is precisely to set yourself apart from the people who trade, being a scholar for pay is out of the question.

None of this prevents a scholar, monk, or learned aristocrat from being, say, more deferential to those in power than to those that are powerless. Here is an action that belongs on the list by which we identify the desire for private gain but also occurs in different settings. But this simply points to the fact that single acts are occasioned by different motives, at various times, or, that we may ascribe more than one motive to a person in the light of only a single action, depending on what other actions we expect that person to perform in the future. One action may occur on more than one list. Entire portions of lists may occur on other lists. Lists specifying the desire for private gain may overlap with lists specifying different motives. But that overlap does not establish the universality of the desire for private gain. On the contrary, as long as large portions of that list can only occur in a capitalist society, it is quite clear that the list by which we identify the desire for private gain is indeed a defining feature of a capitalist economy. Here goods and services are apportioned by the market. This means that people display market behavior pervasively and thus can be said to be motivated by the desire for private gain. This desire is not a universal human trait. It defines capitalist man.

To all of this one may want to reply that the desire for private gain is universal after all, but that in different cultures it manifests itself in very different ways or is, to use the language of this paper, identifiable by reference to very different lists of actions. If one wants to talk this way, one cannot claim, however, that capitalism is defensible for being so peculiarly well adapted to the desire for private gain, because, on the present view, so is every other culture, for it too gives free rein to a list of actions which in that culture, we are told, must be used to identify the desire for private gain. The universality of the desire is here being maintained at the cost of saying that all cultures are equally well suited to its expression.

On the other hand, the defender of capitalism may say that granted there are different lists of actions that identify the desire for private gain in different cultures, nevertheless the motive force behind those actions is always the same. But that claim has been dealt with before. We do not possess any criteria by which to identify that inner force.

NOTES

1. See, e.g., Milton Friedman, *Capitalism and Freedom* (Chicago: University of Chicago Press, 1962).
2. Quoted in David Horowitz, ed., *Containment and Revolution* (Boston: Beacon Press, 1967), p. 28.
3. Quoted in Armen Alchian and William Allen, *University Economics* (Belmont, Calif.: Wadsworth Publishing, 1967), p. 10.
4. John Stuart Mill, *System of Logic* (New York: Harper, 1895), pp. 623-26. para. 3.
5. Frank H. Knight, *The Economic Organization* (New York: A. M. Kelley, 1951), esp. pp. 21, 36, 63, 73 and 77.
6. Ibid., pp. 11-12.
7. See George Dalton, ed., *Primitive, Archaic, and Modern Economics: Essays of Michael Polanyi* (Boston: Beacon Press, 1971).
8. G. E. M. Anscombe, *Intention* (Oxford: Clarendon Press, 1958), p. 18.
9. Ibid., p. 20.
10. The most recent instance of this is Paul M. Churchland's "The Logical Character of Action Explanation," *Philosophical Review* 74 (1970): 214-36.

11. J. J. Valberg in "Some Remarks on Action and Desire," *Journal of Philosophy* 62 (1970): 503-19 appears to argue against the sort of view I am defending here. In his formulation the view asserts that the description of a motive must refer to the action motivated. His refutation of that view rests on a very restrictive sense of *refer:* "A phrase P refers, definitely or indefinitely, only if there is an answer to: 'which thing does P refer to?' " (p. 509). The claim here is that only particular things can be referred to. The thesis that I am defending implies that classes and sorts of things can also be identified and, therefore, referred to.

THOMAS TORRANCE

Capitalism and the Desire for Private Gain

In his paper "The Desire for Private Gain: Capitalism and the Theory of Motives" [the article preceding this one], Richard Schmitt claims to have refuted what he calls "the psychological defense of capitalism." According to him, defenders of capitalism from the time of Adam Smith onwards have contended that since the desire for private gain is a fundamental human trait which in all societies spurs men to productive activity and since capitalism gives full rein to this motive, it is, as a system of economic organization, peculiarly well adapted to human nature and for this reason is liable to lead to a more efficient use of scarce resources than any alternative system.

In criticism of this line of defense, Schmitt complains that in recent years many of those who have engaged in discussion on the nature of motives have not considered the question of identity criteria for motives. This neglect is unfortunate, Schmitt claims, because "a reasonable understanding of the identity criteria for motives shows up the psychological defense of capitalism as a sham." Novel though Schmitt's approach is, I believe that it can be faulted on two counts: (*a*) even as Schmitt presents it, the psychological defense of capitalism cannot be overthrown by an argument concerning the identification of motives; and (*b*) the psychological defense is more subtle and persuasive than Schmitt appears to

Source: *Inquiry,* Vol. 17, 1974. Reprinted with permission of Universitetsforlaget, Oslo, Norway.

acknowledge, and hence his argument is to some extent misdirected. I shall consider both these objections in turn.

Schmitt bases his attack against the psychological defense on the supporting thesis that a motive cannot be identified by introspection, but only by compiling and contrasting lists of actions that a person moved by the motive in question would be expected to perform in a certain set of societal circumstances. In the last sentence, it is important to realize that the word *cannot* should be understood as "logically cannot." For Schmitt himself emphasizes that identifying a motive *logically* requires reference to actual or potential behavior occasioned within the agent's environment; on this point he writes: "It is analytic that identifying a motive is identifying something . . . that is connected to an action." Since few philosophers would wish to quarrel greatly with this thesis, having simply stated it we can turn without comment to the central part of Schmitt's argument.

At the beginning of his paper, Schmitt claims that the psychological defense of capitalism, as he construes it, relies for its plausibility upon the important but implicit assumption that "the desire for private gain is not a consequence of the capitalist social and economic arrangements but, instead, motivates the actions of all mankind." By assailing this assumption, Schmitt hopes to demolish the psychological defense of capitalism. However, in place of this assumption, we must ask which of the following two propositions he is advancing: (1) the desire for private gain is a consequence of capitalism, in the sense that in noncapitalist societies there do not exist the social conditions which causally generate the predominance of this motive in men; or (2) the desire for private gain is a consequence of capitalism, in the sense that in noncapitalist societies there do not exist the social conditions logically necessary for identifying this motive in men.

In reply, it seems that Schmitt's paper argues for proposition (2) rather than (1), if this is not the case, then it is very difficult to see the force or even pertinence of the passages that are about to be quoted. At one point Schmitt writes:

> desiring private gain is not a universal human desire but is, on the contrary, just the sort of thing that people will do in a capitalist society. In fact, we call a society "capitalist" because in it one will do the sorts of things by reference to which we identify peoples' motives as the desire for private gain.

And at another point he asserts:

> to say that a society is capitalist is to say that peoples' behavior conforms to the lists that define the desire for private gain. Seeking private gain, as defined by lists of behavior, is to operate in a market.

It thus appears that Schmitt's argument amounts to the following: the desire for private gain cannot motivate the actions of all mankind, because (given that the criteria for identifying the referent of the concept "society where men are motivated first and foremost by the desire for private gain" presuppose the criteria for identifying the referent of the concept "capitalism") one can only identify a motive as a desire for private gain by reference to the sort of actions performed within a capitalist society.

If, as I recommend, we now concede proposition (2), does this then dispose once and for all of the psychological defense? To allow that Schmitt has demonstrated that the desire for private gain is not a universal human motive, is of course to admit that he has achieved his aim as originally defined. His victory, however, is devoid of any great significance; for it is nevertheless possible to defend capitalism on psychological grounds in a way that places the argument beyond the reach of his criticism. For example as follows: The desire for material improvement is a more general motive than the highly specific desire for private gain, and can therefore be identified as that which occasions a considerable amount of human action in both non-capitalist and capitalist societies; but under capitalism (where the motive can be identified with logical propriety as the desire for private gain), the desire for material improvement can be utilized in order to produce a system of satisfying men's many needs and desires which is more effective in the allocation and use of productive resources than any other known system of economic arrangements. This version of the psychological defense is not, I submit, open to attack from an argument relating to identity criteria for motives; although actions stemming from the desire for private gain can only be identified in capitalist societies, actions occasioned by the desire for material improvement can be identified in almost every kind of society.

At this point it may be complained that I have ridden roughshod over Schmitt's argument, which is concerned with the desire for private gain and not with the desire for material improvement. However, if it is accepted that the desire for private gain is what the desire for material improvement becomes in capitalist societies, it is clear that defenders of capitalism would be both willing and happy to accept Schmitt's argument and conclusion. For nothing his motive-identification argument says or shows, touches the claim (which can be used in support of capitalism) that the desire for material improvement can be employed most effectively in a capitalist society. Thus although Schmitt may indeed have successfully established that the desire for private gain is not a universal human motive, he fails to obtain what he *really* wants: a proof that capitalism cannot be defended on the grounds that "it is so peculiarly adapted to human nature that it will, more than any other system, induce people to make the most efficient use of the productive resources of their nation."

It seems to me that the only way to destroy the above contention (which is the assertion all formulations of the psychological defense seek to buttress), is to prove a slightly altered version of the causal hypothesis advanced by proposition (1). This altered version avoids all reference to the desire for private gain and is simply the claim that the desire for material improvement is not to be widely found in noncapitalist societies but is largely something causally produced in men by the capitalist process itself. I do not propose to argue the pros and cons of the matter, but will content myself with the comment that *if* it could be established that the desire for material improvement is more or less a universal human motive, then this would obviously be of some value for a defense of capitalism.

So much for the first objection against Schmitt. The second objection is that the psychological defense as employed by Adam Smith and his intellectual heirs is more powerful than Schmitt seems to grant. If well stated, the defense does not merely amount to the position that capitalism by giving opportunities for self-interested actions is superior by virtue of its impressive ability to elicit greater productive effort on the part of individuals, but is rather the position that under capitalism (and capitalism alone of all known economic systems) the pursuit of what is in one's own self-interest is not antithetically opposed to service to one's fellow men. That is to say, unlike what takes place in societies whose economic life is not based on the functioning of a market price mechanism, under capitalism one man's gain is not necessarily another's loss; for under capitalism, self-interested actions on one's own part have unintended consequences that are very often beneficial for many others.

The classic exposition of this view is to be found in the following well-known passage from Adam Smith's *The Wealth of Nations* (Bk. IV, Ch. 2):

> ...every individual necessarily labours to render the annual revenue of the society as great as he can. He generally, indeed, neither intends to promote the public interest, nor knows how much he is promoting it. ...he intends only his own gain, and he is in this, as in many other cases, led by an invisible hand to promote an end which was no part of his intention. Nor is it always the worse for the society that it was no part of it. By pursuing his own interest he frequently promotes that of the society more effectually than when he really intends to promote it.[1]

Thus when fully expressed, the psychological argument for the defense of capitalism has two parts. (*a*) under capitalism, the opportunities for self-interested activities are maximized and this provides an enormous incentive for men to work; and (*b*) under capitalism, men's self-interested actions lead to a more efficient deployment of scarce resources than could be achieved by any alternative method, and hence the whole population benefits even though this consequence is no part of the entrepreneur's direct intention. It is to be admitted that the second of these two parts does not belong to what perhaps we would want strictly to call the psychological defense of capitalism; nevertheless it is so closely bound up with the purely psychological part, that the two parts should not be examined in isolation from each other.

Now again, I do not wish to argue for or against the matter in hand. But since what I take to be the second part of the psychological defense when fully developed, has been and is still presented as the most compelling argument in favor of capitalism,[2] it is worth just stating in outline its main tenets. Very briefly, therefore, the second part maintains something like this. A market economy by allowing individuals the freedom to act according to what they take to be their own best interest vis-à-vis such features of the price mechanism as prices, costs, and profit rates (which emerge as the results of the continuous interplay between the self-interested actions of all consumers and producers in the economy) is able to make better use of the huge amount of knowledge in society relating to peoples' needs and desires than an economic system under which all decisions concerning what is to be produced and in what quantities, etc., are made in accordance with the plans laid down by a central planning agency. For the plans of such an agency would be largely arbitrary (i.e., their implementation would result in the production of many goods that were not in demand, and in the nonsupply of many goods that were in demand), because no central authority could even begin to acquire, let alone be able to make use of, all the knowledge which would be required to satisfy the numerous and differing needs of each member of the economy over which it had control.[3]

Even if the various claims comprising the psychological defense could be proved, no one in his right mind would want to conclude that capitalism is perfect; Schmitt correctly mentions the growth of monopolies and the decline of competition as an extremely undesirable feature of present-day capitalism (but a feature, incidentally, whose appearance is not "inevitable" in an historicist sense, but one which could be removed by vigorous governmental action). Indeed, the most that the psychological defense could possibly establish is the modest statement that of all workable economic systems currently available, capitalism (or more accurately, the mixed economy, i.e., private plus some state enterprise) is the least unfavorable.

NOTES

1. Adam Smith, *The Wealth of Nations,* 5th ed., ed. E. Cannan (London: Methuen, 1961), vol. 1, pp. 477-78.
2. See, e.g., F. A. von Hayek, *Individualism and Economic Order* (London: Routledge & Kegan Paul, 1949), esp. pp. 77-91; M. Polanyi, *The Logic of Liberty* (London: Routledge & Kegan Paul, 1951), pp. 111-37; and K. R. Popper, *The Poverty of Historicism* 2nd ed. (London: Routledge & Kegan Paul, 1962), pp. 89 ff.
3. It is interesting to observe that even a few economists in Eastern Europe are prepared to defend this particular point to some degree. In a paper Béla Csikós-Nagy, *Pricing in Hungary* (London: The Institute of Economic Affairs, 1968) published a few years ago on economic reforms in Eastern Europe, the chairman of the Hungarian Board for Materials and Prices writes: "Hungary is trying to transform her economic system from a centrally directed one into a controlled market economy. We proceed from the propositions that without government planning no purposeful development can be achieved *and without market relations no rational allocations can be realised*" (p. 7, emphasis added).

3.

Competition

The pursuit of profit is a fundamental principle of our economic system. Everyone, in theory (and for the most part, in practice), is trying to get more; however, since there is only a limited amount of what everyone wants, competition ensues. As one embarks on one's journey to become a millionaire, one must face a salient, and perhaps disturbing, fact: Others also want to become millionaires, and in the resulting competition, not everyone will be successful.

Not only those who are interested in great wealth have to compete. Our business system is infused with competition at every level. Car companies compete for sales, television networks compete for ratings, giant corporations compete with each other to attract investments, corner gas stations compete for customers, accountants compete for jobs, and individual consumers compete to get scarce items. Every firm and every individual that desires to make any gain must enter the competition.

Those who disapprove of this all-pervading competition have called it the "rat race." What these critics see is a system in which everyone is scurrying, seeking, and fighting in order to collect a few grains of corn. Such a life may be adequate for lowly rodents, but it is not thought to be dignified or beneficial for human beings.

Whether this kind of criticism is justified, and whether the competition of our system is all pervasive and destructive, are the subjects of this section. Many people believe that the "rat-race" view is the truth about this issue; however, in order to see if the system does turn people into combative rats, one must have an idea of what competition is and how it occurs in the business system.

A good place to begin a discussion of competition is with the definition of it given by the English philosopher Thomas Hobbes. In chapter thirteen of the *Leviathan,* his major work, he said that competition occurs when "two men desire the same thing which nevertheless they cannot both enjoy."[1] Underlying Hobbes's view of competition is a certain belief about human nature. For Hobbes, human beings are creatures who continually have new desires and who deem important the satisfaction of these desires. If our desires did not so urgently demand satisfaction, the problem of competition might never arise.

But there is competition, and it occurs in those cases in which the unsharable object of one individual's desire is also the object of desire of another individual. We all have an urgent desire to breathe air, but, for the moment, there is enough available air so that each of us can take his share without interfering with others. However, such abundance is not commonplace. In many areas, there is not sufficient water or land for everyone to have as much as he desires; as people strive to get as much of these items as they want, or as they think they need, competition inevitably results. As Hobbes also pointed out, people compete for nonmaterial things such as honor and glory, which of necessity cannot be shared by everyone. Thus, for Hobbes it is the limited supply of the things that people desire combined with the determination of people to get what they want that causes competition to occur.

This is a general view of competition, and while it provides a framework for thinking about this subject, it also includes a number of different types of competition between which it would be useful to distinguish. The following four cases all fit Hobbes's view about competition; yet they are different in some important respects.

Consider this case: Explorer A is endeavoring to reach the South Pole on horseback. He knows no one has ever done this before; and if he is successful, he will gain a line in the *Guinness Book of World Records,* which he desires very much. A believes that no one else has the same goal; however, unbeknownst to A, explorer B from a different country is approaching the South Pole on horseback from the other way, and he has the very same motive. B also is unaware that he and A desire the same goal. One who knows all these facts can see that A and B are competing though they have no knowledge of each other and do not know that anybody else is pursuing the goal of being the first person to arrive at the South Pole on horseback.

Case two: Scientist C is working in New York on a cure for cancer. He knows that if he is successful he will win the Nobel Prize, and he wants it very much. He knows it is likely that there are other people in other places also working on this problem, but he does not know who they are.

Case three: Scholar D is working in Los Angeles trying to find the answer to some esoteric problem in the understanding of the pre-Socratic philosophers. The thought of the fame in his profession that he will gain if he is successful motivates him. Scholar D knows, however, that scholar E in San Francisco is working on exactly the same problem. D knows that E is getting close to the solution and that if he does not find the answer quickly, scholar E will gain the recognition of the profession.

Case four: Boxer F wants to be the world heavyweight champion. In order to gain this goal, he must defeat boxer G. Boxer G wants to retain the championship, and in order to do so, he must defeat F.

These four cases represent different types of competition. In case one, the competitors are unaware of each other and of the fact that they are competing. In case two, the competitors know they are competing; however, they do not know who their competitors are. In cases three and four the competitors know they are competing and they also know exactly who their competitors are. Case four is different from three and also from the other two, however, because in case four the competitor can only gain his goal by defeating some-one. In the first three cases, the competitors probably would wish that no one had the same goal. The fact that others do have the same goal can be considered as just another obstacle to be overcome. Each competitor in cases one, two, and three would have a better chance of achieving what he wants if his respective competitor were to dis-appear. In the boxer case, however, boxer F would not wish that no one else wanted to be heavyweight champion. If boxer F has already defeated a number of other boxers, so that he is the number-one contender, he may wish that the current champion would retire so that he could become champion by default. But he could have only become the number-one contender by defeating other boxers. If at the very beginning of his career all the other heavyweight boxers coincidentally had retired, boxer F's desire to be champion would not have been enhanced; instead, it would have been seriously ham-pered. In this case other competitors are not incidental obstacles; rather, they must exist if boxer F is to achieve his goal. The boxer case exemplifies the kind of competition I shall call *essential* com-petition. The other three cases are examples of what I shall call *incidental* competition.

There are, therefore, four types of competition. The factors in-volved are whether the competitors have knowledge of each other and whether the existence of the competitors is essential or incidental to the desired goal. As far as knowledge is concerned, there are three different possibilities. First, people can compete without realizing that there are other competitors. Second, people can realize competitors exist but not know who they are. Third, people can know exactly who the other competitors are.

These four cases all fit the general framework Hobbes supplied for competition. The problem now is to consider the ways these various types of competition are exemplified in our economic system.

First, consider the cases in which individuals and firms desire to sell either goods or services to buyers. It is not difficult to think of examples that fit into this category. Salesmen are constantly competing with each other as they try to interest customers in what they have to offer. Companies devise advertising that promotes the good qualities of their own products and emphasizes the negative aspects of their competitors' products. Banks offer all sorts of inducements to get investors to save with them rather than with some other bank. Individuals who are selling their houses or cars fix them up so that they will appear better than other houses or cars on the market.

In broader terms, sellers of all sorts, individuals and firms, compete with each other to get other individuals and firms to buy what they have to sell. For the most part, this type of competition is incidental, because people who are selling something probably wish that at least some of their competitors would disappear. It becomes much easier to sell one's goods, or to get a higher price, when there are not as many others trying to sell the same thing. When the number of competitors becomes smaller, the ability to achieve one's goal is enhanced. Also, in almost all cases, sellers are aware that there are others around who are competing with them. Often, individuals and firms know exactly who their competitors are; and, given modern systems of communication, it is not easy to think of examples in which two individuals (or firms) are unaware that they are in competition.

Another kind of competition between sellers occurs in cases in which workers compete with each other to get jobs. This type of competition occurs throughout our system, from the executive level to the labor level. It is a kind of selling, because in each instance, the competitors are selling their abilities. Competition of this sort is most like cases two and three (the scientist and the scholar examples), because almost all applicants for a job know that there are other applicants. They sometimes may even know who the other applicants are, and, most probably, every job candidate wishes he were the only one applying. Thus, competition between applicants for a job is almost always incidental.

In most cases of competitive selling, the parties know they are competing; however, there are examples in which two individuals might know that they are both selling the same item to the same market but still not think that they are competing with each other. Consider neighboring wheat farmers who are well aware that they are both selling their wheat to the same buyer. In fact, they might even discuss current prices over their back fence. They might not, however, say that they are competing with each other, because they undoubtedly get the same price for their wheat. It is not the case that one farmer will sell his wheat and the other one will not be able to.

To see that they are in competition, one must take a broader view and realize that there are many farmers, all of whom want to sell their wheat. Each one would probably like to sell it at a rate much higher than the market price, but he cannot because other farmers are willing to sell at the market price.

Suppose the current price for wheat is two dollars per bushel. What each farmer would really like is to sell his wheat for four dollars per bushel. Unfortunately, there are many other farmers willing to sell their wheat at the current market price; so, if anyone refuses to sell at this current price, there is the distinct possibility that he will not sell his wheat at all and thus end up with nothing. But if enough of the other farmers were to disappear, the market price would go up because there would no longer be so many willing to sell their wheat for only two dollars per bushel. And if enough farmers disappeared, and a satisfactory substitute for wheat were not found, the remaining lucky ones might even be able to sell their wheat at the highly desirable (for them, at least) price of four dollars per bushel. But because of the existence of many farmers who all desire the goal of high prices, this goal cannot be shared and, in fact, can be gained by none of them. This fits Hobbes's definition of competition, and it is most like, although not exactly like, the two explorers in case one. The two farmers we started with might not realize it; but those who know all the facts of the case, including the requisite part of economic theory, can see that they are competing with each other, as well as with all other wheat farmers.

Finally, there does not seem to be any example of competition between sellers that is like case four (the boxer case). In all probability, most sellers wish they did not have any competition. The goal of selling is to sell a product at the best possible price. If others are also trying to sell the same type of product, competition will result. However, if the competitors were to disappear, a seller's achievement of his goal would be enhanced rather than hindered.

Competition in selling is incidental and usually, but not always, involves knowledge of one's competitors. Competition in buying also has these characteristics. It is not difficult to think of cases in which individuals or firms are aware that they are competing to buy something. Individuals often compete in buying a house, companies compete in buying the right to natural resources, and employers compete in buying (hiring) employees. In these, and in innumerable other cases of competition in buying, the competitors almost always know they are competing; and because they all probably wish they were the only ones buying, the competition is incidental.

Another kind of competition in buying is similar to the wheat-farmer case. Two consumers in a supermarket, standing side by side looking at the tomatoes, might not feel that they are competing with each other, for, after all, there are enough tomatoes in the bin for both of them. But again, for reasons parallel to the wheat-farmer case, one can see that competition is occurring. These two shoppers are members of a very large group, all of whom desire tomatoes at lower than the market price. If the current market price is seventy cents per pound, the tomato sellers know that if a few shoppers refuse to buy at this price they can still sell their tomatoes to all the other consumers who are willing to pay what tomatoes currently cost. Even though all tomato buyers would prefer to pay only fifty cents per pound, because so many buyers exist who are willing to pay seventy cents, none of them can enjoy the low price he really wants. If enough of these buyers, however, were to disappear or lose interest, the price would go down, at least for a little while. The reason for the decline is that the tomato sellers would not then be able to find enough people willing to pay the seventy cents and they would have to lower their price in order to sell all the tomatoes. Again, the broader perspective shows that the original consumers are part of a very large group, all of whom are competing with one another even if the individuals in the group are unaware that they are competing.

So far, the concern has been with competition at the same level, i.e., the competition between sellers and the competition between buyers. However, competition also exists at the contact point between buyer and seller. Buyers and sellers are in competition with each other to get the best deal. The buyer would like to get a low price. The seller would like to get a high price. Both of them cannot get exactly what they would like at the same time, and so there is competition; but unlike the other examples that have been considered, this type of competition is essential. In the relationship between buyer and seller, it makes no sense for either one to wish that his respective competitor did not exist. It is essential that there be sellers; otherwise, the competition to get a good deal cannot occur.

Similarily, a seller of tomatoes cannot achieve his goal of the highest possible price unless he has customers.

Labor-management relationships also have the structure of essential competition. Management, in effect, is the buyer and labor is the seller. Each side is trying to get the best deal. This requires bargaining and negotiation in which each side tries to get as much as it can of what it wants. However, neither side can get what it wants if the other side does not exist. Management wants cheap, efficient labor, but this desire would be frustrated if all the workers were to move to other areas. Labor wants to sell its services for high wages and good benefits; but to get these things, there must be someone willing to pay these prices. If the company leaves the town, the workers are not in a position to get any deal, let alone a good one. In a labor-management relationship the opposing side is not just an incidental unfortunate obstacle that must be overcome in order for the goal to be reached. Each side needs the other before it can even begin to think about how it will achieve its desired result.

In summary, the competition between buyers and the competition between sellers is incidental and can fit into any of the three categories of competitor awareness that were distinguished. A buyer or seller may know exactly with whom he is competing, or he may know that he is competing with some others but not know who they are, or he may not even know he is competing. At the point of contact between buyer and seller, however, the competition is essential. In these cases each competitor needs the other party in order to gain what he wants.

The next question to investigate is what ethical concerns are raised by the different types of competition in the economic system. Again, Hobbes is a good figure to use as a starting point in this discussion. Hobbes thought that competition was the primary cause of violence among men. In *Leviathan* (again in chapter thirteen) he says that when individuals compete for what they cannot share ". . . they become enemies, and in the way to their end, which is principally their own conservation, and sometimes their delectation only, endeavor to destroy, or subdue one another." In this quotation Hobbes is talking about a situation in which there is no authority to control men's actions, but his point is one that concerns any type of competition. In a situation in which A and B want to achieve a goal they cannot· share, is it not the case that they will become enemies and do almost anything to defeat each other? A and B might not resort to violence, but will not the competitive aspects of their situation encourage them to lie, to cheat, and to do all sorts of underhanded things?

These questions also have been raised about competition in the economic system. Ethics is a study, at least in part, of what sorts of actions are morally right or wrong and thus is concerned with the question of what sorts of actions are encouraged by a system of pervasive competition. There is no easy answer to this question; for, as we have seen, there are different kinds of competition in our economy, and each one may be involved with a different set of actions. The kind of competition in which the competitors are unaware that they are competing would not seem to lead to the performance of actions generally considered to be immoral. If a person is unaware that he is competing, it is difficult to see how the fact that he is in a competitive situation can influence him to perform immoral actions.

In those cases in which a person knows he is competing but does not know who his competitors are, there is also no direct way to do anything immoral to harm the other people's chances of winning. Even so, the competitor in this type of case will try to enhance his own prospects, and if he desires this goal fervently but is also worried that his chances of winning are small, is it not likely that he will do something dishonest? Won't a seller try to give a distorted view of what he is selling? Won't a buyer try to give an inflated impression of the price he is willing to pay? And if honesty is one mark of an action which is moral, does not this kind of competition encourage dishonesty?

The temptation to do something immoral would even be stronger in those cases of incidental competition in which one person knows exactly who the competitors are. In this case, there is not only the temptation of dishonesty, but also the possibility of directly harming one's competitors. If a person knows that other specific individuals are obstacles in the way of achieving one's goal, will not the person consider actions that would remove the obstacle? Furthermore, if the goal is very desirable, and the obstacles very frustrating, would not the person be encouraged all the more to do anything to get rid of them?

The case against essential competition is stronger yet. To gain the goal in this case, one must defeat someone. One cannot just concentrate on one's own efforts and ignore the existence of the other competitors as one can in incidental competition. In this sort of situation, one must meet the competitor in order to win. In almost all competitions of the essential type, rules are specified to set limits for what the competitors may do; however, when the goal is to defeat someone, is there not great temptation to violate the rules? Won't the competitors try to discover actions that fit the letter of the rules but not the spirit of them? Won't actions of intimidation, humiliation, aggression, and deception be commonly practiced?

These are some of the questions that have been raised about the kinds of actions that can be expected in competitive situations. To raise these questions is not to suggest that the answers to them are obvious. The writers of the following articles consider these problems from very different perspectives and reach very different conclusions.

Another not completely distinguishable topic that all the writers in this section discuss is the effect of competition on people's characters. The actions that people perform in competitive situations lead to the development of certain character traits. Are these traits desirable from an ethical point of view? Are they the kind of traits that we generally approve of, or are they the kind of character traits that most people would consider undesirable?

This is a complex question. To answer it satisfactorily one must first be able to identify the traits that result from actions performed in situations of competition. This is not an easy matter; for as we have seen, there are different types of competition that occur in business, and each one may lead to different character traits. Another complicating factor is that the same trait is not always considered by everyone to have the same value. Critics of competition usually consider aggressiveness an undesirable trait, while defenders of competition often find it praiseworthy. Although none of the writers in this section concentrates on competition's effect on character in all of its complexity, all of them mention it and have interesting things to say about it.

Another aspect of competition is discussed in the article by Fred Hirsch. As I mentioned, competition takes place not only between sellers in our business system but also between buyers. This point is not often considered; however, Hirsch says that it has some important consequences. If what everybody wants is a "good life," and if a "good life" is characterized by such things as educational advantages, then not everyone can have a "good life." Educational advantages are competitive advantages, and thus not everyone can have them. When examined carefully, other aspects of a "good life" also seem to be competitive; and the results seem to be that our system, in presenting the goal of a "good life" to everyone, is, in effect, encouraging frustration.

Finally, business is not the only area of our life in which competition exists. We play competitive games, become educated in a competitive school system, and have competitive political and legal systems. The fact that competition is so pervasive in our lives probably indicates something about our ultimate ideals. We live in a society that considers competition to be an essential and inescapable fact of life, and we attach tremendous importance to winning the various competitions we participate in. This view of life is not, and has not been, universally accepted, and it is interesting to compare this "competitive ideal" with other ideals that people have held. Frank Knight is the only author in this section who tries to do this. He is fully aware of the problem involved in comparing different ideals. Ideals are used to evaluate actions and traits of character, but there is no clear way of evaluating the ideals themselves, for that would seem to require a higher ideal. This is a difficult problem, but Knight faces it squarely and discusses the ideal of competition in a way that has not been surpassed and has seldom been attempted.

NOTES

1. Thomas Hobbes, *Leviathan,* ed. Michael Oakeshott (London: Collier Macmillan, Ltd., 1962), p. 98.

H. B. ACTON

The Ethics of Competition

COMPETITION STRIFE AND RIVALRY

Critics of competitive markets often contrast the competition that is essential to such markets with noncompetitive cooperation. They believe that competition goes along with such characteristics as aggression, emulation, rivalry, conflict, and strife, and that cooperation belongs with mutual aid, benevolence, modesty, and harmony. In their view it follows, therefore, that economic competition is morally inferior to cooperative, noncompetitive modes of commercial and industrial organization. Right-minded people, it is assumed, are against strife and in favor of harmony and mutual aid. Modestly conducted cooperation, therefore, is superior to aggressive competition, and hence collectivist organization is to be preferred to what these

Source: *The Morals of Markets.* Copyright © 1971 by Longman Group, London, England. Reprinted by permission of the publisher.

critics call "the law of the jungle." Collectivists are on the side of the angels while supporters of competitive markets are the devil's disciples, helping him to bring misfortunes on the hindmost. Some, even, of those who support capitalism do so in a shamefaced way,[1] as they are convinced that in itself collectivism, being a form of cooperation and harmony, is morally superior to capitalism, even though, alas, human egoism makes capitalism inevitable.

We must now ask whether competition in free markets does have the morally obnoxious features we have just mentioned. Is it a species of strife, rivalry, emulation? Is it opposed to altruism, cooperation, and harmony? Is the only moral justification for competitive markets and capitalism that socialism is an ideal beyond human capacity to realize?

According to Dr. Samuel Johnson, competition is "the action of endeavouring to gain what another endeavours to gain at the same time." Johnson expresses this definition in morally neutral terms and brings out the central idea that in competition two or more people want and try to get what only one can have. He does not say anything about *how* they try to get it, since this depends upon what it is that they want and how it *can* be got. There certainly are what we might call competitive jungle situations in which animals seize food and run away with it or fight among themselves for it. Human beings sometimes do similar things, as when the members of a bingo club jostled each other as they pillaged presents intended for children at a Christmas party. Those who gain them do so as a result of strength or agility, but although some animals fight to the death, human beings generally confine their scramble within rules. With animals there may be no rules at all, and no conception of what is fair or unfair.* When "all's fair in love or war" human beings approach the jungle situation.

But let us now consider the sort of situation in which human beings compete for a prize or a job. In such situations the competitors may not meet one another and may not even know one another. When a prize is offered, say, for the best essay on Balzac or for the first correct solution of a mathematical problem, the winner of the competition is the competitor who does the required thing best or first. There has to be an awarding authority which makes the award according to certain rules. The essay has to be of such and such a length and has to be sent in by such and such a date. Applicants for

---

* Animals do generally confine their fights within rules, and so may be said to have some conception of what is permissible.

a job have to submit accounts of their qualifications, specimens of their work, and so on. If there is only one prize or only one job, then at least one competitor has to be unsuccessful.

We may now compare prize-competition situations with competitive jungle situations. In the latter, let us suppose, there are no rules and no awarding authorities. In the absence of rules, jungle competition may take place when there is enough for all, even though it is intensified when there is a scarcity. In price-competition situations, there is never enough for all, and there must be losers. Jungle competition often takes place by means of fighting, but this is not necessary to it, since by eating its food or occupying its space, a group of animals may destroy another group it does not come into contact with. For competition of either sort to involve rivalry, the competitors have to know one another, for when "rivalry" does not mean the same thing as "competition," it means the attempt of individuals or groups to outdo other individuals or groups, and this requires the rivals to have some knowledge of one another. It is possible to compete without knowing that one is competing, for someone might endeavor to obtain a prize or job without knowing that others are after it too. The essence of competition is that each competitor strives after what he wants. The essence of rivalry is that each competitor strives to outdo the others. In competition, the failure of the losers is a consequence of the success of the winners, not something that the winners aim to secure. Rivals, on the other hand, set out to *defeat each other* as well as to win the prize. To aim at defeating someone else comes somewhat closer to malevolence than mere competition does. Someone who endeavors to write the best essay in order to win the prize may have no desire to defeat anyone else, but rivals do endeavor to defeat one another. Friendly rivalry is possible, as in games, but even this can easily spill over into hostility.

In jungle competition, then, the competing parties may fight, and may act as rivals to one another. But even in this primitive kind of competition, fighting *need* not occur, and does not when a species of animal unwittingly destroys the food of another species. In prize or job competition, there is an awarding authority proceeding according to rules, as there is not in jungle competition. As in some sorts of jungle competition, the competitors for prizes or jobs may not know one another or have any personal contact with one another. If they know one another they can behave as rivals. Rivals can be friends, as in games, but rivalry has kinship with hostility and malevolence, because rivals endeavor to outdo one another as well as to do what will win them the prize. The existence of rules for competitions for prizes and jobs limits the things that can be done to win. Competitors at local flower shows have been known to destroy their rivals' blooms. But this sort of behavior is against the rules.

How, then, is economic competition related to the forms of competition we have now considered? It shares one important presupposition with them, that there is not an abundance of everything for everybody. If everyone could always get everything that he wanted, there would be no economic activity and no competition. Competition of all sorts presupposes scarcity, or at any rate a *belief* that what is wanted is scarce. (There might be enough food for all the animals who fight for it, but they fight because they do not know this.) Now competitive markets are not places where people fight, nor places where they pursue their rivalries. We have already seen that the attempts to outwit one another in what is called "oriental" bargaining are not features of developed markets, but can only make sense for parties who are ignorant of conditions of supply and demand. Rivalry comes in when political considerations are important, as with preemptive purchases in time of war. But in general, economic behavior in competitive markets is a peaceful sort of thing. Piracy and confiscation are uncommercial activities, and trade flourishes when goods can be inspected and moved about without danger from marauding bands. Exchange, as we have seen, is morally preferable to spoliation or entreaty.

These, however, are very general considerations, and we must now consider some forms of economic activity in more detail, in order to see what morally relevant forms economic competition may take. Let us consider, then, competition between firms for a contract, competition in the labor market, and competition to sell to ultimate consumers.

Competition for Contracts

When firms compete for a contract they are in a situation analogous to that between competitors for a prize or a job. Each firm tries to get the order for itself by considering its own technical resources and probable costs in relation to what it considers the ordering firm is willing to pay. Its knowledge that other firms are tendering discourages it from asking too much, and its desire to make as good a profit as possible makes it unwilling to ask too little. Knowledge, intelligence, and luck all affect the success of the enterprise. Rivalry need not enter into the situation at all, although, of course, it often does.

A spirit of rivalry could cloud the judgment of a firm or individual and lead to unprofitable courses. In trying to obtain an order, of course, the tendering firm does more than quote its price, it will laud its product. Its representative may entertain the potential buyer and flatter him. But a buyer who signs a contract because of the charm of the salesman rather than because of the economic merits of the deal may come to regret it and certainly will do so if he makes a practice of acting in that way. Both parties will judge the success of the contract in terms of eventual profit or loss and, in a competitive situation, are led by the hope of profit to cut their costs as much as they can.

It should be noted that there is impersonal competition between firms, just as there is impersonal competition between animals in the jungle. We have said that a group or species of animal, even without fighting, may deprive another group or species of its food or space, and in so doing may lead to its extinction. In the process of natural selection those animals which do not succeed in adapting themselves to their circumstances eventually die out. They may be devoured by others, or they may just be deprived of what they need by others which do not ever meet or recognize them. Something analogous happens between firms. A firm which makes and uses a new invention may cause other firms to go out of business or even bring about the extinction of a whole industry. The defeated firms or industries are not assaulted or threatened; they just cease to get orders. But the extinction of a firm or an industry is not the same sort of thing as the extinciton of an animal or a species. When the last are rendered extinct, particular animal organisms die and have no descendants. Physical death occurs. But the extinction of firms and industries does not necessarily involve the physical death of human organisms, even though a stockbroker may jump from the roof or handloom weavers die of hunger.* Bankruptcy may be described as economic death, but it is quite different from physical death. Firms themselves, indeed, may survive by changing the scope of their activities, and even if they are extinguished, the men who direct the work for them go elsewhere and work for other firms. Herbert Spencer's phrase "the survival of the fittest" applies, therefore, to firms as well as to animals and animal species, but in its economic application it does not imply the physical death of those that fail to survive, but only the cessation of some groupings and activities and the assumption and organization of new ones.

---

* The bankrupt stockbroker is generally "hammered" and the employees of dying industries are nowadays retrained, redeployed, or pensioned.

Competition between Suppliers of Labor

We may now consider some moral implications of competition in the market for labor. When workmen compete with one another for jobs and firms compete with one another for workmen, wages vary in terms of its supply and of the demand for labor. It is well known that for several generations from the end of the eighteenth century employers in industrial countries had the upper hand over those who worked for them. The population was increasing, new industrial methods were making traditional skills useless to those who had them, and combinations among workmen were legally regarded as criminal conspiracies. Furthermore, the society within which the industrial revolution was taking place was already divided into classes and accustomed to the exercise of authority from above. In these circumstances workmen tended to be the losers in wage bargaining, and their situation was improved when legal obstacles to the formation of trade unions were removed, and improved still more when trade unions were given legal immunity from claims for damages.

Nowadays groups of employers negotiate with trade unions, and in many industries no workman can get a job if he does not belong to a union, and may lose it if he does not strike when his union gives the order. Furthermore, it is a function of unions to prohibit unusually productive or efficient workmanship on the part of its members, and in this way competition between more efficient and less efficient workmen is prevented. Because of their need for votes, democratic political parties dare not seem to falter in advocating full employment. When there are more jobs than there are workmen to fill them, employers bid among one another for skilled men and in this way the total wages paid are often much higher than those negotiated between unions and employers' associations. At the same time there has been a growth of egalitarian sentiment, so that workmen are less inclined to fall in with their employers' wishes than they were in the nineteenth-century aftermath of aristocratic society.

Competition between Employers of Labor

When there is full employment and unions bargain on behalf of men who have little fear of losing their jobs, there is competition between firms for the skilled labor they find it difficult to obtain, but little competition between workmen applying for jobs. If competition promotes efficiency, then the absence of competition among workers is likely to lessen their working efficiency. Trade unions, furthermore, tend to discourage speed and efficiency of work, and in so doing they tend to diminish pride in achievement and workmanship. In such conditions unions are not the protectors of the workers against grasping employers—the employers may *want* to grasp, but they just cannot do so—but aggressive fomenters of increased claims. If they did not act in this way they would not retain their members, since the terms of trade favor the workers in any case. The trade unions are thus tempted to require all workers to become union men and to regard themselves as united claimants from what the employers willfully withhold from them. It is no longer a question of individuals competing for jobs as if they were prizes, but of the whole group extorting a collective prize for everyone. Bargaining comes into its own again, and the employers do well if they manage to settle for something less than the original demand. Instead of individuals competing with one another for scarce jobs, there are large organizations, maneuvering, compromising, bluffing, and striking to secure collective transfers of wealth. Instead of competing with one another, the workers support organizations which threaten and fight for them.

Under conditions of full employment, then, employers compete for labor, even when they do not compete with one another in other ways. Employees, however, do not compete among themselves, but pay spokesmen to bargain for collective benefits on their behalf. It is not a situation of emulation and rivalry between individuals, but one of conflicting collectivities. But even in these conditions the *impersonal* competition I mentioned above still continues. As invention proceeds, for example, some industries decline by comparison with others. Thus oil and gas gain by comparison with coal, and road transport by comparison with the railways. Declining private industries may get state subsidies, declining nationalized industries may get both subsidies and other privileges. But unless they can be kept in being as museum pieces, like the Swiss Guards at the Vatican, they are reduced or eliminated just like the unsuccessful firms in competitive market conditions. This competition is inseparable from the attempt to improve. Whenever someone tries to do something in a better way than it has been done before, others are faced with the choice of doing likewise or of being squeezed out. There may be no rivalry, no emulation, no struggle, no fighting, but just an exercise of originality or ingenuity by someone who has no intention of competing with or outdoing anyone.

Competition to Sell to Consumers

We now come to competition to sell to ultimate consumers and the ethics of the relationships involved. There is a sense in which the ultimate consumers compete among themselves, in that a buyer who is unwilling to buy at the price that is asked may realize that there are others who will pay that price. The sellers, of course, compete with one another in providing what the consumers want at prices they will pay. The sellers also compete with one another in offering the consumers commodities they had not thought of before.

Competition between sellers is not unlike competition between firms for contracts and raises no new issues except those connected with advertising. Competition between buyers is hardly felt as such in competitive markets. This is because most consumers arrange their purchases according to their means, and go to those shops where the things they can afford are on sale. In societies divided into classes, few individuals think much about expenditures outside or beyond their ability to pay. But the situation is rather different when everyone thinks it possible or thinks it right that he should buy everything that is on offer. Then he may come to regard the rich man who pays high prices as competing against him, with superior buying power, for goods that he would like to have but is prevented from affording. When there is a single, classless market, the feeling of being, so to say, "out-bought" by others is engendered. This encourages both demands for higher pay and demands for reductions in the spending power of the richer consumers. I suggest that competition between consumers is not emulative when they think of their budgets in terms of their resources. It tends to become emulative when they take seriously the idea of expenditure beyond the limits of their present income. In the nineteenth century and earlier twentieth, those who had such ambitions aimed first to acquire the money necessary to satisfy them. They tried to get better-paid jobs and they saved. But many consumers now hope for these results by collective measures exerted through trade unions and political parties. This is the reason why hopes and demands outrun resources and intensify the struggle for them. Whereas in the earlier forms of free competition individuals were encouraged to rely on their own efforts and abilities, in the system of cooperative conflict that has now emerged individuals hope to satisfy their desires by collective protection and pressure groups. The activities of individuals are merged into those of groups and masses.

Opponents of competitive markets often criticize the part played by advertisements in stimulating desire and demand. They assert that when competing firms advertise in order to encourage expenditure on their goods they stimulate a materialistic outlook and mold men's lives in doing so. It is true that advertisement can lead to increased sales,[2] but commercial advertisement is only part of the apparatus of persuasion that operates so massively in contemporary society. Ever since the eighteenth century, political leaders have been saying that each individual has the right to pursue his happiness, and the results of this belief are being experienced in our day. The "scramble" for consumption goods is due to the misleading belief that there is increased wealth to be had effortlessly for all rather than to economic competition. Individuals would be less willing to buy what advertisers tell them if they were more inclined to accept limitations on their desires. When, furthermore, governments encourage inflation, thrift becomes pointless except for those with very large incomes or very small outgoings or both. The inflation characteristic of our day results from the happiness-seeking moral outlook of our time as well as from clumsy attempts to apply Keynesian economic theories in democratic societies. Indeed, Keynes's economic theory was in part an expression of his opposition to the strenuous moralism of the Victorian era when it was generally considered right first to save and then to spend. This comes out in a passage of *The General Theory of Employment, Interest, and Money* where he writes, with reference to Mandeville's criticisms of the evils of saving:

> No wonder that such wicked sentiments called down the opprobrium of two centuries of moralists and economists who felt much more virtuous in possession of their austere doctrine that no sound remedy was discoverable except in the utmost of thrift and economy both by the individual and the state. Petty's "entertainments, magnificient shows, triumphal arches, etc." gave place to the penny-wisdom of Gladstonian finance, and to a state system which "could not afford" hospitals, open spaces, noble buildings, even the preservation of its ancient monuments, far less the splendours of music and the drama, all of which were consigned to the private charity or magnanimity of improvident individuals.[3]

In *The Fable of the Bees,* Mandeville called prodigality "that noble sin," and elaborated this by saying: "I mean the unmixed prodigality of heedless and voluptuous men, that being educated in plenty, abhor the vile thoughts of lucre." Keynes, like his friend (and rival) Lytton Strachey, disliked the puritanism inculcated in Victorian times, and Mandeville's easygoing hedonism was congenial to him. It has now become congenial to large sections of the population and in doing so has served to increase both the effective demand for consumer goods and the belief that they ought to be available for the asking. It is in this moral climate that advertisers of consumer goods operate, and there will be a "scramble" for them as long as this fundamental weather does not change. There is no consistency, and little honesty, in criticizing competitive advertising and at the same time proclaiming the right of everyone to as much as they can enjoy.

NOTES

1. H.F.R. Catherwood, *Britain with the Brakes Off.* In *The Christian in Industrial Society* (London: Tyndale, 1964). Mr. Catherwood had proposed the setting up of what were later called "Little Neddies" (p. 37).
2. Ralph Harris and Arthur Seldon, *Advertising in Action* (London: Hutchinson for the Institute of Economic Affairs, 1962).
3. J. M. Keynes, *The General Theory of Employment, Interest, and Money* (London: Macmillan, 1936), p. 362.

ALBERT Z. CARR

Is Business Bluffing Ethical?

A respected businessman with whom I discussed the theme of this article remarked with some heat, "You mean to say you're going to encourage men to bluff? Why, bluffing is nothing more than a form of lying! You're advising them to lie!"

I agreed that the basis of private morality is a respect for truth and that the closer a businessman comes to the truth, the more he deserves respect. At the same time, I suggested that most bluffing in business might be regarded simply as game strategy—much like bluffing in poker, which does not reflect on the morality of the bluffer.

I quoted Henry Taylor, the British statesman who pointed out that "falsehood ceases to be falsehood when it is understood on all sides that the truth is not expected to be spoken"—an exact description of bluffing in poker, diplomacy, and business. I cited the analogy of the criminal court, where the criminal is not expected to tell the truth when he pleads "not guilty." Everyone from the judge down takes it for granted that the job of the defendant's attorney is to get his client off, not to reveal the truth; and this is considered ethical practice. I mentioned Representative Omar Burleson, the Democrat from Texas, who was quoted as saying, in regard to the ethics of

Congress, "Ethics is a barrel of worms"[1] —a pungent summing-up of the problem of deciding who is ethical in politics.

I reminded my friend that millions of businessmen feel constrained every day to say yes to their bosses when they secretly believe no and that this is generally accepted as permissible strategy when the alternative might be the loss of a job. The essential point, I said, is that the ethics of business are game ethics, different from the ethics of religion.

He remained unconvinced. Referring to the company of which he is president, he declared: "Maybe that's good enough for some businessmen, but I can tell you that we pride ourselves on our ethics. In thirty years not one customer has ever questioned my word or asked to check our figures. We're loyal to our customers and fair to our suppliers. I regard my handshake on a deal as a contract. I've never entered into price-fixing schemes with my competitors. I've never allowed my salesmen to spread injurious rumors about other companies. Our union contract is the best in our industry. And, if I do say so myself, our ethical standards are of the highest!"

He really was saying, without realizing it, that he was living up to the ethical standards of the business game—which are a far cry from those of private life. Like a gentlemanly poker player, he did not play in cahoots with others at the table, try to smear their reputations, or hold back chips he owed them.

But this same fine man, at that very time, was allowing one of his products to be advertised in a way that made it sound a great deal better than it actually was. Another item in his product line was notorious among dealers for its "built-in obsolescence." He was holding back from the market a much-improved product because he did not want it to interfere with sales of the inferior item it would have replaced. He had joined with certain of his competitors in hiring a lobbyist to push a state legislature, by methods that he preferred not to know too much about, into amending a bill then being enacted.

In his view these things had nothing to do with ethics; they were merely normal business practice. He himself undoubtedly avoided outright falsehoods—never lied in so many words. But the entire organization that he ruled was deeply involved in numerous strategies of deception.

PRESSURE TO DECEIVE

Most executives from time to time are almost compelled, in the interests of their companies or themselves, to practice some form of deception when negotiating with customers, dealers, labor unions, government officials, or even other departments of their companies. By conscious misstatements, concealment of pertinent facts, or exaggeration—in short, by bluffing—they seek to pursuade others to agree with them. I think it is fair to say that if the individual executive refuses to bluff from time to time—if he feels obligated to tell the truth, the whole truth, and nothing but the truth—he is ignoring opportunities permitted under the rules and is at a heavy disadvantage in his business dealings.

But here and there a businessman is unable to reconcile himself to the bluff in which he plays a part. His conscience, perhaps spurred by religious idealism, troubles him. He feels guilty; he may develop an ulcer or a nervous tic. Before any executive can make profitable use of the strategy of the bluff, he needs to make sure that in bluffing he will not lose self-respect or become emotionally disturbed. If he is to reconcile personal integrity and high standards of honesty with the practical requirements of business, he must feel that his bluffs are ethically justified. The justification rests on the fact that business, as practiced by individuals as well as by corporations, has the impersonal character of a game—a game that demands both special strategy and an understanding of its special ethics.

The game is played at all levels of corporate life, from the highest to the lowest. At the very instant that a man decides to enter business, he may be forced into a game situation, as is shown by the recent experience of a Cornell honor graduate who applied for a job with a large company.

This applicant was given a psychological test which included the statement. "Of the following magazines, check any that you have read either regularly or from time to time, and double-check those which interest you most. *Reader's Digest, Time, Fortune, Saturday Evening Post, The New Republic, Life, Look, Ramparts, Newsweek, Business Week, U.S. News & World Report, The Nation, Playboy, Esquire, Harper's, Sports Illustrated.*"

His tastes in reading were broad, and at one time or another he had read almost all of these magazines. He was a subscriber to *The New Republic*, an enthusiast for *Ramparts*, and an avid student of the pictures in *Playboy*. He was not sure whether his interest in *Playboy* would be held against him, but he had a shrewd suspicion that if he confessed to an interest in *Ramparts* and *The New Republic*, he would be thought a liberal, a radical, or at least an intellectual, and his chances of getting the job, which he needed, would greatly diminish. He therefore checked five of the more conservative magazines. Apparently it was a sound decision, for he got the job.

He had made a game player's decision, consistent with business ethics.

A similar case is that of a magazine-space salesman who, owing to a merger, suddenly found himself out of a job. This man was fifty-eight, and, in spite of a good record, his chance of getting a job elsewhere in a business where youth is favored in hiring practice was not good. He was a vigorous, healthy man, and only a considerable amount of gray in his hair suggested his age. Before beginning his job search he touched up his hair with a black dye to confine the gray to his temples. He knew that the truth about his age might well come out in time, but he calculated that he could deal with that situation when it arose. He and his wife decided that he could easily pass for forty-five, and he so stated his age on his résumé.

This was a lie; yet within the accepted rules of the business game, no moral culpability attaches to it.

THE POKER ANALOGY

We can learn a good deal about the nature of business by comparing it with poker. While both have a large element of chance, in the long run the winner is the man who plays with steady skill. In both games ultimate victory requires intimate knowledge of the rules, insight into the psychology of the other players, a bold front, a considerable amount of self-discipline, and the ability to respond swiftly and effectively to opportunities provided by chance.

No one expects poker to be played on the ethical principles preached in churches. In poker it is right and proper to bluff a friend out of the rewards of being dealt a good hand. A player feels no more than a slight twinge of sympathy, if that, when—with nothing better than a single ace in his hand—he strips a heavy loser, who holds a pair, of the rest of his chips. It was up to the other fellow to protect himself. In the words of an excellent poker player, former president Harry Truman, "If you can't stand the heat, stay out of the kitchen." If one shows mercy to a loser in poker, it is a personal gesture, divorced from the rules of the game.

Poker has its special ethics, and here I am not referring to rules against cheating. The man who keeps an ace up his sleeve or who marks the cards is more than unethical; he is a crook, and can be punished as such—kicked out of the game or, in the Old West, shot.

In contrast to the cheat, the unethical poker player is one who, while abiding by the letter of the rules, finds ways to put the other players at an unfair disadvantage. Perhaps he unnerves them with loud talk. Or he tries to get them drunk. Or he plays in cahoots with someone else at the table. Ethical poker players frown on such tactics.

Poker's own brand of ethics is different from the ethical ideals of civilized human relationships. The game calls for distrust of the other fellow. It ignores the claim of friendship. Cunning deception and concealment of one's strength and intentions, not kindness and open-heartedness, are vital in poker. No one thinks any the worse of poker on that account. And no one should think any the worse of the game of business because its standards of right and wrong differ from the prevailing traditions of morality in our society.

DISCARD THE GOLDEN RULE

This view of business is especially worrisome to people without much business experience. A minister of my acquaintance once protested that business cannot possibly function in our society unless it is based on the Judeo-Christian system of ethics. He told me:

"I know some businessmen have supplied call girls to customers, but there are always a few rotten apples in every barrel. That doesn't mean the rest of the fruit isn't sound. Surely the vast majority of businessmen are ethical. I myself am acquainted with many who adhere to strict codes of ethics based fundamentally on religious teachings. They contribute to good causes. They participate in community activities. They cooperate with other companies to improve working conditions in their industries. Certainly they are not indifferent to ethics."

That most businessmen are not indifferent to ethics in their private lives, everyone will agree. My point is that in their other lives they cease to be private citizens; they become game players who must be guided by a somewhat different set of ethical standards.

The point was forcefully made to me by a midwestern executive who has given a good deal of thought to the question:

"So long as a businessman complies with the laws of the land and avoids telling malicious lies, he's ethical. If the law as written gives a man a wide-open chance to make a killing, he'd be a fool not to take advantage of it. If he doesn't, somebody else will. There's no obligation on him to stop and consider who is going to get hurt. If the law says he can do it, that's all the justification he needs. There's nothing unethical about that. It's just plain business sense."

This executive (call him Robbins) took the stand that even industrial espionage, which is frowned on by some businessmen, ought not to be considered unethical. He recalled a recent meeting of the National Industrial Conference Board where an authority on marketing made a speech in which he deplored the employment of spies by business organizations. More and more companies, he pointed out, find it cheaper to penetrate the secrets of competitors with concealed cameras and microphones or by bribing employees than to set up costly research and design departments of their own. A whole branch of the electronics industry has grown up with this trend, he continued, providing equipment to make industrial espionage easier.

Disturbing? The marketing expert found it so. But when it came to a remedy, he could only appeal to "respect for the golden rule." Robbins thought this a confession of defeat, believing that the golden rule, for all its value as an ideal for society, is simply not feasible as a guide for business. A good part of the time the businessman is trying to do unto others as he hopes others will *not* do unto him.[2] Robbins continued:

"Espionage of one kind or another has become so common in business that it's like taking a drink during Prohibition—it's not considered sinful. And we don't even have Prohibition where espionage is concerned; the law is very tolerant in this area. There's no more shame for a business that uses secret agents than there is for a nation. Bear in mind that there already is at least one large corporation—you can buy its stock over the counter—that makes millions by providing counterespionage service to industrial firms. Espionage in business is not an ethical problem; it's an established technique of business competition."

"We Don't Make the Laws"

Wherever we turn in business, we can perceive the sharp distinction between its ethical standards and those of the churches. Newspapers abound with sensational stories growing out of this distinction:

- We read one day that Senator Philip A. Hart of Michigan has attacked food processors for deceptive packaging of numerous products.[3]
- The next day there is a congressional to-do over Ralph Nader's book, *Unsafe at Any Speed,* which demonstrates that automobile companies for years have neglected the safety of car-owning families.[4]
- Then another senator, Lee Metcalf of Montana, and journalist Vic Reinemer show in their book, *Overcharge,* the methods by which utility companies elude regulating government bodies to extract unduly large payments from users of electricity.[5]

These are merely dramatic instances of a prevailing condition; there is hardly a major industry at which a similar attack could not be aimed. Critics of business regard such behavior as unethical, but the companies concerned know that they are merely playing the business game.

Among the most respected of our business institutions are the insurance companies. A group of insurance executives meeting recently in New England was startled when their guest speaker, social critic Daniel Patrick Moynihan, roundly berated them for "unethical" practices. They had been guilty, Moynihan alleged, of using outdated actuarial tables to obtain unfairly high premiums. They habitually delayed the hearing of lawsuits against them in order to tire out the plaintiffs and win cheap settlements. In their employment policies they used ingenious devices to discriminate against certain minority groups.[6]

It was difficult for the audience to deny the validity of these charges. But these men were business game players. Their reaction to Moynihan's attack was much the same as that of the automobile manufacturers to Nader, of the utilities to Senator Metcalf, and of the food processors to Senator Hart. If the laws governing their businesses change, or if public opinion becomes clamorous, they will make the necessary adjustments. But morally they have in their view done nothing wrong. As long as they comply with the letter of the law, they are within their rights to operate their businesses as they see fit.

The small business is in the same position as the great corporation in this respect. For example, in 1967 a key manufacturer was accused of providing master keys for automobiles to mail-order customers, although it was obvious that some of the purchasers might be automobile thieves. His defense was plain and straightforward. If there was nothing in the law to prevent him from selling his keys to anyone who ordered them, it was not up to him to inquire as to his customers' motives. Why was it any worse, he insisted, for him to sell car keys by mail, than for mail-order houses to sell guns that might be used for murder? Until the law was changed, the key manufacturer could regard himself as being just as ethical as any other businessman by the rules of the business game.[7]

Violations of the ethical ideals of society are common in business, but they are not necessarily violations of business principles. Each year the Federal Trade Commission orders hundreds of companies, many of them of the first magnitude, to "cease and desist" from practices which, judged by ordinary standards, are of questionable morality but which are stoutly defended by the companies concerned.

In one case, a firm manufacturing a well-known mouthwash was accused of using a cheap form of alcohol possibly deleterious to health. The company's chief executive, after testifying in Washington, made this comment privately:

"We broke no law. We're in a highly competitive industry. If we're going to stay in business, we have to look for profit wherever the law permits. We don't make the laws. We obey them. Then why do we have to put up with this 'holier than thou' talk about ethics? It's sheer hypocrisy. We're not in business to promote ethics. Look at the cigarette companies, for God's sake! If the ethics aren't embodied in the laws by the men who made them, you can't expect businessmen to fill the lack. Why, a sudden submission to Christian ethics by businessmen would bring about the greatest economic upheaval in history!"

It may be noted that the government failed to prove its case against him.

Cast Illusions Aside

Talk about ethics by businessmen is often a thin decorative coating over the hard realities of the game.

Once I listened to a speech by a young executive who pointed to a new industry code as proof that his company and its competitors were deeply aware of their responsibilities to society. It was a code of ethics, he said. The industry was going to police itself, to dissuade constituent companies from wrongdoing. His eyes shone with conviction and enthusiasm.

The same day there was a meeting in a hotel room where the industry's top executives met with the "czar" who was to administer the new code, a man of high repute. No one who was present could doubt their common attitude. In their eyes the code was designed primarily to forestall a move by the federal government to impose stern restrictions on the industry. They felt that the code would hamper them a good deal less than new federal laws would. It was, in other words, conceived as a protection for the industry, not for the public.

The young executive accepted the surface explanation of the code; these leaders, all experienced game players, did not deceive themselves for a moment about its purpose.

The illusion that business can afford to be guided by ethics as conceived in private life is often fostered by speeches and articles containing such phrases as, "It pays to be ethical," or, "Sound ethics is good business." Actually this is not an ethical position at all; it is a self-serving calculation in disguise. The speaker is really saying that in the long run a company can make more money if it does not antagonize competitors, suppliers, employees, and customers by squeezing them too hard. He is saying that oversharp policies reduce ultimate gains. That is true, but it has nothing to do with ethics. The underlying attitude is much like that in the familiar story of the shop-keeper who finds an extra twenty-dollar bill in the cash register, de-bates with himself the ethical problem—should he tell his partner?—and finally decides to share the money because the gesture will give him an edge over the s.o.b. the next time they quarrel.

I think it is fair to sum up the prevailing attitude of businessmen on ethics as follows:

We live in what is probably the most competitive of the world's civilized societies. Our customs encourage a high degree of aggression in the individual's striving for success. Business is our main area of competition, and it has been ritualized into a game of strategy. The basic rules of the game have been set by the government, which attempts to detect and punish business frauds. But as long as a com-pany does not transgress the rules of the game set by law, it has the legal right to shape its strategy without reference to anything but its profits. If it takes a long-term view of its profits, it will preserve amicable relations, so far as possible, with those with whom it deals. A wise buinessman will not seek advantage to the point where he generates dangerous hostility among employees, competitors, cus-tomers, government, or the public at large. But decisions in this area are, in the final test, decisions of strategy, not of ethics.

THE INDIVIDUAL AND THE GAME

An individual within a company often finds it difficult to adjust to the requirements of the business game. He tries to preserve his pri-vate ethical standards in situations that call for game strategy. When he is obliged to carry out company policies that challenge his con-ception of himself as an ethical man, he suffers.

It disturbs him when he is ordered, for instance, to deny a raise to a man who deserves it, to fire an employee of long standing, to prepare advertising that he believes to be misleading, to conceal facts that he feels customers are entitled to know, to cheapen the quality of materials used in the manufacture of an established product, to sell as new a product that he knows to be rebuilt, to exaggerate the curative powers of a medicinal preparation, or to coerce dealers.

There are some fortunate executives who, by the nature of their work and circumstances, never have to face problems of this kind. But in one form or another the ethical dilemma is felt sooner or later by most businessmen. Possibly the dilemma is most painful not when the company forces the action on the executive but when he originates it himself—that is, when he has taken or is contemplating a step which is in his own interest but which runs counter to his early moral conditioning. To illustrate:

• The manager of an export department, eager to show raising sales, is pressed by a big customer to provide invoices which, while containing no overt falsehood that would violate a U.S. law, are so worded that the customer may be able to evade certain taxes in his homeland.

• A company president finds that an aging executive, within a few years of retirement and his pension, is not as productive as formerly. Should he be kept on?

• The produce manager of a supermarket debates with himself whether to get rid of a lot of half-rotten tomatoes by including one, with its good side exposed, in every tomato six-pack.

• An accountant discovers that he has taken an improper deduction on his company's tax return and fears the consequences if he calls the matter to the president's attention, though he himself has done nothing illegal. Perhaps if he says nothing, no one will notice the error.

• A chief executive officer is asked by his directors to comment on a rumor that he owns stock in another company with which he has placed large orders. He could deny it, for the stock is in the name of his son-in-law and he has earlier formally instructed his son-in-law to sell the holding.

Temptations of this kind constantly arise in business. If an executive allows himself to be torn between a decision based on business considerations and one based on his private ethical code, he exposes himself to a grave psychological strain.

This is not to say that sound business strategy necessarily runs counter to ethical ideals. They may frequently coincide; and when they do, everyone is gratified. But the major tests of every move in business, as in all games of strategy, are legality and profit. A man who intends to be a winner in the business game must have a game player's attitude.

The business strategist's decisions must be as impersonal as those of a surgeon performing an operation—concentrating on objective and technique, and subordinating personal feelings. If the chief executive admits that his son-in-law owns the stock, it is because he stands to lose more if the fact comes out later than if he states it boldly and at once. If the supermarket manager orders the rotten tomatoes to be discarded, he does so to avoid an increase in consumer complaints and a loss of good will. The company president decides not to fire the elderly executive in the belief that the negative reaction of other employees would in the long run cost the company more than it would lose in keeping him and paying his pension.

All sensible businessmen prefer to be truthful, but they seldom feel inclined to tell the *whole* truth. In the business game, truth telling usually has to be kept within narrow limits if trouble is to be avoided. The point was neatly made a long time ago (in 1888) by one of John D. Rockefeller's associates, Paul Babcock, to Standard Oil Company executives who were about to testify before a government investigating committee: "Parry every question with answers which, while perfectly truthful, are evasive of *bottom* facts."[8] This was, is, and probably always will be regarded as wise and permissible business strategy.

For Office Use Only

An executive's family life can easily be dislocated if he fails to make a sharp distinction between the ethical systems of the home and the office—or if his wife does not grasp that distinction. Many a businessman who has remarked to his wife, "I had to let Jones go today" or "I had to admit to the boss that Jim has been goofing off lately," has been met with an indignant protest. "How could you do a thing like that? You know Jones is over fifty and will have a lot of trouble getting another job." Or, "You did that to Jim? With his wife ill and all the worry she's been having with the kids?"

If the executive insists that he had no choice because the profits of the company and his own security were involved, he may see a certain cool and ominous reappraisal in his wife's eyes. Many wives are not prepared to accept the fact that business operates with a special code of ethics. An illuminating illustration of this comes from a southern sales executive who related a conversation he had had with his wife at a time when a hotly contested political campaign was being waged in their state:

"I made the mistake of telling her that I had had lunch with Colby, who gives me about half my business. Colby mentioned that his company had a stake in the election. Then he said, 'By the way, I'm

treasurer of the citizens' committee for Lang. I'm collecting contributions. Can I count on you for a hundred dollars?'

"Well, there I was. I was opposed to Lang, but I knew Colby. If
he withdrew his business I could be in a bad spot. So I just smiled
and wrote out a check then and there. He thanked me, and we
started to talk about his next order. Maybe he thought I shared his
political views. If so, I wasn't going to lose any sleep over it.

"I should have had sense enough not to tell Mary about it. She hit
the ceiling. She said she was disappointed in me. She said I hadn't
acted like a man, that I should have stood up to Colby.

"I said, 'Look, it was an either-or situation. I had to do it or risk
losing the business.'

"She came back at me with, 'I don't believe it. You could have
been honest with him. You could have said that you didn't feel you
ought to contribute to a campaign for a man you weren't going to
vote for. I'm sure he would have understood.'

"I said, 'Mary, you're a wonderful woman, but you're way off the
track. Do you know what would have happened if I had said that?
Colby would have smiled and said, "Oh, I didn't realize. Forget it."
But in his eyes from that moment I would be an oddball, maybe a
bit of a radical. He would have listened to me talk about his order
and would have promised to give it consideration. After that I
wouldn't hear from him for a week. Then I would telephone and
learn from his secretary that he wasn't yet ready to place the order.
And in about a month I would hear through the grapevine that he   ·
was giving his business to another company. A month after that
I'd be out of a job.'

"She was silent for a while. Then she said, 'Tom, something is
wrong with business when a man is forced to choose between his
family's security and his moral obligation to himself. It's easy for me
to say you should have stood up to him—but if you had, you might
have felt you were betraying me and the kids. I'm sorry that you did
it, Tom, but I can't blame you. Something is wrong with business!' "

This wife saw the problem in terms of moral obligation as conceived in private life; her husband saw it as a matter of game strategy.
As a player in a weak position, he felt that he could not afford to
indulge an ethical sentiment that might have cost him his seat at
the table.

Playing to Win

Some men might challenge the Colbys of business—might accept
serious setbacks to their business careers rather than risk a feeling of
moral cowardice. They merit our respect—but as private individuals,

not businessmen. When the skillful player of the business game is compelled to submit to unfair pressure, he does not castigate himself for moral weakness. Instead, he strives to put himself into a strong position where he can defend himself against such pressures in the future without loss.

If a man plans to take a seat in the business game, he owes it to himself to master the principles by which the game is played, including its special ethical outlook. He can then hardly fail to recognize that an occasional bluff may well be justified in terms of the game's ethics and warranted in terms of economic necessity. Once he clears his mind on this point, he is in a good position to match his strategy against that of the other players. He can then determine objectively whether a bluff in a given situation has a good chance of succeeding and can decide when and how to bluff, without a feeling of ethical transgression.

To be a winner, a man must play to win. This does not mean that he must be ruthless, cruel, harsh, or treacherous. On the contrary, the better his reputation for integrity, honesty, and decency, the better his chances of victory will be in the long run. But from time to time every businessman, like every poker player, is offered a choice between certain loss or bluffing within the legal rules of the game. If he is not resigned to losing, if he wants to rise in his company and industry, then in such a crisis he will bluff—and bluff hard.

Every now and then one meets a successful businessman who has conveniently forgotten the small or large deceptions that he practiced on his way to fortune. "God gave me my money," old John D. Rockefeller once piously told a Sunday-school class. It would be a rare tycoon in our time who would risk the horselaugh with which such a remark would be greeted.

In the last third of the twentieth century even children are aware that if a man has become prosperous in business, he has sometimes departed from the strict truth in order to overcome obstacles or has practiced the more subtle deceptions of the half-truth or the misleading omission. Whatever the form of the bluff, it is an integral part of the game, and the executive who does not master its techniques is not likely to accumulate much money or power.

NOTES

1. *New York Times,* 9 March 1967, p. 1.
2. See Bruce D. Henderson, "Brinkmanship in Business," *Harvard Business Review,* vol. 45, March-April 1967, p. 49.

3. *New York Times,* 21 November 1966, p. 36.
4. Ralph Nader, *Unsafe or Any Speed* (New York: Grossman Publishers, 1965).
5. Lee Metcalf and Vic Reinemer, *Overcharge* (New York: David McKay, 1967).
6. *New York Times,* 17 January 1967, p. 19.
7. Cited by Ralph Nader in "Business Crime," *New Republic,* vol. 157, 1 July 1967, p. 7.
8. Babcock in a memorandum to Rockefeller (Rockefeller Archives).

FRED HIRSCH

Competitive Consumption

The structural characteristic in question is that as the level of average consumption rises, an increasing portion of consumption takes on a social as well as an individual aspect. That is to say, the satisfaction that individuals derive from goods and services depends in increasing measure not only on their own consumption but on consumption by others as well.

To a hungry man, the satisfaction derived from a square meal is unaffected by the meals other people eat or, if he is hungry enough, by anything else they do. His meal is an entirely individual affair. In technical terms it is a pure private good. At the other extreme, the quality of the air that the modern citizen breathes in the center of a city depends almost entirely on what his fellow citizens contribute toward countering pollution, whether directly by public expenditure or indirectly through public regulation. Clean air in a metropolis is a social product. In technical terms, it is close to a pure public good.

These polar cases, however, are relatively few in number. It has recently become recognized by economists who specialize in these matters that the major part of consumption is neither purely private nor purely public. What is generally referred to as private or personal consumption is nonetheless affected in its essence—that is, in the satisfaction or utility it yields—by consumption of the same goods

Source: Reprinted by permission of the publishers from *Social Limits to Growth* by Fred Hirsch, Cambridge, Mass. Harvard University Press. Copyright © 1976 by the Twentieth Century Fund.

or services by others; and in that specific sense it can be said to contain a social element. Correspondingly, what is generally referred to as public consumption contains some of the characteristics of private goods, in the sense that its costs and benefits are or can be confined to a limited group.

The range of private consumption that contains a social element in the sense described is much wider than is generally recognized. In textbooks on economics, public goods are discussed in the context of goods and facilities that can be provided only, or most economically, on a collective basis, open to all and financed by all. City parks and streets and national defense are prominent examples. In addition, elements of public goods are recognized in side effects of private transactions such as pollution and congestion occurring in particular identifiable situations. But a more general public-goods element can be attributed to a wide range of private expenditures. Thus the utility of expenditure on a given level of education as a means of access to the most sought-after jobs will decline as more people attain that level of education. The value to me of my education depends not only on how much I have but also on how much the man ahead of me in the job line has. The satisfaction derived from an auto or a country cottage depends on the conditions in which they can be used, which will be strongly influenced by how many other people are using them. This factor, which is social in origin, may be a more important influence on my satisfaction than the characteristics of these items as "private" goods (on the speed of the auto, the spaciousness of the cottage, and so forth). Beyond some point that has long been surpassed in crowded industrial societies, conditions of use tend to deteriorate as use becomes more widespread.

Congestion is most apparent in its physical manifestation, in traffic jams. But traffic congestion can be seen as only a special case of the wider phenomenon of social congestion, which in turn is a major facet of social scarcity. Social scarcity is a central concept in this analysis. It expresses the idea that the good things of life are restricted not only by physical limitations of producing more of them but also by absorptive limits on their use. Where the social environment has a restricted capacity for extending use without quality deterioration, it imposes social limits to consumption. More specifically, the limit is imposed on satisfactions that depend not on the product or facility in isolation but on the surrounding conditions of use.

What precisely is *new* about this situation? The limits have always been there at some point, but they have not until recent times become obtrusive. That is the product, essentially, of past achievements in material growth not subject to social limits. In this sense, the concern with the limits to growth that has been voiced by and through the Club of Rome[1] is strikingly misplaced. It focuses on distant and uncertain physical limits and overlooks the immediate if less apocalyptic presence of social limits to growth.

So long as material privation is widespread, conquest of material scarcity is the dominant concern. As demands for purely private goods are increasingly satisfied, demands for goods and facilities with a public (social) character become increasingly active. These public demands make themselves felt through individual demands on the political system or through the market mechanism in the same way as do the demands for purely private goods. Individuals acquire both sets of goods without distinction, except where public goods are provided by public or collective action; even there, individuals may seek to increase their own share by private purchases.

These demands in themselves appear both legitimate and attainable. Why should the individual not spend his money on additional education as a means to a higher-placed job, or on a second home in the country, if he prefers these pleasures to spending on a mink coat or whiskey or to a life of greater leisure? That question was being loudly voiced in the mid-1970s as part of a middle-class backlash in both Britain and the United States. It can be answered satisfactorily only by reference to the public goods or social content of the expenditures involved.

Considered in isolation, the individual's demand for education as a job entrée, for an auto, for a country cottage, can be taken as genuinely individual wants, stemming from the individual's own preferences in the situation that confronts him. Acting alone, each individual seeks to make the best of his or her position. But satisfaction of these individual preferences itself alters the situation that faces others seeking to satisfy similar wants. A round of transactions to act out personal wants of this kind therefore leaves each individual with a worse bargain than was reckoned with when the transaction was undertaken, because the sum of such acts does not correspondingly improve the position of all individuals taken together. There is an "adding-up" problem. Opportunities for economic advance, as they present themselves serially to one person after another, do not constitute equivalent opportunities for economic advance by all. What each of us can achieve, all cannot.

A break between individual and social opportunities may occur for a number of reasons; excessive pollution and congestion are the most commonly recognized results. A neglected general condition that produces this break is competition by people for place, rather than competition for performance. Advance in society is possible only by moving to a higher place among one's fellows, that is, by improving one's performance in relation to other people's performances. If everyone stands on tiptoe, no one sees better. Where social interaction of this kind is present, individual action is no longer a sure means of fulfilling individual choice: the preferred outcome may be attainable only through collective action. (We all agree explicitly or implicitly not to stand on tiptoe.) The familiar dichotomy between individual choice and collective provision or regulation then dissolves. Competition among isolated individuals in the free market entails hidden costs for others and ultimately for themselves. These costs are a dead-weight cost for all and involve social waste, unless no preferable alternative method of allocation is available. But the same distortion may result from public provision where this responds to individual demands formulated without taking account of subsequent interactions.

A conspicuous example is provided in certain aspects of education. People possessing relatively high educational qualifications are seen to enjoy attractive professional and social opportunities. This situation induces a strong latent demand for access to such qualifications. Such demand may flow through the market, in the willingness of individuals to pay higher fees for educational services supplied by private institutions without public support. In our own times, the demand more often is directed to the state, to broaden access to the higher strata of the educational pyramid. The state is expected to foster equality of educational opportunity and perhaps also equality of educational outcome. But these concepts present a number of difficulties, some well known and some less so.

The concept of equal opportunity, or equality at the starting gate, is not much less question-begging when applied to education than when applied to life chances in general, the central ambiguity being which starting handicaps are to be removed. At the limit, the criterion of an equal start is an equal finish. Worse, equal outcome in education would be impeded not only by differences in individual talent and inclination; the concept also fails to allow for an important function education performs in modern society, that is, sorting or screening. In its own way education is a device for controlling social scarcity.

To the extent that education in fact functions so as to sort out those who can best survive and master an educational obstacle course, improved performance by some worsens the position of those who would otherwise be ahead. The "quality" of schooling, in effect, exists in two dimensions. There is an *absolute* dimension, in which quality is added by receptive students, good teachers, good facilities, and so on; but there is also a *relative* dimension, in which quality consists of the differential over the educational level attained by others. The enormous resistance induced in both the United States and Britain by public attempts to integrate previously inferior schools with previously superior schools cannot be fully understood without reference to both these aspects of educational quality. Even if complete assurance could be given that absolute quality would be fully preserved, the previous incumbents of the superior schools would still lose their edge. This loss in turn can be expected to induce them to demonstrate their proficiency in a tougher or longer course of study. To the extent that education is a screening device (a qualification that must be kept firmly in mind), then the possibility of general advance is an illusion.

What is possible for the single individual is not possible for all individuals—and would not be possible even if they all possessed equal talent. Individuals, whether shopping for educational advance in the marketplace or pushing for educational advance through political demands, do not see the break between individual and social opportunity; that is, they do not see that opportunities open to each person separately are not open to all. It follows that response to individual demands of this kind, whether in market processes or in public provision, cannot deliver the order.

Consumers, taken together, get a product they did not order; collectively, this result involves potential social waste. Consumers individually find that their access to socially scarce goods and facilities, where these are attainable even in part through market processes, is determined in accord not with absolute but with relative real income. The determining factor is the individual's position in the distribution of purchasing power. Frustration of individual expectations then results from both these characteristics: from social waste, which cuts into the level of welfare* available to all; and from an imposed hierarchy that confines socially scarce goods to those on the highest rungs of the distributional ladder, disappointing the expectations of those whose position is raised through a lift in the ladder as a whole.

So the distributional struggle returns, heightened rather than relieved by the dynamic process of growth. It is an exact reversal of what economists and present-day politicians have come to expect growth to deliver.

---

* In the sense of some concept of ultimate consumer satisfaction.

The compelling attraction of economic growth in its institutional-ized modern form has been as a superior substitute for redistribution. Whereas the masses today could never get close to what the well-to-do have today, even by expropriating all of it, they can, in the con-ventional view, get most if not all the way there with patience in a not-too-distant tomorrow, through the magic of compound growth. But, as outlined above, once this growth brings mass consumption to the point where it causes problems of congestion in the widest sense—bluntly, where consumption or job holding by others tends to crowd you out—then the key to personal welfare is again the ability to stay ahead of the crowd. Generalized growth then increases the crush.

Thus the frustration in affluence results from its very success in satisfying previously dominant material needs. This frustration is usually thought of as essentially a psychological phenomenon, a matter of our subjective internal assessment. What we previously had to struggle for now comes easily, so we appreciate it less. The analysis of this book fastens on a separate consequence of general-ized material growth that is independent of any such psychological revaluation; it affects what individuals get as well as the satisfaction it brings them. What they get, in the growing sphere of social scarcity, depends to an increasing extent on their relative position in the economic hierarchy. Hence, the paradox of affluence. It embodies a distributional compulsion, which in turn leads to our reluctant collectivism.

These sources of frustration with the fruits of economic growth are concealed in the economist's standard categorization. Strictly speaking, our existing concept of economic output is appropriate only for truly private goods, having no element of interdependence between consumption by different individuals. The bedrock is valuation by individuals of goods and opportunities in the situation in which they find themselves. At any moment of time and for any one person, standing on tiptoe gives a better view, or at least prevents a worse one. Equally, getting ahead of the crowd is an effective and feasible means of improving one's welfare, a means available to any one individual. It yields a benefit, in this sense, and the measure of the benefit is what individuals pay to secure it. The individual benefit from the isolated action is clear-cut. The sum of benefits of all the actions taken together is nonetheless zero.

This reckoning, it should be emphasized, is still made on the measure of the individual's own valuation, the same valuation that imputes a positive benefit to the individual action. Since individual benefits of this kind simply do not add up, the connection between individual and aggregate advance is broken. Yet the modern concepts of economic output, and of growth in that output, are grounded on individual valuations and their addition. Individual preference is assumed to be revealed implicitly in market behavior—in the consumer's choice between products at their given market prices, in the worker's choice between jobs and between different opportunities of job training at the going rates of pay and conditions. If individual valuations do not add up, then the aggregated valuations based upon them become biased measures.

Unfortunately no better quantitative measure of economic output has yet been found. The need for a flanking set of social indicators is now widely accepted, at least in principle. The end product of such a system would be an integrated system of numbers comparable with the national income accounts. This objective is far from being realized. There is no social performance indicator that can be systematically calculated and easily understood.

The national accounts have been developed into an elaborate ground plan of the economy that is used for a large variety of purposes. The gross national product and its components are the best indicators of personal and national prosperity we have, if only because they are the only such indicators. They thereby maintain a strong hold on public attention. Inevitably, this attention has given its own validity to the analytical categorization which lies at the base of national accounting, as well as of the older, related economic concepts from which it grew. The products of the economics numbers factory enjoy a brisk demand; and the economic inducement to cater to effective demand is not suspended for economics itself. Nor are economists immune from the instinct of trade unionists; they too judge the social worth of their performance by the prosperity and prestige it brings to their craft.

The ambiguity in the concept of economic output pointed out here is of secondary or even negligible significance in making use of the conventional measures of national accounts for the formulation of official policy designed to regulate or stabilize the short-term performance of the economy. For comparisons of welfare over extended periods of time, in estimates of long-term economic growth, and in league tables of living standards among countries in different situations at a given period of time, national accounting measures are notoriously less suitable.

What is stressed here is a different limitation, one almost wholly neglected by economists: the problem of translating individual economic improvement into overall improvement. In the standard model of thinking, if the fruits of aggregate advance appear inadequate or disappointing, the deficiency merely reflects inadequate economic effort or excessive demands by individuals, or poor organization or inadequate capital equipment currently available to them. Too much has been expected too soon. This conceptual framework adopted by economists concerned with policy has penetrated the thinking, expectations, and performance criteria of politicians and electorates of all western countries. As a consequence, conventional wisdom thinks in terms of "excessive expectations." The populace wants it now. It cannot have it now. It is too impatient. The implication is that the gathering of the fruit must await exercise of the necessary virtues—essentially, effort and restraint. Yet for those aspects of individual welfare where the connection between individual and aggregate advancement does not exist, or is broken under the stress of widening access to limited availabilities, the established conceptual framework is invalid. Its application to ultimate consumer satisfaction in this sector operates as a frustration machine.

Thus to see total economic advance as individual advance writ large is to set up expectations that cannot be fulfilled, ever. It is not just a matter of scaling down demand and expectations that are extravagant in relation to effort by workers or to the availability of technology or the use made of it. This view has become the conventional one on problems of excess demand and inflation. The appropriate solution to the problem so conceived is simple, at least in principle: to adjust expectations down and/or performance up. The necessary adjustment is purely quantitative. If all put a little more into the pool and take a little less out for a while, then present expectations can in time be fulfilled. So runs the predominant message of politicoeconomic managers in the postwar generation. Only hold back a little, and the good things you rightly crave will come to you or, at least, to your children. The inflationary explosion of the early 1970s and the severe world recession that followed attempts to contain it have been widely interpreted in this vein—as a painful interruption in a progressive improvement in living standards that could be restored and sustained once the public was prevailed upon to exercise the necessary restraint.

It follows from this line of thought that the chief culprits responsible for derailing the train of technological advance are those institutions that inflate economic demands beyond the steady but limited growth in capacity to fulfill them. Trade unions exercising the bargaining power of their collective strength stand out as such culprits. It is the collective element in their activities—the mobilization of economic strength greater than the sum of the individual parts—that is seen to intrude on the balance and viability of an individualistic economy. The unquestioned premise of this approach is that competitive individualistic advance can ultimately deliver the goods. If it cannot, which participants in collective activity may instinctively feel and as the present analysis explicitly argues, then defensive collective expedients must be looked at in a new light.

To the extent that the mismatch between current expectations and resources is qualitative rather than quantitative, the restraint necessary would be not patience but stoicism, acceptance, and social cooperation—qualities that are out of key with our culture of individualistic advance. Yet without such qualities, the traditional response by the public to the prospect of satisfaction as reward for extra effort or temporary abstinence will worsen the problem. For addition to the material goods that can be expanded for all will, in itself, increase the scramble for those goods and facilities that cannot be so expanded. Taking part in the scramble is fully rational for any individual in his own actions, since in these actions he never confronts the distinction between what is available as a result of getting ahead of others and what is available from a general advance shared by all. The individual who wants to see better has to stand on tiptoe. In the game of beggar your neighbor, that is what each individual must try to do, even though not all can. The only way of avoiding the competition in frustration is for the people concerned to coordinate their objectives in some explicit way, departing from the principle of isolated individual striving in this sphere. That is to say, only a collective approach to the problem can offer individuals the guidance necessary to achieve a solution they themselves would prefer. The principle is acknowledged in the standard liberal analysis, but confined to the exceptional case.

How a satisfactory collective view is to be arrived at, and then implemented, remains a large and mostly unresolved problem of its own. Collective action can involve familiar distortions and inefficiencies. The means to a collective solution may be inadequate. To the extent that this is so, the analysis put forward here carries no clear-cut implications for immediate policy. The distortions and frustrations entailed in uncoordinated individual actions may still appear as the lesser evil. However, a change in the nature of a problem is not undone by deficiencies in the tools available for tackling it. Correct diagnosis is likely to yield some implications for policy, if only to stop banging into the wall.

By collapsing individual and total opportunities for economic advance into a single process grounded on individual valuations, the standard view has obscured a significant change in the nature of the economic problem. It has thereby overstated the promise of economic

growth. It has understated the limitations of consumer demand as a
guide to an efficient pattern of economic activity. It has obscured
the extent of the modern conflict between individualistic actions and
satisfaction of individualistic preferences. Getting what one wants is
increasingly divorced from doing as one likes.

NOTES

1. The Club of Rome is an informal international association, styling itself as
   an invisible college, which is best known for its "world model" representing
   the interconnections of resources, population, and environment in the mode
   of systems dynamics. The message, which received worldwide popular
   acclaim and widespread professional criticism, was contained in Donella H.
   Meadows, et al., *The Limits to Growth: A Report for the Club of Rome's
   Project on the Predicament of Mankind* (London: Earth Island Limited,
   1972).

FRANK KNIGHT

The Ethics of Competition

In an earlier paper[1] the writer undertook to argue against the view of
ethics most commonly accepted among economists. The argument
was not directed against hedonism as such, but against "scientific"
ethics of any kind, against any view which sets out from the assumption that human wants are objective and measurable magnitudes and
that the satisfaction of such wants is the essence and criterion of
value, and which proceeds on the basis of this assumption to reduce
ethics to a sort of glorified economics. It was pointed out that any
such view consistently reduces the "higher" wants to a secondary
position as compared with "lower," and interprets human life in
biological terms. But the fact is that human beings do not regularly
prefer their lower and more "necessary" needs to those not easily

Source: *Quarterly Journal of Economics*, Vol. 37, 1923.

justified in terms of subsistence or survival value, but perhaps rather the contrary; in any case what we call progress has consisted largely in increasing the proportion of want gratification of an aesthetic or spiritual as compared to that of a biological utilitarian character, rather than in increasing the "quantity of life." The facts, as emphasized, are altogether against accepting any balance-sheet view of life; they point rather toward an evaluation of a far subtler sort than the addition and subtraction of homogeneous items, toward an ethics along the line of aesthetic criticism, whose canons are of another sort than scientific laws and are not quite intellectually satisfying. We cannot accept want satisfaction as a final criterion of value because we do not in fact regard our wants as final; instead of resting in the view that there is no disputing about tastes, we dispute about them more than anything else; our most difficult problem in valuation is the evaluation of our wants themselves and our most troublesome want is the desire for wants of the "right " kind.

The purpose of the present paper is to develop and supplement the argument already given, first by reemphasizing the necessity of a defensible criterion of values as a basis for passing judgment on questions of policy; and secondly by inquiring into the standards of value implicit in the laissez faire or individualistic social philosophy and raising certain questions in regard to them. On the first head, fortunately, we can be brief. It is a thesis which calls for no elaborate demonstration that social policy must be based upon social ideals. An organized system must operate in accordance with a *social* standard. This standard will of course be related in some way to the values of the individuals making up the society, but it cannot be merely identical with them; it presupposes some process of organizing the various individual interests, weighing them against each other and adjudicating conflicts among them.

It is impossible to form any concept of "social efficiency" in the absence of some general measure of value. Even in physics and engineering, "efficiency" is strictly a value category; there is no such thing as mechanical efficiency. It follows from the fundamental laws of the indestructibility of matter and of energy that whatever goes into any apparatus or process comes out *in some form.* In purely mechanical terms, all efficiencies would be equal to 100 percent. The efficiency of any machine means the ratio between the *useful* output and the total output. In simple cases the distinction between useful and useless may be so sharp and clear as to give rise to no discussion—as in the case of the mechanical energy and the heat generated by an electric motor. But when more than one form of useful output (or costly input) is involved, the necessity arises for having a measure of usefulness, of value, before efficiency can be discussed. The efficiency relations of a steam engine may be much changed when the exhaust steam is applied to heating. In so complicated a problem as that of social efficiency, where the elements of outlay and of return are both infinitely numerous and diverse, it is no wonder that the process of valuation has become the heart and core of the study. It must ultimately be recognized that only within rather narrow limits can human conduct be interpreted as the creation of values of such definiteness and stability that they can serve as scientific data, that life is fundamentally an exploration in the field of values itself and not a mere matter of producing given values. When this is clearly seen, it will be apparent why so much discussion of social efficiency has been so futile.

Perception of these obvious fundamental principles at once cuts the ground from under one of the lines of criticism of the economic order which has attracted wide attention. It is an idea sponsored especially by Dr. Thorstein Veblen and copied by others, that there is some distinction between "pecuniary" and "industrial" employments[2] and that society ought to take the control of industry out of the hands of "financiers" and put it into the hands of "technicians."[3]

This notion rests on the same obvious fallacy, the idea that society has a choice between producing more goods and producing more value, and that it is the part of wisdom to prefer the former. It is difficult to take either part of the proposition seriously. The quantity of goods, if there is more than one kind, must so obviously be measured in value units. The proposal of leaving it to technicians in the respective fields to say how much social productive power shall be expended in each is merely grotesque; military experts would use it all for the army and navy, the medical men could usefully employ it all, and more, for health, and so on. There is no more important function of a first course in economics than to make the student see that the whole problem of social management is a *value* problem; that mechanical or technical efficiency is a meaningless combination of words.

Indeed there can be no question, as the course of the argument will show, that the valid criticisms of the existing economic order relate chiefly to its value standards, and relatively much less to its efficiency in the creation of such values as it recognizes. We shall furthermore insist that not merely a measure of value but ideals of value are prerequisite to any intelligent criticism of social processes or results. This is not, like the proposition regarding efficiency, a self-evident truth. It is quite arguable that the determination or criticism of policy involves only a comparison of alternative possibilities and a choice of that which is considered preferable. It is arguable, and the contention is in fact often put forward, that values are purely relative, that it means nothing to say that anything is good or bad except in comparison with a worse or better alternative. It is a practical question: does the judging faculty actually work by reasoning out alternatives and deciding which is preferable, or does it not rather formulate ideals and compare actuality and potentiality with these, and with each other indirectly, by so comparing them with an ideal? No doubt both methods are used, and are useful; but we contend that in regard to the larger and higher questions, the ultimate problems of moral and social life, the formulation of ideals is a necessary step. There is a place, and a vital place, for an "absolute" science of ethics. Its dicta will not be really absolute, for they never cut loose entirely from the real world and its possibilities of growth and transformation, and they will always grow and change. But at least they are not "merely" relative; they must be beyond the immediately attainable, and will often lie in the field of the actually impossible, patterns to be approached rather than objectives to be achieved.

We contend not merely that such ideals are real to individuals, but that they are a part of our culture and are sufficiently uniform and objective to form a useful standard of comparison for a given country at a given time. Normal common sense does judge in terms of ideals, of absolute ethics in the sense indicated, and not merely in terms of the best that can be done; else it would be linguistically equivalent to call a situation hopeless and to call it ideal, which is clearly not in accordance with usage. In what follows we shall appeal to what we submit to be the common-sense ideals of absolute ethics in modern Christendom. No pretense will be made of drawing up a code of such principles; they are frequently not of a character to fall readily into propositions. There will be no attempt to "settle" moral questions or set up standards, but only to bring out the standards actually involved in making some familiar moral judgments in regard to the economic system, and to examine them critically. The argument will therefore be negative in tone, and the need for brevity may occasionally give it something of the flavor of an "attack"; but let it be stated here that we are not advocating or proposing change. The question of *policy* is a question of alternatives, a purely relative matter; we are concerned here with the question of *ideals,* which we assume may be carried further, into the realm of considerations at least "relatively" absolute. Even if the competitive system is better than any available substitute, a clear view of its shortcomings in comparison with conceivable ideals must be of the highest value in making it better than it is.

An examination of the competitive economic order from the standpoint of its ethical standards will fall naturally into three parts. In the first place, the contention already put forward, that wants are not ultimate data or to be identified with values, does not mean that they are not real and important. We can never get entirely away even from physical needs, requirements for life, for health, and for comfort, small as such motives really bulk in civilized behavior. Moreover, at any given time and place the existing stage of culture sets minimum requirements which are imperative in character. It is true within limits that the purpose of economic activity is to satisfy wants, and the fact raises a group of questions for consideration in an appraisal of any system of economic organization. We must inquire first into its value standards, in the economic or quasi-mechanical sense, its manner of dealing with wants as they exist, its mechanism for comparing and equating and perhaps selecting among the various wants of the various persons and classes of persons which make up the society. It is hardly necessary to remark that the questions *which* wants and *whose* wants are to be satisfied are in fact closely bound up together. The system's answer to this twofold question constitutes its social economic value scale; and very different social value scales may be formed from the same set of individual wants by different methods of selection, equation, and combination. The more distinctly ethical aspect of this issue is of course the old problem of social justice, relating to the system's treatment of the wants of persons and classes; but that is by no means separable from the question of ranking different wants of the same person. A second inquiry under the same head, of a more mechanical sort but still distinctly a problem of values, deals with the *efficiency* of the system in using its available resources in creating the values which it recognizes, that is, in producing the largest quantity of "goods" as measured by the standard which it sets up.

Another question, ethically more fundamental than these but inseparable from them, and one which must be considered in the first section of the inquiry, follows directly from recognizing the provisional character of wants and the obvious fact that the wants which an economic system operates to gratify are largely produced by the workings of the system itself. In organizing its value scale, the economic order does far more than select and compare wants for exchangeable goods and services: its activity extends to the formation and radical transformation, if not to the outright creation, of the wants themselves; they as well as the means of their gratification are largely products of the system. An examination of the ethics of the economic system must consider the question of the kind of wants which it tends to generate or nourish as well as its treatment of wants as they exist at any given time.

The second of the three main standpoints to be considered corresponds to an aspect of economic life which is rapidly securing more adequate recognition among economists, the fact that the motive of business is to such a large extent that of emulation as such. Industry and trade is a competitive game, in which men engage in part from the same motives as in other games or sports. This is not a matter of want satisfaction in any direct or economic sense; the "rewards" of successful participation in the game are not wanted for any satisfying power dependent on any quality which they possess as things, but simply as insignia of success in the game, like the ribbons, medals, and the like which are conferred in other sorts of contests. Our second main task will therefore be to raise the question, *what kind of game* is business? Is there anything to be said about games from an ethical point of view, any basis for judging them or ranking them as games, and if so, is business a relatively good, bad, or indifferent game?

The third part of the paper will deal briefly with the more fundamental aspects of the problem of values from the standpoint of absolute ethics. Economic activity is a large part of life, and perhaps tends to grow in relative magnitude. The issue as to the influence of the economic system on character can be treated only superficially, but should at least be raised. Emphasis will be placed on the particular phase of competitive emulation as a motive and of success in a contest as an ethical value. The competitive economic order must be partly responsible for making emulation and rivalry the outstanding quality in the character of the Western peoples who have adopted and developed it. The modern idea of enjoyment as well as of achievement has come to consist chiefly in keeping up with or getting ahead of other people in a rivalry for things about whose significance, beyond furnishing objectives for the competition itself, little question is asked. It is surely one function of ethical discussion to keep the world reminded that this is not the only possible conception of value and to point out its contrast with the religious ideals to which the Western world has continued to render lip service—a contrast resulting in fundamental dualism in our thought and culture.

Throughout the discussion it will be necessary to keep in mind the close interconnection among these several aspects of the economic system. Economic activity is *at the same time* a means of want satisfaction, an agency for the want and character formation, a field of creative self-expression, and a competitive sport. While men are "playing the game" of business, they are also molding their own and other personalities, and creating a civilization whose worthiness to endure cannot be a matter of indifference.

Discussion of the merits of free competition, or "laissez faire," takes on an especial interest in view of the contrast between the enticing plausibility of the case for the "obvious and simple system of natural liberty," and the notoriously disappointing character of the results which is has tended to bring about in practice.* In the later eighteenth and early nineteenth centuries, under the influence of the "classical economists," of the Manchester liberals, of the political pressure of the rising bourgeoisie, and the general force of circumstances, rapid progress was made toward the establishment of individual liberty in economic affairs. But long before complete individualism was closely approached, its consequences were recognized to be intolerable, and there set in that countermovement toward social interference and control which has been going on at an accelerating pace ever since. The argument for individualism, as developed by its advocates from Adam Smith down, may be summarized in a sentence as follows: a freely competitive organization of society tends to place every productive resource in that position in the productive system where it can make the greatest possible addition to the total social dividend as measured in price terms, and tends to reward every participant in production by giving it the increase in the social dividend which its cooperation makes possible. In the writer's opinion such a proposition is entirely sound; but it is not a statement of a sound ethical social ideal, the specification for a utopia. Discussion of the issue between individual freedom and socialization, however, has largely centered around the truth of the proposition as a statement of the tendencies of competition, rather than around its ethical significance if true. Those who do not like

---

* It should be stated that for simplicity we shall speak of "the" competitive system, though the discussion relates to a "purely" competitive system, as understood by the economic theorist. It is superfluous to remark that such a system has never been closely approximated in reality, or perhaps advocated by any writer taken seriously by any large group—certainly it was not advocated by Adam Smith. The idea of a purely individualistic order is a logical device, necessary to separate for study the tendencies of individualism from those of socialism. It would go a long way toward clarifying discussion if it were generally recognized on both sides that there are no 100 percent individualists and no 100 percent socialists; that the issue is one of degree and proportion.

the actual tendencies of the system as they appear to work out when it is tried—and that is virtually everybody—attack the scientific analysis. We propose to argue in the first place that the conditions of life do not admit of an approximation to individualism of the sort necessarily assumed by the theory, and secondly that there are in the conditions of actual life no ethical implications of the kind commonly taken for granted as involved in individualism insofar as it is possible of realization.

The careful statement of the meaning of individualism falls within the province of the economic theorist rather than that of the ethical critic. It is an accident of the way in which economic science has developed, and especially of the peculiar relation between science and practice in this field, that so little serious effort has been made to state with rigor and exactitude the assumptions involved in the notion of perfect competition, the premises of pure economics. Literary writers on economics have been interested in administrative problems, for which the results of any exact treatment of principles are too abstract to be of direct application, and have not generally been trained to use or appreciate rigorous methods. The mathematical economists have commonly been mathematicians first and economists afterward, disposed to oversimplify the data and underestimate the divergence between their premises and the facts of life. In consequence they have not been successful in getting their presentation into such a form that it could be understood, and its relation to real problems recognized, by practical economists. The critical reader of general economic literature must be struck by the absence of any attempt accurately to define that competition which is the principal subject under discussion. A clear formulation of the postulates of theoretical individualism will bring out the contrast with practical laissez faire, and will go far to discredit the latter as a policy. In the present paper the attempt to state the presuppositions of a competitive system cannot be carried beyond a bare outline; it will be developed with reference to our special purpose of showing that in the conditions of real life no possible social order based upon a laissez faire policy can justify the familiar ethical conclusions of apologetic economics.

1. In the first place, an individualist competitive system must be made up of freely contracting individuals. As a matter of fact, a rather small fraction of the population of any modern nation enter into contracts on their own responsibility. Our "individualism" is really "familism"; all minors, the aged, and numerous persons in other classes, including for practical purposes the majority of adult women, have their status-determining bargains made for them by other per-

sons. The family is still the unit in production and consumption. It is hardly necessary to point out that all arguments for free contract are nullified or actually reversed whenever one person contracts on behalf of another.

2. Moreover, the freest individual, the unencumbered male in the prime of life, is in no real sense an ultimate unit or social datum. He is in large measure a product of the economic system, which is a fundamental part of the cultural environment that has formed his desires and needs, given him whatever marketable productive capacities he has, and which largely controls his opportunities. Social organization through free contract implies that the contracting units know what they want and are guided by their desires, that is, that they are "perfectly rational," which would be equivalent to saying that they are accurate mechanisms of desire satisfaction. In fact, human activity is largely impulsive, a relatively unthinking and undetermined response to stimulus and suggestion. Moreover, there is truth in the allegation that unregulated competition places a premium on deceit and corruption. In any case, where the family is the social unit, the inheritance of wealth, culture, educational advantages, and economic opportunities must tend toward the progressive increase of inequality, with bad results for personality at both ends of the scale. It is plainly contrary to fact to treat the individual as a datum, and it must be conceded that the lines along which a competitive economic order tends to form character are often far from being ethically ideal.

3. It is universally recognized that effective competition calls for "fluidity," the perfect divisibility and mobility of all goods and services entering into exchange. The limited extent to which this assumption fits the facts of life sets limits to the "tendency" of actual competition, which in many cases nullify the principle. Here, as in the case of other assumptions, it is illegitimate to draw practical conclusions from a "tendency," however real, without taking account of contradictory tendencies also, and getting the facts as to their relative strength. One of the dangers of reasoning from simplified premises is the likelihood that the abstracted factors may be overlooked in drawing conclusions and formulating policies based thereon.

4. One of the most important prerequisites to perfect competition is complete knowledge on the part of every competing individual of the exchange opportunities open to him. A "perfect market" would involve perfect, instantaneous, and costless intercommunication among all the traders. This condition is really approximated quite closely in the case of a few commodities dealt in on the organized exchanges, but the market for most consumption goods is very crude in its workings. As regards the productive services, abstract

pecuniary capital does indeed flow through a highly developed market; but the market for labor, land, and real capital, and their uses, leaves wide margins for "bargaining power" and accidental aberrations. Both the organization of production and the distribution of the product diverge correspondingly from the theoretically ideal results.

5. Competition further requires that every actual or potential buyer of every saleable good or service shall know accurately its properties and powers to satisfy his wants. In the case of productive goods this means knowledge of their technical significance. In an industrial civilization as complex as that of the modern world it is clear that the divergences from this "tendency" must often be more important than the tendency. Indirect knowledge is available to offset direct ignorance in many subtle ways, and yet no individual can know enough to act very closely according to the ideal of perfect intelligence. Moreover, perfect competition does not stop at requiring knowledge of things as they are; the competitor must foresee them as they will be, often a very considerable distance in the future, and the limitations of foreknowledge are of course more sweeping than those of knowledge.

6. The results of intelligent action are the purposes to which it is directed, and will be ethically ideal only if these ends are true values. Under individualism this means that the wants of individuals must be ideal, as well as their knowledge perfect. We have commented enough on the fact that the social order largely forms as well as gratifies the wants of its members, and the natural consequence that it must be judged ethically rather by the wants which it generates, the type of character which it forms in its people, than by its efficiency in satisfying wants as they exist at any given time.

7. Another sweeping limitation to the actual workings of free competition arises from the fact that men do not have free access to such imperfect markets as exist. No error is more egregious than that of confounding freedom with free competition, as is not infrequently done. As elementary theory itself shows, the numbers of any economic group can always make more by combining than they can by competing. Under freedom all that would stand in the way of a universal drift toward monopoly is the fortunate limitations of human nature, which prevent the necessary organization from being feasible or make its costs larger than the monopoly gains which it might secure. But universal monopoly is self-contradictory, and against any such tendency social action is the only recourse. The workings of competition educate men progressively for monopoly, which is being achieved not merely by the "capitalist" producers of

more and more commodities, but by labor in many fields, and in many branches of agriculture, while the producers of even the fundamental crops are already aspiring to the goal.*

8. The individualistic competitive organization of want-satisfying activity presupposes that wants and the means of satisfying them are individual, that is, that wants attach to things and services which gratify the wants of the person consuming them without affecting other persons. As a matter of fact, what is desired is more largely a matter of human relations than goods and services as such; we want things because other people have them, or cannot have them, as the case may be. Then, too, the appurtenances of civilized life can be furnished to an individual only by providing them for the community, and we want to live in a civilized community as well as to live in a civilized way ourselves. With rare exceptions, exchanges or contracts between individuals affect for good and for ill persons not represented in the bargain itself, and for these the bargain is not "free." Social action is necessary to promote the exchanges which diffuse benefits on others for which the parties cannot collect payment in the market, and to suppress those which diffuse evils for which the contracting parties do not have to pay. A typical illustration is the improvement or use of property in ways which add value to or subtract value from neighboring property. In a developed social order hardly any "free exchange" between individuals is devoid of either good or bad results for outsiders.

9. An exchange system cannot work at all according to "theory" without a scientific unit for measuring values. Society has to take over or carefully control activities which have to do with the circulating medium. With the use of credit highly developed, the control of banking and currency involves a large measure of control over all business, but really free banking would soon reduce all exchange relations to chaos.

10. An economic organization must employ its available productive power in part to provide for current needs of society and in part to provide for future growth. If this second function is to be performed intelligently through individual initiative under competitive organization, each member of the system must make a correct comparison and choice between his own present wants and future social requirements. The weakness of competitive individualism in this field is

---

* The resemblance of this argument to that of Marx is evident. There seems to be ground for treating Marx's conclusions seriously even though his supporting logic, based on the alleged universal superiority of large scale methods of production, must be repudiated.

well recognized, since manifestly progress is essentially a social fact. In an individualistic system, provision for progress depends upon the interest of present individuals in future individuals—engendered to an uncertain extent and with uncertain consequences on the form of progress by the family system—or upon their interest in progress itself or some form of it as an ideal value, or upon some accidental connection which makes progress a by-product of activities directed toward other ends. None of these, nor all together, produce results invulnerable to criticism; but the problems of social action in the same field are likewise so difficult and the ideal of progress itself so vague that it is impossible in short compass to say anything of value about the relation of different forms of social organization to the solution of the problem. It is a fact that social interference has gone further in this field than in that of controlling current production and consumption, as witness especially the social provision for education and scientific research.

11. All human planning and execution involve uncertainty, and a rational social order can be realized through individual action only if all persons have a rational attitude toward risk and chance. But the general human attitude is proverbially irrational, and much social limitation of individual freedom is called for. Not only is it necessary to prohibit gambling, but provision has to be made for placing control of resources and the direction of wealth production in the hands of persons reasonably fit and competent to take responsibility; and the freedom of these individuals to take chances has to be further restricted by general regulations. Thus no society has in fact ever treated productive resources as private property in any strict sense. It seems likely, however, that a socialistic society would err rather on the side of overconservatism than on that of recklessness.

12. The last heading in this list of reasons why individualism and competition cannot bring about an ideal utilization of social resources will be the ethics of distribution. In a competitive system distribution is effected by a marketing process, the evaluation of productive services, and is of course subject to all the limitations of marketing in general. . . . But that is not the main point. It is a common assumption—for which the exponents of the "productivity theory" are partly responsible—that productive contribution is an ethical measure of desert. This has improperly tended to bring the theory itself, as a causal explanation of what happens in distribution, into disrepute; because those who are misled into accepting the standard, but cannot approve of the result realized, react by attacking the theory. An examination of the question will readily show that productive contribution can have little or no ethical significance

from the standpoint of absolute ethics. (The question of practicability, it must be kept in mind, is eliminated by the boundaries set for this discussion; we are dealing with ideals and not inquiring whether or in what respects the possibilities of the real world may be harmonious with our moral cravings.) The examination of productivity as a standard of desert must again be handled in outline.*

a. In the first place, as already noted, there is only a "general tendency" to impute to each productive agency its true product. The factor of ignorance is especially important here, since correct imputation would require perfect technological knowledge and foresight. Human beings do not live on averages, and it is only to a very limited extent that a system of free exchange can make it possible for one to live this year on what he may (or may not) earn next year. To a still more limited extent, if at all, can the particular individual whom the tendency passes over live, through free exchange, on the compensating extra share of a more favored person?

b. The tendency to place each productive agency in the position where it will make the greatest contribution is far less effective even than the force which adjusts remuneration to actual contribution. A social system which sets artists to shining shoes and pays them what they are worth in that occupation is no less open to condemnation than one that sets them to work at their art and pays them what they would be worth as bootblacks.

c. The product or contribution is always measured in terms of price, which does not correspond closely with ethical value or human significance. The money value of a product is a matter of the "demand," which in turn reflects the tastes and purchasing power of the

---

* The "specific product" of any agency is what it enables society to produce more than could be produced without it, with no reference to what it could produce by itself. We assume that this is a correct use of the word *product,* since it is generally true in cause-and-effect relations that "the cause" is only the deciding factor in the antecedent situation, and that which factor is regarded as deciding is largely a matter of point of view.

We recognize also that specific productivity is the only possible basis for organizing productive resources intelligently, since maximum specific contribution all round is the condition of maximum total product.

It should be kept in mind also that the absolute ethics of distribution are not affected by the fact of organization and the interconnection of the products of different agencies. In a society characterized by individual self-efficiency, but recognizing the same ethical principles, the obligation of the more efficient or more industrious or more lucky individual who secured a superior share to divide up with others would be as great and as small as it is in a developed system of free enterprise.

buying public and the availability of substitute commodities. All these factors are largely created and controlled by the workings of the economic system itself, as already pointed out. Hence their results can have in themselves no ethical significance as standards for judging the system. On the contrary, the system must be judged by the conformity to ethical standards of these facts of demand rather than by the conformity to demand of the actual production and distribution of goods. And the final results diverge notoriously from the ethical standards actually held. No one contends that a bottle of old wine is ethically worth as much as a barrel of flour, or a fantastic evening wrap for some potentate's mistress as much as a substantial dwelling house, though such relative prices are not unusual. Ethically, the whole process of valuation is literally a "vicious" circle, since price flows from demand and demand from prices.

d. The income does not go to "factors," but to their owners, and can in no case have more ethical justification than has the fact of ownership. The ownership of personal or material productive capacity is based upon a complex mixture of inheritance, luck, and effort, probably in that order of relative importance. What is the ideal distribution from the standpoint of absolute ethics may be disputed, but of the three considerations named certainly none but the effort can have ethical validity. From the standpoint of absolute ethics most persons will probably agree that inherited capacity represents an obligation to the world rather than a claim upon it. The significance of luck will be discussed below in connection with the conception of business as a game. We must contend that there is a fallacy in the common position which distinguishes between the ethical significance of the income from labor and that from other factors. Labor in the economic sense may represent either a sacrifice or a source of enjoyment, and the capacity to labor productively derives from the same three sources as property ownership, namely, inheritance, luck, and effort of acquisition, and with no obvious general difference from the case of property in their relative importance.

e. The value of any service or product varies from zero to an indefinite magnitude, according to the demand. It is hard to see that, even when the demand is ethical, possession of the capacity to furnish services which are in demand, rather than other capacities, constitutes an ethical claim to a superior share of the social dividend, except to the extent that the capacity is itself the product of conscientious effort.

f. The value of a productive service varies from zero to an indefinite magnitude, according to its scarcity. The most vital ministrations become valueless if offered in superabundance, and the most trivial performance becomes exceedingly valuable if sufficiently unique and rare, as when a human monstrosity satisfies an economic demand by letting people look at him. It is hard to see how it is more meritorious merely to be different from other people than it is to be like them— except again, possibly, if the capacity has been cultivated by an effort which others refused to put forth.

g. Finally, it may be pointed out that modern society does accept and honor the claim of the entirely helpless to a tolerable human existence, and that there is no difference in principle between this recognition in the extreme case and admitting that differences in degree of competence form no valid basis for discriminatory treatment in distribution. But, after all, does anyone really contend that "competence," as measured by the price system, corresponds to ethical merit? Is it not obvious that "incompetence" follows just as surely if not quite so commonly from being too good for the world as from being blameworthy in character?

Thus the competitive system, viewed simply as a want-satisfying mechanism, falls far short of our highest ideals. To the theoretical tendencies of perfect competition must be opposed just as fundamental limitations and countertendencies, of which careful scrutiny discloses a rather lengthy list. Its standards of value for the guidance of the use of resources in production are the prices of goods, which diverge widely from accepted ethical values; and if the existing order were more purely competitive, if social control were reduced in scope, it seems clear that the divergence would be enormously wider still. Moreover, untrammeled individualism would probably tend to lower standards progressively rather than to raise them. "Giving the public what it wants" usually means corrupting popular taste. The system is also inefficient in utilizing resources to produce the values which it sets up, as brought out with startling force by the report on waste in industry, by a committee of the Confederated Engineering Societies. It distributes the produce of industry on the basis of power, which is ethical only in so far as right and might are one. It is a confessed failure in the field of promoting many forms of social progress, and its functions in this regard are being progressively taken over by other social agencies. Left to itself, such a system "collapses" at frequent intervals through dilution of its value unit and through other causes which produce violent oscillation instead of the equilibrium of theory.

It is expressly excluded from the field of the present paper to pass any practical judgment upon the competitive system in comparison with any possible alternative. But in view of the negative tone of the discussion, it seems fair to remark that many of these problems are exceedingly difficult and that many of the evils and causes of trouble are inherent in all large-scale organization as such, irrespective of its form. It must be said also that radical critics of competition as a general basis of the economic order generally underestimate egregiously the danger of doing vastly worse. Finally, let us repeat that practically there is no question of the exclusive use or entire aboliton of any of the fundamental methods of social organization, individualistic or socialistic. Economic and other activities will always be organized in all the possible ways, and the problem is to find the right proportions between individualism and socialism and the various varieties of each, and to use each in its proper place.

In turning from the want-satisfying aspect of economic activity to consider other of its value problems we enter upon a much harder task. There is little in the way of an established tradition for guidance, and the material is far less amenable to detailed subdivision or to treatment with scientific definiteness. All that can be attempted here is to raise questions and suggest lines of investigation.

It is an essential point in our criticism of established dogma that it has accepted in too narrow and final a sense the view of the economic system as merely a mechanism for satisfying those wants which are dependent upon exchangeable goods and services. Economists have given a belated and even yet not general and adequate recognition to the want-creating side of the system, and to wants as economic products at the same time that they serve as ends and guides of production. Still less attention has been paid to aspects of the organization problem which do not fall naturally under the subject of the satisfaction of wants at all, in the ordinary sense of wants for goods and services. But when we consider that productive activity takes up the larger part of the waking lives of the great mass of mankind, it is surely not to be assumed without investigation or inquiry that production is a means only, a necessary evil, a sacrifice made for the sake of some good entirely outside the production process. We are impelled to look for ends in the economic process itself, other than the mere consumption of the produce, and to give thoughtful consideration to the possibilities of participation in economic activity as a sphere of self-expression and creative achievement.

As soon as the question is raised, it becomes apparent that there are other values involved in production besides the consumption of the goods produced. Since the light of psychological criticism has been turned upon economic theory there has been a growing recognition of the inadequacy of the old treatment of production as mere sacrifice or pain undergone exclusively for the sake of consuming the product. The satisfaction derived from consumption itself is seen to be derived largely from the social situation rather than from the intrinsic qualities of the goods, while the mere fact that wealth is so largely accumulated, or devoted to all sorts of purposes manifestly not in view when its production was undertaken, is sufficient to prove that consumption is not the only motive of production. On the contrary, the persons most actively and successfully engaged in creating wealth not untypically limit their consumption to the point of living rather abstemious personal lives, which they must do to keep fit to meet the physical and mental demands which their business interests make upon them. At the bottom of the social economic scale, the satisfaction of physical needs is undoubtedly the dominant motive in the mind of the unskilled laborer. Higher up, consumption becomes less and less a matter of physiology and more a matter of aesthetics or the social amenities. Still higher, this in turn becomes mixed with a larger and larger proportion of the joy of activity not dependent on any definite use to be made of its results. Traditionally, economics has been vague on the character of economic motives, implying at one time wealth possession and at another wealth consumption as fundamental, and never working out clearly the relations between these essentially contradictory impulses or between them and other possible motives.

Turning to look for motives attached to production as an activity rather than to the product, the most obvious is its appeal as a competitive game. The desire for wealth takes on more or less of the character of the desire to capture an opponent's pieces or cards in a game. An ethical criticism of the industrial order must therefore consider it from this point of view. Insofar as it is a game, what kind of game is it? There is no doubt that a large amount of radical opposition to the system arises in this connection. The propertyless and ill-paid masses protest not merely against the privations of a low scale of living, but against the terms of what they feel to be an unfair contest in which being defeated by the stacking of the cards against them is perhaps as important to their feelings as the physical significance of the stakes which they lose. In a higher social class, resentment is aroused in the hearts of persons who do not like the game at all, and rebel against being compelled to play it and against being estimated socially and personally on the basis of their success or failure at it.

Increasing attention to this "human side" in economic relations is familiar to all in the demands of labor leaders, who talk much more than formerly of "control" and much less of wages and hours.

The same shift in emphasis is manifest in the entire literature of economic discontent. When the sentiment grows strong enough, the personnel problem begins to interfere seriously with business operations, and the ruling classes are forced to pay heed to it. It is probably within the truth to say that inequality in the enjoyment of the produce is now less important as a source of opposition to the competitive system than is the far greater inequality in the distribution of economic power, opportunity, and prestige. The feeling of antagonism is no doubt accentuated by the contrast between the political rhetoric about liberty and equality, on which our citizens are so largely fed, and the facts of autocracy and servitude which laboring people (rightly or wrongly) feel to characterize their actual lives.

Economists and publicists are coming to realize how largely the efficiency of business and industry is the result of this appeal to intrinsic interest in action; how feeble, in spite of the old economics, is the motivation of mere appetite or cupidity; and how much the driving power of our economic life depends on making and keeping the game interesting. A rapidly growing literature on "incentive" is a witness to this awakening. As long as we had the frontier and there was not only "room at the top" but an open road upward, the problem was not serious. But in a more settled state of society, the tendency is to make the game very interesting indeed to a small number of "captains of industry" and "Napoleons of finance," but to secure this result by making monotonous drudgery of the lives of the masses who do the work. There are limits beyond which this process cannot be carried without arousing a spirit of rebellion which spoils the game for the leaders themselves, not to mention the effect on the output of products upon which people have become dependent.

The problem of an ethical standard or ideal in terms of which to judge the economic order is of a different and far more difficult sort when we leave the field of more or less comparable burdens and quantitites of goods, to consider power and prestige as ends. In a competitive game it is absurd to speak of equality as an ideal, a fact which much radical discussion overlooks. Some of the criticisms brought against existing society amount to condemning a foot race as unfair because someone has come out ahead. We must bear in mind, too, that the system is a want-satisfying agency at the same time that it is a competitive game, and that the two functions are inseparable, while the two sets of ideals are different. For efficiency in the production of goods a large concentration of authority is necessary. But this concentration violates the principle of equality of opportunity in the game; and when power of control carries with it the right to consume product accordingly, as it actually does, the result is flagrant inequality in this respect also. There appears to be a deep-seated conflict between liberty and equality on the one hand and efficiency on the other. There is little comfort for democratic, equalitarian idealism in the study of evolutionary biology, in which the highly centralized or "cephalized" forms have always come out ahead. Yet apparently human society is different in some degree at least, for there appears to be a tendency for autocracies, aristocracies, and systems approaching a caste organization to be beaten out in history by the apparently less efficient "democracy," though democracies have not in practice approached closely to the equalitarian ideal.

In a system which is at the same time a want-satisfying mechanism and a competitive game we seem to find three ethical ideals in conflict. The first is the principle already mentioned, of distribution according to effort. The second is the principle of "tools to those who can use them." This is a necessary condition of efficiency, but involves giving the best player the best hand, the fastest runner the benefit of the handicap, and thus flagrantly violates the third ideal, which is to maintain the conditions of fairness in the game.

An attempt to formulate accurately the conditions of a fair and interesting game leads into difficult problems. The difference between play and work is subtle, and remains obscure after all the attempts of psychologists to deal with it. It is an old and ever-fascinating dream that all work might be converted into play under the right conditions. We know that almost any kind of work may become infused with the play spirit, as is more or less typically true of the creative arts, the higher professions to some extent, and notably business itself, as already observed. Yet definitions of play carry us little beyond the statement that it is enjoyable activity. It is usually defined as activity which constitutes its own end, is performed for its own sake. But this view will hardly stand examination. We cannot think of any human activity, however "playful," which is entirely spontaneous and self-contained. Perhaps the random movements of a baby's hands and feet fit the description; but the games and recreative activities of an adult or a child look more or less beyond the mere bodily movements; they have an objective, if nothing more than to build a block house to be immediately torn down, and on it they are dependent for their peculiar interest. Perhaps we can say that in play the objective usually follows so closely upon the activity that the two are naturally thought of as a unit, or that the result occupies the attention so fully as to exclude the effort from consciousness altogether, while in work they are contrasted and the activity is presented to the mind as a means, over against the end. At least, the feeling tone of play can often be imparted to work more or less voluntarily by fixing attention upon the objective, thus crowding the effort out of consciousness. The power to induce this shift of attention in other persons seems to be an important factor in leadership.

We are here concerned rather with the special psychology of competitive games than with the general problem of play, which includes noncompetitive social ceremonial as well as solitary random play and formal games played solitaire. A few general statements may be made with some confidence in regard to the difference between a good competitive game and a poor one. In the first place, there are three elements which affect the question of who is to win and thus contribute to the interest: these are ability to play, effort, and luck. It is also significant that the ability to play brought to the game on any particular occasion is, like all human capacity, a compound of innate endowment and "education" acquired from the previous expenditure of effort in play or practice, or perhaps in some closely related activity of either a recreative or a serious character. A good game must test the capacity of the players, and to do this it must compel them to exert effort. At the same time, it must involve more than a purely objective measure of capacity (assuming maximum effort). The result must be unpredictable: if there is no element of luck in it there is no game. There is no game in lifting weights, after one once knows how much can be lifted, even though the result measures capacity. Where "records" are made, the interest centers in the unpredictable fluctuations in the powers of men (or horses, etc.) from one trial to another.

A good game calls for some reasonable, though far from definite, proportion among the three elements, capacity, effort and luck— except that apparently most human beings are susceptible to fascination by pure chance, in spite of the obvious fact that a competitive game of pure chance involves a logical contradiction. Certainly there is general agreement that games of skill are "superior" to games of chance. Effort is called forth by interest, and intelligent interest is dependent on the fact that effort makes some difference in the result. But effort is futile or superfluous if there is too great a difference in the abilities of the players, and the game is spoiled. Even the hunter who considers himself a sportsman always gives his quarry a chance. Finally, it will no doubt be admitted that some games are "higher class" than others, depending presumably on the human qualities necessary to play them successfully and to enjoy them. The actual ranking of games would, it is true, raise the same problems of value standards which beset the path to objectivity in all fields of artistic criticism; and here also we should have to appeal to a general consensus and perhaps admit within limits the equal validity of opposing judgments.

No doubt different judges would disagree in their ranking of business as a competitive game, but the principles sketched above suggest some shortcomings. Its outcome is a very inaccurate test of real ability, for the terms on which different individuals enter the contest are too unequal. The luck element moreover is so large—far larger than fairly successful participants in the game will ever admit— that capacity and effort may count for nothing. And this luck element works cumulatively, as in gambling games generally. The effects of luck in the first hand or round, instead of tending to be evened up in accord with the law of large numbers in the further progress of the game, confer on the player who makes an initial success a differential advantage in succeeding hands or rounds, and so on indefinitely. Any particular individual may be eliminated by the results of his first venture, or placed in a position where it is extraordinarily difficult to get back into the game.*

Again, differences in the capacity to play the business game are inordinately great from one person to another. But as the game is organized, the weak contestants are thrown into competition with the strong in one grand mêlée; there is no classification of the participants or distribution of handicaps such as is always recognized to be necessary to sportsmanship where unevenly matched contestants are to meet. In fact the situation is worse still; there are handicaps, but, as we have seen, they are distributed to the advantage of the strong rather than the weak. We must believe that business ability is to some extent hereditary, and social institutions add to inherited personal superiority the advantages of superior training, preferred conditions of entrance into the game, and even an advance distribution of the prize money.

---

* In the matter of luck it is even more difficult than in the case of want satisfaction to measure the relative strength of different tendencies. Opinions will differ as to the ideal amount of luck in a game as well as in regard to the amount which there actually is in business. The cumulative working of the luck element will probably be more generally acknowledged to be a real evil. It is worth observing that the excessively crucial character of single decisions is a common phenomenon in all phases of life, a leading source of its tragedy and pathos. Rarely are we given enough "trials" in planning any feature of our careers to test the judgment which we actually possess. And when one thinks of the possibilities of developing better judgment, one is face to face with the essential tragedy of the brevity of life itself.

The distribution of prizes diverges from the highest ideal of sports-manship in another way. In a competition where the powers of the contestants are known to be unequal but the inequalities are not well enough determined to permit the classification of the players or an equalization of chances by means of handicaps, it is possible to sus-tain interest by offering a larger number of prizes less unequal in value. This method brings about an automatic classification of the contestants by the progress of the game itself. But in the business game the tendency is to multiply inequalities of performance in the inequality of distribution of the stakes. Let us suppose that we are organizing a foot race among a thousand men taken at random from the general population. At one extreme they might be all lined up on a mark and made to race for a single first prize; at the other, the prize money might be distributed equally, irrespective of the results of the race. From the standpoint of sport, the one proceeding would be as absurd as the other. If the critics of competition tend to make a fetish of equality, the system itself does undoubtedly go very far to the opposite extreme.

Admitting that business success tends in the large to go with business ability, we must face the question of the abstract merit of such capacity as a human trait, and hence of business as a game. It can hardly be denied that there is a preponderance of cultivated opinion against it. Successful businessmen have not become pro-verbial for the qualities that the best minds and most sensitive spirits of the race agree in calling noble. Business as it is and has been does not commonly display a very high order of sportsmanship, not to mention the question which will be raised presently as to whether sportsmanship itself is the highest human ideal. As to the human qualities developed by business activity and requisite to enjoyment of and successful participation in it, there is no objective measure, and no opinion will be accepted as free from "prejudice" by those who disagree with it. We shall dismiss the subject by quoting a state-ment by Ruskin, which can hardly be waived aside as valueless or unrepresentative. "In a community regulated by laws of demand and supply, but protected from open violence," he says, "the persons who become rich are, generally speaking, industrious, resolute, proud, covetous, prompt, methodical, sensible, unimaginative, insensitive and ignorant. The persons who remain poor are the entirely foolish, the entirely wise, the idle, the reckless, the humble, the thoughtful, the dull, the imaginative, the sensitive, the well-informed, the im-provident, the irregularly and impulsively wicked, the clumsy knave, the open thief, the entirely merciful, just and godly person."[4]

However favorable an opinion one may hold of the business game, he must be very illiberal not to concede that others have a right to a different view and that large numbers of admirable people do not like the game at all. It is then justifiable at least to regard as unfortunate the dominance of the business game over life, the virtual identification of social living with it, to the extent that has come to pass in the modern world. In a social order where all values are reduced to the money measure in the degree that this is true of modern industrial nations, a considerable fraction of the most noble and sensitive characters will lead unhappy and even futile lives. Everyone is compelled to play the economic game and be judged by his success in playing it, whatever his field of activity or type of interest, and has to squeeze in as a sideline any other competition, or noncompetitive activity, which may have for him a more intrinsic appeal.

We must treat still more inadequately our third main question, which from the point of view of pure ethics is the most important of all—the question of the ethics of competition as such. Is emulation as a motive ethically good or base? Is success in any sort of *contest*, as such, a noble objective? Are there no values which are real in a higher sense than the fact that people have agreed to strive after them and to measure success in life by the result of their striving? It seems evident that most of the ends which are actually striven after in the daily lives of modern peoples are primarily of this character; they are like the cards and checkermen, worthless (at best) in themselves, but the objects of the game; and to raise questions about the game is to make one's self disagreeable. To "play the game" is the current version of accepting the universe, and protest is blasphemy; the good man has given place to the "good sport." In America particularly, where competitive business, and its concomitant, the sporting view of life, have reached their fullest development, there have come to be two sorts of virtue. The greater virtue is to win; and meticulous questions about the methods are not in the best form, provided the methods bring victory. The lesser virtue is to go out and die gracefully after having lost.

We do not mean to beg the question whether the spirit of rivalry is ethically good, but only to state it in a form which raises it sharply. It cannot be denied that appeal to the competitive motive may be a source of interest in activity. The issue raised is in part the old and doubtless scientifically unanswerable one of pleasure versus discipline as the fundamental moral value. The hedonist would say that, as a matter of course, whatever adds to the pleasure adds to the value, and would ask only whether more is added than is taken away.

But here we appear to run into the obverse of Mill's paradox of hedonism, which is perhaps the paradox of life. It is in fact much easier to argue that the introduction of the contest motive into economic life has made it more efficient than that it has made it more pleasurable! Candid observations of industrial operatives at work, and of their frenzied, pathetic quest for recreation when off duty, alike fail to give the impression of particularly happy existence. As already observed, economic production has been made a fascinating sport *for the leaders*, but this has been accomplished by reducing it to mechanical drudgery for the rank and file. In the large is the competitive urge a lure, or is it rather a goad? Is it positive or negative, especially when we recall that for the masses the competition is in the field of consumption, with production regarded purely as a means? From the standpoint of pleasure, does the normal human being prefer a continuous, unquestioning, and almost deadly competition, or the less strenuous atmosphere of activity undertaken for ends that seem intrinsically worthwhile, with a larger admixture of the spectator attitude of appreciation? Current comment on the rush of life and the movement toward guilds and medievalism indicate a widespread feeling of opposition to the competitive tendency.

If on the other hand one adopts the view that the end of life is to get things done, the case for competition becomes much stronger; but even here misgivings arise. It is hard to avoid asking *what things*. If it is thought to be important which things are done, competition may be entirely indifferent and unselective, equally effective as a drive toward worthy and unworthy ends. If so, the selection of ends must be left to accident or to some other principle. There seems to be a tendency, however, for competition to be selective, and not in a very exalted sense. It is hard to believe that emulation is as effective in the "higher" fields of endeavor as it is in relation to material concerns or mere trivialities.

It is possible to hold that it does not matter what is done, that all activity develops personality equally, or that action and change as such are what make life worth living. From the point of view of mere interested activity, if we are to bring into question neither the character of the result nor that of the interest (beyond the fact that it is an "intelligent" interest, the result a foreseen result), the organization of life on a competitive basis would seem to be abundantly justified. Perhaps the organization tends to foster a philosophic attitude which will justify itself; and if so, we have a sufficient "economic interpretation" of the vogue of pragmatism. Interpreting life in terms of power as such, including "intelligence" as a form of power, there can be little question that competitive business has been an effective agency in bringing the forces of nature under human control and is largely responsible for the material progress of the modern era.

It is in terms of power, then, if at all, that competitive economics and the competitive view of life for which it must be largely accountable are to be justified. Whether we are to regard them as justified at all depends on whether we are willing to accept an ethics of power as the basis of our world view. And as Fichte said, "Was für eine Philosophie man wählt hangt davon ab was für ein Mensch man ist." But like most aphorisms this may be turned around without ceasing to be equally true: the sort of person one is depends on the sort of philosophy one chooses. It is the eternal law of reciprocal cause and effect; as just suggested, the system tends to mold men's minds in the channels which will justify the system itself, and in this sense there is a partial truth in the "economic interpretation," which we have gone to such lengths to attack and repudiate.[5] But the matter does not, cannot, rest there. The whole question is, are we to accept an "ethics of power" à la Nietzsche, or does such an acceptance involve a contradiction in terms and really mean the rejection of any true "ethics" altogether? Most of us have been taught in various connections not only that there is some sort of contrast between ethics and power, between right and might, but that the contrast is fundamental to the nature of morality. In these days it is eminently respectable to hold that all ideas of this sort belong to those childish things which one must put away on becoming a man. It is a part of the modern scientific world view, and a legitimate part. To many of its 'tough-minded" advocates, one who calls it in question must class himself as not merely "tender-minded," but "feeble-minded" as well.

And "logically" they are inevitably right! A strictly scientific discussion of general world problems leads inexorably to fatalism, to a mere question of power, to the relegation to a land of dreams of any ethics which involves questions of another sort than that as to which of two forces is the greater in magnitude. The question at issue must be clearly recognized to be precisely this: whether the logic of science itself is universally valid; whether there is or is not a realm of reality which is not comprehended in factual categories and describable in terms of definite meaning combined in propositions subject to empirical verification. Or, more accurately, it is the question whether knowledge of any such reality is possible, or whether it can be intelligently discussed. The tough-minded scientist, if candid, will admit that there *may be* such a reality, but will insist

that we cannot talk about it "intelligently." Which of course is true,
in the nature of the case, if to talk intelligently means to talk scientifically, which are to him equivalent terms. To the modern mind
any attempt to argue such a question is fraught with the greatest
difficulty, since the modern mind itself is molded into conformity
with the scientific view of what is meant by intelligent discourse.
Two facts, however, must apparently be accepted. The first is that
one may also find "respectable" company in the belief that the
scientific world view not only finds no place for many of the most
fundamental data of human experience, but that, tested by the
canons of its own logic, it is ultimately riddled with contradictions;
numerous minds of demonstrated competence in the field of science
itself hold this view. The second fact is that people do manage to
"understand each other" more or less, in conversation about things
which are not matters of scientific fact, but of interpretation, as in
discussions of art and of character or personality.

Assuming that all ethical standards other than that of quantity
of accomplishment, the ideal generated by the institution itself, are
not to be dismissed a priori as manifestations of incompetence to
discuss the question, we may close the discussion by referring briefly
to the relation of some historic types of ethical theory to the problem of the evaluation of competition. From the standpoint of
hedonism, the question would be simply whether competition has
added to the pleasure of living. This question has been raised above,
and we shall recur to it presently. In our view the nineteenth-century
hedonists were not ethical hedonists anyway. They held, or assumed,
the position of psychological hedonism, which involves the question-
begging procedure of using pleasure as a synonym for motive in
general, and to attack or criticize it at this day would be to slay the
slain. They were really utilitarians in the sense in which the term
was used by Paulsen, referring to the judgment of human actions by
their consequences and not in accordance with formal rules. On the
crucial question, how to judge the consequences, they were commonly silent or vague. But examination will show that nineteenth-
century utilitarianism was in essence merely the ethics of power, the
"glorified economics" to which we have referred before. Its outcome
was to reduce virtue to prudence, its ideal the achievement of the
greatest *quantity of desired results*. It was scientific, intellectual, in
the naturalistic, pragmatic conception of knowledge as instrumental
to power, that is, as power itself. As to the purposes for which power
ought to be used, the true problem of ethics, they had nothing to
say in any definite or systematic way; the fact of desire was tacitly
accepted as the essence of value. Spencer bravely reduced the whole

system to an ethical absurdity by explicitly carrying desire back to an ultimate justification in the desire to live, postulating that any species "must" desire what is good for it in a biological sense; and for all the group, survival power was in fact the final measure of rightness.

It seems to the writer almost superfluous to deny the appropriateness of the term "ethics" to any such conception. The conditions of survival are merely the laws of biology. It may well be the part of prudence to act in accordance with them, assuming that one *wants* to survive, but it can hardly be associated with the notions of right or duty, and if these have no meaning beyond prudence the whole realm of ethics is illusory.* Ethics deals with the problem of choosing between different kinds of life, and assumes that there is real choice between different kinds, or else there is no such thing as ethics. The ethical character of competition is not decided by the fact that it stimulates a greater amount of activity; this merely raises the question of the ethical quality of what is done or of the motive itself.

With this so-called ethics of scientific naturalism may be contrasted, as general types of ethical thought, true ethical hedonism or eudemonism, the Greek and the Christian views. From the standpoint of the first, the happiness philosophy, little need be added to what has already been said. Competition may form an added source of pleasure in activity, especially to the winner or, in the progress of the game, to those who stand some chance to win. But it is more likely to become a goad, especially when participation in the contest is compulsory. There is a fairly established consensus that happiness depends more on spiritual resourcefulness, and a joyous appreciation of the costless things of life, especially affection for one's fellow creatures, than it does on material satisfaction. A strong argument for cooperation, if it would work, would be its tendency to teach people to like each other in a more positive sense than can ever be bred by participation in a contest—certainly in a contest in which the means of life, or of a decent life, are felt to be at stake. The dominance of salesmanship in the business world, as well as the spirit of economic rivalry, must also tend to work against the appreciation of the "free goods."

It should be observed also that while the principle of "whom the Lord loveth he chasteneth" is hard to apply as a maxim of practical morality, it is generally admitted that human nature is likely to show up morally finer under adversity than in security and ease; also that

---

* These writers could find no place for and would have to reject an ethical obligation to live.

few people can be trusted with much power without using it to the physical damage of others and their own moral discredit.

Surely no justification of competition as a motive is to be found in the Aristotelian conception of the good as that which is intrinsically worthy of man as man, or the Platonic idea of archetypal goodness. The outstanding characteristic of Greek ethical thought was the conception of the good as objective, and of the moral judgment as a cognition. A thing should be done because it is the thing to do, not because it is or is not being done by others. Virtue is knowledge, and the good is intellectually conceived, but the meaning of these statements contrasts as widely as possible with the modern reduction of virtue to prudence and of choice to a calculation of advantage. The intellectual quality in Greek ethics is the capacity of discrimination between true and false values, which is a wholly different thing from the ability to foresee changes and adapt means to ends. The one runs in terms of appreciation as the other runs in terms of power. The ideal in the one case is perfection, in the other that of bigness. To be sure, the Greeks were far from indifferent to recognition and glory, and the contest spirit played a large role in the life of the people, as shown in the national games. But the ideal seems always to have been the achievement of perfection, and the education of the people to recognize superior merit, not merely to win. Certainly it was not the mere winning of power.

Christianity has been interpreted in so many conflicting ways that one must hesitate to bring it into a scientific discussion; yet even this wide range of uncertainty will not admit competitive values into Christian thought. If there is anything on which divergent interpretations would have to agree, it would be the admission that the Christian conception of goodness is the antithesis of competitive. We are by no means forced to believe that the central figure of the Gospels was an ascetic; he never condemned pleasure as such, and seems to have had his own pleasure in life. But his participation in any sort of competitive sport is not to be imagined. Among his most characteristic utterances were the fervent exhortations that the last should be first and that he who would be chief should be the servant of all. The Christian ethical ideal contrasts as sharply with the Greek as either does with modern ideas derived from natural science and political economy. We have said that any *ethical* judgment of activity must be based not upon its efficiency, the quantity of results accomplished, but on either the character of those results or the character of the motive which led to the action. The Greek view fixes attention upon the character of the result, and gives an essentially aesthetic conception of ethical value; Christianity centers attention upon the motive, and its ideal of life may be summed up in the word *spirituality*, as the Greek ideal is summed up in *beauty* or *perfection*. As the Greek identified virtue with knowledge, assuming it to be inconceivable that one should recognize true values and not act in accordance with them, Christianity (more explicitly as formulated by Paul—Romans 7:15; Galatians 5:19–23) makes virtue consist in conscientiousness, in doing what one believes to be right, rather than in the correct perception of objective goodness. It must be admitted that if it is hard to describe or define beauty, it is enormously more difficult to discuss spirituality in terms that seem at all intelligible to a scientific age. Both ideals agree in differing from economic (scientific, pragmatic) ethics in that they are *qualitative* in their ideals, whereas the last is merely quantitative. It seems fairly clear to the writer that it is from Christianity (and from Kant, who merely systematized Christian, or Pauline, principles) that modern common sense derives its conceptions of what is ethical when that point is explicitly under discussion.

The striking fact in modern life is the virtually complete separation between the spiritual ethics which constitutes its accepted theory of conduct and the unethical, uncriticized notion of efficiency which forms its substitute for a practical working ideal, its effective values being accepted unconsciously from tradition or the manipulations of commercial sales managers, with a very slight admixture of aesthetic principles. For "spirituality" is reserved in practice a smaller and smaller fraction of the seventh day, by a smaller and smaller fraction of the population; and even that is more and more transformed by organizations into a mere contest in membership and display, with a larger or smaller admixture of the element of aesthetic diversion and a smaller or larger admixture of pure commercialism. The spirit of life in the "Christian" nations and the spirit of Christianity offer an interesting study in the contrast between theory and practice. And all the while there are multiplying evidences of a genuine spiritual hunger in the modern peoples. They have got away from the spiritual attitude toward life, and do not know how to get back. Science is too strong for old beliefs, and competitive commercialism too strong for old ideals of simplicity, humility, and reverence.

Thus we appear to search in vain for any really ethical basis of approval for competition as a basis for an ideal type of human relations, or as a motive to action. It fails to harmonize either with the pagan ideal of society as a community of friends or the Christian ideal of spiritual fellowship. Its only justification is that it is effective in getting things done; but any candid answer to the question, "What things," compels the admission that they leave much to be desired. Whether for good or bad, its aesthetic ideals are not such as command the approval of the most competent judges, and as for spirituality, commercialism is in a fair way to make that term incomprehensible to living men. The motive itself has been generally condemned by the best spirits of the race. In academic life, for example, though every (American) institution feels itself compelled to use credits, marks, and honors, they are virtually never defended as intrinsically worthy incentives to effort.

Whether it is possible to bring about improvement by substituting some other basis of social organization for competitive individualism is beyond the scope of this paper. Its purpose has been merely to bring out fundamental weaknesses of competition from the standpoint of purely ideal standards, and so to establish bases for comparison with any other possible system. Summarizing the argument, it was first emphasized by way of introduction that any judgment passed upon a social order is a value judgment and presupposes a common measure and standard of values, which must be made as clear and explicit as possible if the judgment is to be intelligent. Efficiency is a value category and social efficiency an ethical one. Now the standards which underlie a competitive system, according to orthodox economic theory, are the actual desires of the individual members of society. Competition is supposed to effect a comparison of these, and to organize the resources of society in such a way as to satisfy them to the greatest possible extent in order of magnitude— that is, it is supposed to "tend" to do so. The first main task of the paper was therefore to enumerate the more fundamental and obvious limitations on this tendency, or countertendencies which are in many cases quite as important as the tendency itself. Economic theory must isolate the ideal tendencies with which it can deal most readily; but no practical conclusions as to the real beneficence of the system can be drawn until the actual relative importance of the tendencies recognized by the general theory—which in endeavoring to explain always seems to justify—are measured in comparison with divergent tendencies and taken into account.

In the next part of the paper it was pointed out that the competitive economic life has value implications on the production side, the most notable of which is its appeal as a competitive game. An examination from this point of view reveals notable shortcomings of business considered purely as a game. There is also a certain ethical repugnance attached to having the livelihood of the masses of the people made a pawn in such a sport, however fascinating the sport may be to its leaders.

Finally, we have called in question from the standpoint of ideal ethics the predominance of the institution of sport, or action motivated by rivalry, and in particular have contrasted it with the pagan ethics of beauty or perfection and the Christian ideal of spirituality.

NOTES

1. "Ethics and the Economic Interpretation," *Quarterly Journal of Economics,* vol. 36, pg. 454–481.
2. Thorstein Veblen, "Industrial and Pecuniary Employments" in *Publications of the American Economics Association,* 3rd series, vol. 2, 1901.
3. Thorstein Veblen, "The Vested Interests and the Common Man," (New York: Huebsch, 1920).
4. John Ruskin, "Ad Valorem," *The Cry of Justice: An Anthology of Social Protest* ed. Upton Sinclair (Philadelphia: John C. Winston, 1915).
5. See the paper above referred to: "Ethics and the Economic Interpretation," in the *Quarterly Journal of Economics,* vol. 36 (May 1922), pp. 454–481.

4.

Justice

The issue of the justice of an economic system appears to be an abstract, philosophical problem beyond the interest and concern of most ordinary people. But, in actuality, this issue is probably given more attention than any other ethical problem of the business system. Everyone is constantly debating, in one way or another, the justice of the system.

There are numerous manifestations of this debate. One can even find it in many sections of the daily newspaper. In the sports section appears a report that star athlete X receives $800,000 a year for performing for six months. This kind of fact is not only reported in the sports pages, it is also analyzed and discussed. Is someone really worth $800,000 to a team? Is it right to pay an athlete so much? Do sports stars make a contribution equivalent to the enormous salaries that some of them receive?

Turning to the entertainment section, we find similar reports. Someone has agreed to perform in Las Vegas for $100,000 per week, and someone else is being paid $2 million to appear in a movie. For some reason, the discussion of whether any entertainer deserves that kind of money is not as intense and widespread as it is for athletes. Still, articles that ask this kind of question are not unusual.

The everyday discussions of justice, however, are not confined to why some athletes and entertainers are so rich. Other aspects of this issue more directly touch most people. One of these aspects is taxes. Although death may be a taboo subject for general discussion according to current American mores, this is not true for its supposedly inevitable partner. Talk about taxes goes on and on. Is it right that married people should pay more than those who are living together? Is it fair, as is often currently being asked, that business-men can deduct their three-martini lunches while laborers cannot deduct their salami sandwiches? Is it just that a homeowner who improves his house has his taxes raised, while a slum landlord who lets his property deteriorate does not? Is it fair when rich people who can afford to invest in tax-free municipal bonds pay no income tax at all?

Another area in which discussions of justice are rampant is labor-management relations. When there is a strike, or the threat of one, talk always centers on how much each side should get. Labor might claim it deserves more because it is doing the hard work, or because the cost of living has gone up, or because profits of the company have risen due to higher productivity. Management might claim that the workers are getting as much as they should because any more would hurt the company financially, or because productivity has gone up because of management-introduced innovations. The argu-ment about who should get what is the basic issue.

The argument about justice also arises over fundamental aspects of the business system. Critics have formulated many complaints about the system, but most of these come down to the view that the American business system is unjust. Some of the familiar cri-ticisms, which are basically accusations of injustice, focus on the exploitation of workers, on the lack of proportion between social contribution and reward, or on the special advantages given to the descendants of the wealthy. These criticisms, and the defenders' answers to them, have constituted a good deal of the past discussion of the ethics of the American business system.

In order to see what is involved in the issue of justice, it will be useful to understand how justice is related to the issue of competi-tion, which was examined in the previous section. Competition, as we have seen, occurs when two or more individuals desire what they cannot share. The consequence of competition is that at least one of the competitors will lose. Most likely, but not necessarily, one of them will win by gaining the desired object. These are, in essence, the bare facts of competition, but they raise an ethical question: Does the winner deserve to win and does the loser deserve to lose? This is the problem of desert, and it is the main point in discussions of the justice of the business system.

The question of desert, however, needs to be clarified: What is meant when one asks whether the winner and the loser in a com-petition deserved their lot? In many ordinary situations, the question of deserving what one gets in competition usually concerns whether the competitors obeyed the rules. It is usually thought that a candidate in an election does not deserve to win if his victory was based on illegal actions. The rules of elections, though changing, are still quite specific. Candidates are not permitted to intimidate those who they think will vote against them. They are not allowed to have their cohorts vote in the names of registered voters who are now dead. They are not allowed to collect certain kinds of contributions. A candidate who is later found out to have won because he violated one of these prohibitions is usually considered not to have deserved the victory.

Similarly, in athletic competitions the rules of what is permissible are usually very explicit. Winners who are found to have broken a rule are sometimes, and appropriately so, deprived of their victory. A boxing champion who is discovered to have won his matches because he soaked his bandaged hands in cement before every fight will have his title taken away. If his career is over when the discovery is made, posterity will no longer give him the honor he had while the fraud was unknown.

In general, when asking if a winner deserved to win or whether a loser deserved to lose, what is being asked is whether the rules of the competition were followed. In cases where it can be shown that this has happened, the results, whatever they are, are considered to be deserved.

Applying this to business, consider the question of whether Mr. So-and-so deserves to be rich. Mr. So-and-so is the son of wealthy parents who sent him to prestigious schools. On his twenty-first birthday they gave him a present of $100,000 and told him to go seek his fortune. Of course, some might think that So-and-so had been given a fortune, but he was not satisfied with what he had and so he contacted a shrewd financial advisor, who drew up a list of investments. So-and-so followed this advice, and his bank account expanded until it reached the millions. Does he deserve to be so rich? The kind of answer that was given for the election example and the athletic-competition case would emphasize that So-and-so did nothing illegal to gain his money. He broke no laws and could not be accused of doing anything even remotely shady. Therefore, some might say that he did deserve to be a millionaire.

This kind of answer is satisfactory in one respect, but it leads naturally to another question: Is business competition itself set up in a proper manner? One can admit that Mr. So-and-so obeyed all the rules, but there is still a feeling that something is wrong because the rules themselves are unfair. This is the point at which the philosophical question of justice is raised. To think that a competitor deserves his lot because he followed the rules is one thing, but to ask whether the rules themselves are just is a question of a different level.

But how does one determine what factors are relevant to deciding whether a set of competitive rules is just or unjust? What standards are there for judging a whole competitive system? Is there any way to make a reasonable assessment of something as complex as the business and economic system? These questions are perplexing, but an examination of what philosophers have had to say about justice shows that the discussion has coalesced around two major issues. Both of them are suggested in Mannison's article, and together they form the basis of most discussions of the justice of the economic system.

The first is the issue of equality of opportunity. One's belief about the justice of a competition depends to a great extent upon whether one thinks all of the contestants had an equal opportunity to win. In the most obvious case, a race is considered to be unfair if some of the contestants have their legs tied together, if some are given a head start, or if some have to jump over hurdles along the way. It also would be difficult to say that a boxing match was fair if one of the fighters weighed 200 pounds and the other only weighed 100 pounds. Even if the referee were scrupulously fair in applying the rules during the fight, it is agreed that this sort of contest does not provide the contestants with an equal opportunity to win. That is the reason why there are different weight classifications in boxing. Finally, in a nonathletic example, one would have doubts about the fairness of a trial if the state were represented by a battery of well-trained, experienced lawyers, and the defendant had a nervous young man, fresh out of law school.

These are examples in which most people would admit there is an element of injustice. In these examples, the contestants do not seem to have an equal opportunity to win, either because some competitors have unfair advantages or because some are saddled with special handicaps. In order to make these contests really fair, the handicaps and the advantages should be removed. However, removing those features is by no means a simple matter. Consider the race example again. Among the contestants in a race, some undoubtedly have more natural talent than others. There are some people who are born fast runners. Should these naturally talented people be made to run the race carrying a weight of twenty pounds on their backs? If this attempt is made in an effort to remove the advantage of natural talent, is a special handicap, which makes the race unfair again, being introduced?

Another feature that plays an important role in determining who will win the race is the amount of training each contestant has undergone. Training in an intelligent manner improves a runner's chances of winning a race. But then the same question arises. Is being well trained an unfair advantage? In order to ensure equal opportunity, should the well-trained contestants begin the race twenty yards behind the others? But if those who have the training are given some special obstacle, will they not be justified in protesting that they are being treated unfairly?

The idea of equal opportunity is not an easy one to make precise. That everyone should have equal opportunity is something most people would agree with, at least at first. But when one tries to specify exactly what "equal opportunity" means in any particular case, the easy agreement falls apart. What is one person's equal opportunity is another person's unfair advantage. The source of the problem is that one must specify exactly what features should be made equal in order to give all the contestants an equal opportunity to win.

Even upon a superficial examination, it becomes obvious that every individual is different from every other individual in at least some respects. In any group of people some will be taller, some heavier, some more intelligent, some more disciplined, and some more determined. It is impossible to have a competition in which all of the contestants are equal in every respect. The problem is to select those characteristics that must be made equal in order to keep the contest fair, and the philosophical problem is to provide an argument that will justify why just these particular features are the relevant ones in the particular case. In a race, the features usually considered to be the ones that must be equal in order for equal opportunity to exist are: the contestants should all have to cover the same distance, and the contestants should all have displayed roughly similar achievement in the past. The philosophically inclined would argue why just these two features are important in most races and why natural talent and training should be ignored.

The problem of equal opportunity is not only of great philosophical interest; it is also one of the most disturbing issues facing our society today. The matter of preferential treatment of disadvantaged groups, an issue that has crystallized in the Bakke case, is really a debate about what should be done in order to ensure equal opportunity; and the confusion and disagreement over this issue are signs of the unsolved philosophical problem. There is not, at the present time, a clear understanding of how to justify, in any particular case, the selection of features that have to be made equal in order for equal opportunity to be said to exist.

Another problem of equal opportunity is the matter of inheritance. This problem is raised and discussed by all the writers of the following articles. Permitting people to pass their estates on to their heirs seems to violate the equal-opportunity aspect of justice. A person who has inherited a fortune has an enormous advantage in any sort of economic competition. But is it an unfair advantage? The inheritors of natural talent also have a great advantage in contests in which they can use their special talent, but as was mentioned above, this kind of advantage does not necessarily mean the contest is unfair. What is needed in order to solve this problem is an argument that conclusively shows whether the obvious advantage provided by inherited wealth is an unfair advantage. Is inheritance the kind of feature that can be compared to giving some contestants in a race a head start, and is it, for that reason, unjust? Or is it more like being a naturally fast runner—an advantage, no doubt, but one that does not mean that those who possess it have made the competition unfair.

The writers in the following selections argue on both sides of this problem, and there is also a third possible view that receives some support. This is the view that equal opportunity is only one standard by which to judge inheritance. According to this view, other matters should also be considered; and when they are, one will see that there are certain benefits to the institution of inheritance that far outweigh any negative aspects of it. It is interesting to notice, however, that this view implicitly accepts the idea that inheritance is a violation of equal opportunity.

The second major issue is called the problem of *distributive justice*. In this issue the focus is not on the start of the competition as it is with the issue of equal opportunity; instead, the concern is directed more at the end, or the results, of the competition. In competitions, some will win and some will lose, and the winners will gain rewards that the losers will have to forego. The question of distributive justice is whether the winners deserve the kind of rewards they get even if they followed all the rules and if all the contestants started out equally.

To illustrate this issue, consider first some examples that are not directly related to business. Students in some law schools have complained that the grading system used is unfair. The complaint is not that the equal-opportunity requirement has been violated because some students have been given special advantages or handicaps. Nor is the complaint the claim that some students have been cheating. The complaint is that it is unfair that so much depends on one's grades when the grades are established in a haphazard manner. In many cases, one's future career in law (and in today's market, whether one will have a career at all) depends to a great extent on the grades one receives in the first year. In many law schools, these grades are completely determined by the examinations one takes at the end of the year. The rewards for doing well can be great, but the results of doing poorly can be quite depressing. How well one does can be affected by any number of factors besides one's knowledge of the law. Happening to study the right material, not being nervous, or simply being lucky could all determine the result. There is no way to say that equal opportunity did not apply, but still there seems to be something unjust about having so much ride on so little.

Elections provide another example. Two candidates for an office might start out equally in terms of experience and resources. They also might follow all of the rules. But one candidate concentrates his energy on shaking hands and kissing babies, and the other tries to make substantive proposals on the problems of the community. We might not be satisfied that the winner really deserved the office if the "shaking-kissing" candidate received the most votes.

In order to see how the issue of distributive justice arises in a business context, consider the following example. Investor A is a kind, warm-hearted person who has worked hard all his life and has saved a little money. He buys stock in a small furniture company with the hope that he will get a modest return on his investment so that he can afford to send his children to college. Investor B is a mean, nasty, and lazy person who happens to inherit a little money. He invests it in another small furniture company. B hopes to make enough money to finance a trip to Monte Carlo where he can indulge his passion for gambling among the upper crust. Neither A nor B has any good evidence about the prospects of these two companies. One day B's company discovers a cheap substitute for wood and can then make furniture at a much lower cost than any of the competitors. A's company goes bankrupt and A loses his money. B's company becomes one of the Fortune 500 and B becomes a millionaire.

It would certainly seem that A and B started out equally and that no rules were broken, but many people would think that the results are unjust. B did nothing to deserve to gain such a great reward. His success was not due to any effort on his part or to any morally praiseworthy motives. He just happened to be lucky. Nice guy A did nothing to deserve losing. He was a fine citizen and had an unselfish reason for wanting to make some more money, but he was unlucky.

Consider another example: C and D are people of equal ability and training. C decides that as his lifework he will try to find a cure for a rare, but fatal and painful, childhood disease. D decides to try to invent a way to maintain the carbonation in soda pop after a bottle has been opened and the top has not been replaced. Both C and D are successful in their endeavors, but C earns a modest amount for his discovery, whereas D becomes extremely wealthy. Are these results just?

Another example: E and F are friends who both become plumbers. Plumber E decides that he wants to live close to his sick grandmother. This area, however, has a number of other fine plumbers living there, and as a result, even though E works very hard to do quality work, he can only scrape by. Plumber F has no family obligations, and so he moves to an area in which very few plumbers happen to be available. F becomes a shoddy workman, and while he never does a poor enough job to be sued, his work never lasts as long as it would had he been more careful. F's prices are high and so he lives very well in spite of his half-hearted efforts. Are these results just?

These examples, which could, and do, occur in our economic system, raise the issue of distributive justice. In all of them, the people involved seem to have an equal opportunity to win a large economic reward. However, these examples all illustrate the fact that equal opportunity, although an important factor, is not the only matter one considers in thinking about the justice of the results. One also considers the moral qualities of the contestants—their needs, their efforts, and their social contribution—as well as other factors.

However, to consider these other matters does not mean one will conclude that they should be taken into account in assessing the justice of the results of competition. Of the writers of the articles in this section, Nozick and Hayek, for very different reasons, would say that the results in each of the last three examples were just. Mannison would probably claim they were all unjust, and Rawls would say that the results in the example involving C and D were unjust.

What is involved in the disagreement about these examples is a difference of opinion over what factors should be taken into account in judging the justice of the results. All the writers in this section are concerned with the problem of distributive justice, and, structurally, it is a similar problem to the question of equal opportunity. In both cases there are a number of different factors involved, and the problem is to pick out those that are relevant to considerations of justice.

Involved in the results of any distribution are factors concerning qualities of the recipients as well as events that have happened in the past. All the writers in this section are trying to determine which of these factors should be taken into account in deciding if the results of competition are just. Furthermore, they are all trying to provide an argument to justify their particular selection of relevant factors. That there is no agreement between them about this perplexing issue is not surprising.

These then are the two problems of justice: equal opportunity and just rewards. They have generated a great amount of discussion concerning the American business system; and one of the system's prominent defenders, Irving Kristol, has conceded that the problem of justice is the criticism that is the hardest to answer.*

DONALD MANNISON

Remarks on Justice in American Society

Am I correct in characterizing this country as a plutocracy? I.e., is it empirically the case that wealth and political power are systematically linked? This allegation would not, of course, be justified if the attainment of political power by the economically disadvantaged were as probable as it is for the wealthy. American law schools are, notoriously, kindergartens for future political leaders. In recent years, the successful businessman has been increasingly breathing down the lawyer's political neck.

Is it not true that the ranks of lawyers and businessmen are filled almost exclusively by individuals who have at least moderately affluent backgrounds? Of course, it will be argued that many of these are "self-made men," people who have pulled themselves out of poverty, out of the ghetto, and out of the barrio. But the very fact that we can point to a few such people supports the contention that

---

* Irving Kristol, "When Virtue Loses All Her Loveliness—Some Reflections on Capitalism and 'the Free Society' " in *Capitalism Today,* Daniel Bell and Irving Kristol, eds. (New York: Basic Books, 1971).

Source: *The Personalist,* vol. 52, 1971. Reprinted with permission of the editor.

one "normally" expects political leaders to be drawn from a quite different economic class.

It might be noted in passing that those who cite "individualism" as a primary social (and moral) value are not, normally, in the forefront of a fight to eliminate the inheritance laws, tax dodges, and trust funds designed and maintained by the wealthy to bestow wealth upon those who did not contribute in any way to its production. The inheritance of wealth seems to me the most blatant and indefensible case of the "parasitism" decried by social egoists. It is curious to find that social institutions such as trade unions and welfare programs are condemned as instances of "sentimental altruism," while the inheritance of millions, causally justified only by an accident of birth, is condoned and encouraged. Such practices conflict with the principle of justice adumbrated under the rubric of rational egoism articulated by Nathaniel Branden. Branden writes: "Justice is the practice of identifying men for what they *are*, and treating them accordingly—of rewarding actions and traits of character in men which are pro-life and condemning those which are anti-life."[1] But since "the least productive member of our society" can designate one and the same individual as "the only son of Paul Getty," the only way that inheritance could be justified in this case would be to introduce a plutocratically biased premise.

How true is the contention that the poor have "equal opportunity" to participate in political power as the wealthy? The average income of the parents of students attending tertiary educational institutions increases directly with the "quality" of the school attended. I.e., the average income of parents of junior-college students is less than that of state-college students, which in turn is less than that of state-university students, and finally, the last group is less than that of prestigious private schools. It is not strange or surprising that attention has not been focused on junior colleges for their lack of black and Mexican-American students. If the likelihood of a successful political career is greatly increased by having attended a quality university, then it follows that any economic bar to admission ultimately operates to maintain a plutocracy.

Given the general economic pressures on poor families, it is not a principle of rational egoism that dictates the continuance of plutocracy in American political life, but rather, the unspoken (but, perhaps, whispered) dictum that the sins of the father shall be visited upon the sons. The "sin" of the father is, of course, his poverty; and to remain in poverty, then, is the "just desert" of his successors.

Some form of "economic collectivism" is the traditional counterforce to plutocracy. Historically, this has taken the form of guilds

and trade unions. It is, in its simplest terms, a pitting of the collective
strength of productive individuals against the wealth-derived strength
of a single individual. The etymological root of *democracy* involves a
"collectivity" with respect to political power. Where it is a plutocracy that one opposes, democracy can only be restored (or initially
achieved) through altering the systematic interrelationship of wealth
and political power. N.B.: It is not being argued here that the existence of a "capitalist" economic system in a society is a sufficient
condition for that society's being a political plutocracy.*

A healthy body may not be a logically necessary condition for a
healthy mind, but it can scarcely be denied that ill health contributes
significantly to the quality and quantity of a man's productive
efforts. The United States is one of the few "western democracies"
that has failed to provide substantially equal health care for both rich
and poor. This is but another instance of how a plutocratic orienta-
tion tends to maintain itself institutionally. Although no nation is
technologically and scientifically superior to us, U.S. Department of
Health statistics show us to rank fourteenth in infant mortality.
Every country that ranked above us had some government-supported
medical program; including Australia, a U.S. economic satellite.

If Branden is correct in his suggestion that justice pertains to the
actions and *character traits* of people, then in order to protect his
observation from the charge of biased vacuity it is necessary to make
some corollary comments. There is no *point* (here, "point" is being
employed to mark what some philosophers have intended to mark
by "meaning") in the comment "John did not. . . ." (where the
blank is filled by some act-identifying expression) unless the context
is one in which it can be presupposed or understood that John had
the opportunity to perform the action in question. It is only when
one is playing a game (perhaps with words) that it would make sense
to say that someone who lacked opportunity did not (or "failed to")
do something. In most cases a young black from Watts neither does
nor does not enter Harvard University; nor does it, normally, make
sense to say that he did not amass a $5 million fortune. One would
be speaking less than candidly if, knowing that I never gambled, one
told a mutual acquaintance that I had not lost any money in Reno
last weekend.**

---

* I must confess, however, that I cannot imagine economic power entirely
unaccompanied by political power (and privilege).
** The issue that is being touched upon here; viz. that there are semantically
significant "rules of candor" embedded in the use of a natural language, is, of
course, far more complex than these remarks would indicate.

A similar consideration must be entered concerning the idea of a trait of character. Since character traits are expressed or manifested only through action, the ascription of a character trait to a person makes sense only if the individual has had opportunity to execute the kinds of acts appropriate to the trait in question. It can be said of me that I have pride or lack pride in myself only if I have had the opportunity to engage in the kind of activity in which one could be reasonably expected to take pride.

Consequently, in a society in which the range of activities (and achievements) in which the poor have opportunity to participate is severly circumscribed, to speak of what the poor do not do, or what they fail to achieve, or of the character traits they lack, is to violate the rules of candor which give point to speech performances in a natural language.

I have spoken up to now only about justice in a society in a very broad way. The following remarks will be devoted to some rather less general considerations.

I will not here propose either an analytical or phenomenological account of the concept of justice. There is, however, quite general agreement amongst writers on the subject that the notion of justice with which we operate (and, presumably, have always, to some extent, operated) involves a version or formulation of the principle "Treat similar cases similarly, and dissimilar cases dissimilarly." What I shall undertake to do now is to raise difficulties and perplexities about the idea of cases being "similar" or "dissimilar." What I shall contend, in conclusion, is that injustice is widespread; a situation generated and maintained, in part by presuppositions derived from tacit or overt plutocratic biases.

Before continuing, however, I want to make some observations concerning things which are frequently said in connection with the notion of "distributive justice," i.e., where the idea of justice pertains to equitable distribution of products and the means for the acquisition of products. It's been commonly noted that an equitable distribution of things cannot reasonably be understood to be on "equal" distribution, since, e.g., if medicine were distributed equally to all, then someone who *needed* more to survive would either have to be deprived of it, or alternatively, he (or another) would have to violate the principle of justice to obtain it. This is an interesting argument against "equality of distribution" because: (1) I think few would insist that an acceptable principle of just distribution would be one which would sanction the denial of medicine to a sick person; and (2) the principle which is here being appealed to is not one to which appeal is often made.

Apart from shamefully inadequate welfare programs, the idea of distribution according to *need* is entirely ignored in our society. When two people are employed to do the same job (typically), their salaries are not determined, say, by the number of dependents each has. (An interesting countercase is that this is, to a certain extent, true of the military services. I am here thinking of dependents' allowances.) If need were considered, in general, to be a relevant factor in the distribution of goods and money, then it would be the common (or universal) practice to pay a proportionately higher salary to a person with more dependents than to a worker with only himself to support.

Other kinds of cases, of course, could be cited. It might be argued that most people having reached a certain age do not need as much money, say, as a young couple starting out in life. Suppose that one suggested that instead of giving pay raises to people after age fifty-five, one would receive a 5 percent decrease each subsequent year? Once again the justification proffered would be in terms of differential needs.

It will be to no avail to reject these suggestions as being "silly" on the ground that, e.g., if the first were adopted, then employers would favor single people with respect to hiring. The innate or acquired "meanness" of people is irrelevant to the logic of the argument I'm examining. The point here is that while need seemed to be intuitively (and, I might add, morally) acceptable ground in the initial case for not identifying distributive justice with equality of distribution, one is, perhaps, inclined to find bizarre these other cases in which differential distribution was based upon need. It is not obvious, then, that need is a *logically* sufficient condition for rejecting an identification between equality and distributive justice as one principle of justice.

It will be no objection to point out or suggest that a system of remuneration based upon need would be immeasurably complex, and hence, generate its own inequities out of the resultant chaos. The calculation of some instantiations and relevant parameters of the formula "If greater need, then greater remuneration" would be trivially easy, while others, clearly, would be more difficult. The sole reason, I think, that one is inclined to believe that wealth in our society is allocated without difficulty is the disarmingly simple fact that we have no principle or system in accord with which it is distributed. A jungle is not a system, but a precarious balance of forces and counterforces.

If one wonders why a medical practitioner earns more than a garbage collector, one is apt to get the reply that the former needs more education than the latter. (I will ignore the presupposition in this response that raising one's earning power is a logically necessary condition for wanting an education.) But length of education is surely not, in our society, a determining factor of income. The professor of history has, normally, far more education than a truck driver and still often receives less salary. An engineer with an initial degree or a chap with an M.A. in business administration will often receive more money than the people who taught him his trade. At any rate, if education is to be so rewarded, then why not pay the truck driver additional money for gaining more education? (Of course, the time for him to avail himself of this must be made available.)

Nobody, of course, believes that education is a prime determinant of income. Some will speak of "public service," but then it is difficult to see why a dentist earns so much more than a garbage collector. It would need to be explained, as well, how an entertainer provides ten times as much service to the public in a single hour than a schoolteacher does in a year.

The question here has been: What is a just wage? Is the answer readily given by the principle "Treat like cases alike and unlike cases unlike"? Clearly not, since we have not yet articulated criteria for initially determining the likeness or unlikeness of cases. I am not here arguing that the way we are distributing wealth now is unjust; but rather, suggesting that it more resembles a "prejust" Hobbesian state of nature. Whatever the principle of distributive justice we have (if we do have one), it is not needs, education, or public service.

It might be suggested that we have a kind of self-regulating free market when it comes to distributing wealth; i.e., people receive whatever *others* are prepared to part with. But how many "others" have been consulted about this? Has that multimillion audience somewhere out there in television land ever been asked if they would sacrifice an hour of Johnny Cash for an increase in their undermanned fire department? If we do, indeed, have such a market, then I suggest that it's neither free nor self-regulating.

NOTES

1. Nathaniel Brandon, "Rational Egoism: A Reply to Professor Emmons," in *The Personalist*, vol. 51 (Spring 1970), pp. 202-3.

F. A. VON HAYEK

Equality, Value, and Merit

The great aim of the struggle for liberty has been equality before the law. This equality under the rules which the state enforces may be supplemented by a similar equality of the rules that men voluntarily obey in their relations with one another. This extension of the principle of equality to the rules of moral and social conduct is the chief expression of what is commonly called the democratic spirit—and probably that aspect of it that does most to make inoffensive the inequalities that liberty necessarily produces.

Equality of the general rules of law and conduct, however, is the only kind of equality conducive to liberty and the only equality which we can secure without destroying liberty. Not only has liberty nothing to do with any other sort of equality, but it is even bound to produce inequality in many respects. This is the necessary result and part of the justification of individual liberty: if the result of individual liberty did not demonstrate that some manners of living are more successful than others, much of the case for it would vanish.

It is neither because it assumes that people are in fact equal nor because it attempts to make them equal that the argument for liberty demands that government treat them equally. This argument not only recognizes that individuals are very different but in a great measure rests on that assumption. It insists that these individual differences provide no justification for government to treat them differently. And it objects to the differences in treatment by the state that would be necessary if persons who are in fact very different were to be assured equal positions in life.

Modern advocates of a more far-reaching material equality usually deny that their demands are based on any assumption of the factual equality of all men.[1] It is nevertheless still widely believed that this is the main justification for such demands. Nothing, however, is more damaging to the demand for equal treatment than to base it on so obviously untrue an assumption as that of the factual equality of all men. To rest the case for equal treatment of national or racial minorities on the assertion that they do not differ from other men is implicitly to admit that factual inequality would justify unequal treatment; and the proof that some differences do, in fact, exist would not be long in forthcoming. It is of the essence of the demand for equality before the law that people should be treated alike in spite of the fact that they are different.

The boundless variety of human nature—the wide range of differences in individual capacities and potentialities—is one of the most distinctive facts about the human species. Its evolution has made it probably the most variable among all kinds of creatures. It has been well said that "biology, with variability as its cornerstone, confers on every human individual a unique set of attributes which give him a dignity he could not otherwise possess. Every newborn baby is an unknown quantity so far as potentialities are concerned because there are many thousands of unknown interrelated genes and gene-patterns which contribute to his make-up. As a result of nature and nurture the newborn infant may become one of the greatest of men or women ever to have lived. In every case he or she has the making of a distinctive individual. . . . If the differences are not very important, then freedom is not very important and the idea of individual worth is not very important."[2] The writer justly adds that the widely held uniformity theory of human nature, "which on the surface appears to accord with democracy . . . would in time undermine the very basic ideals of freedom and individual worth and render life as we know it meaningless."[3]

It has been the fashion in modern times to minimize the importance of congenital differences between men and to ascribe all the important differences to the influence of environment.[4] However important the latter may be, we must not overlook the fact that individuals are very different from the outset. The importance of individual differences would hardly be less if all people were brought up in very similar environments. As a statement of fact, it just is not true that "all men are born equal." We may continue to use this hallowed phrase to express the ideal that legally and morally all men ought to be treated alike. But if we want to understand what this ideal of equality can or should mean, the first requirement is that we free ourselves from the belief in factual equality.

From the fact that people are very different it follows that, if we treat them equally, the result must be inequality in their actual position,[5] and that the only way to place them in an equal position would be to treat them differently. Equality before the law and material equality are therefore not only different but are in conflict with each other; and we can achieve either the one or the other, but not both at the same time. The equality before the law which freedom requires leads to material inequality. Our argument will be that, though where the state must use coercion for other reasons, it should treat all people alike, the desire of making people more alike in their condition cannot be accepted in a free society as a justification for further and discriminatory coercion.

We do not object to equality as such. It merely happens to be the case that a demand for equality is the professed motive of most of those who desire to impose upon society a preconceived pattern of distribution. Our objection is against all attempts to impress upon society a deliberately chosen pattern of distribution, whether it be an order of equality or of inequality. We shall indeed see that many of those who demand an extension of equality do not really demand equality but a distribution that conforms more closely to human conceptions of individual merit and that their desires are as irreconcilable with freedom as the more strictly egalitarian demands.

If one objects to the use of coercion in order to bring about a more even or a more just distribution, this does not mean that one does not regard these as desirable. But if we wish to preserve a free society, it is essential that we recognize that the desirability of a particular object is not sufficient justification for the use of coercion. One may well feel attracted to a community in which there are no extreme contrasts between rich and poor and may welcome the fact that the general increase in wealth seems gradually to reduce those differences. I fully share these feelings and certainly regard the degree of social equality that the United States has achieved as wholly admirable.

There also seems no reason why these widely felt preferences should not guide policy in some respects. Wherever there is a legitimate need for government action and we have to choose between different methods of satisfying such a need, those that incidentally also reduce inequality may well be preferable. If, for example, in the law of intestate succession one kind of provision will be more conducive to equality than another, this may be a strong argument in its favor. It is a different matter, however, if it is demanded that, in order to produce substantive equality, we should abandon the basic postulate of a free society, namely, the limitation of all coercion by equal law. Against this we shall hold that economic inequality is not one of the evils which justify our resorting to discriminatory coercion or privilege as a remedy.

Our contention rests on two basic propositions which probably need only be stated to win fairly general assent. The first of them is an expression of the belief in a certain similarity of all human beings: it is the proposition that no man or group of men possesses the capacity to determine conclusively the potentialities of other human beings and that we should certainly never trust anyone invariably to exercise such a capacity. However great the differences between men may be, we have no ground for believing that they will ever be so great as to enable one man's mind in a particular instance to comprehend fully all that another responsible man's mind is capable of.

The second basic proposition is that the acquisition by any member of the community of additional capacities to do things which may be valuable must always be regarded as a gain for that community. It is true that particular people may be worse off because of the superior ability of some new competitor in their field; but any such additional ability in the community is likely to benefit the majority. This implies that the desirability of increasing the abilities and opportunities of any individual does not depend on whether the same can also be done for the others—provided, of course, that others are not thereby deprived of the opportunity of acquiring the same or other abilities which might have been accessible to them had they not been secured by that individual.

Egalitarians generally regard differently those differences in individual capacities which are inborn and those which are due to the influences of environment, or those which are the result of "nature" and those which are the result of "nurture." Neither, be it said at once, has anything to do with moral merit.[6] Though either may greatly affect the value which an individual has for his fellows, no more credit belongs to him for having been born with desirable qualities than for having grown up under favorable circumstances. The distinction between the two is important only because the former advantages are due to circumstances clearly beyond human control, while the latter are due to factors which we might be able to alter. The important question is whether there is a case for so changing our institutions as to eliminate as much as possible those advantages due to environment. Are we to agree that "all inequalities that rest on birth and inherited property ought to be abolished and none remain unless it is an effect of superior talent and industry"?[7]

The fact that certain advantages rest on human arrangements does not necessarily mean that we could provide the same advantages for all or that, if they are given to some, somebody else is thereby deprived of them. The most important factors to be considered in this connection are the family, inheritance, and education, and it is against the inequality which they produce that criticism is mainly directed. They are, however, not the only important factors of environment.

Geographic conditions such as climate and landscape, not to speak of local and sectional differences in cultural and moral traditions, are scarcely less important. We can, however, consider here only the three factors whose effects are most commonly impugned.

So far as the family is concerned, there exists a curious contrast between the esteem most people profess for the institution and their dislike of the fact that being born into a particular family should confer on a person special advantages. It seems to be widely believed that, while useful qualities which a person acquires because of his native gifts under conditions which are the same for all are socially beneficial, the same qualities become somehow undersirable if they are the result of environmental advantages not available to others. Yet it is difficult to see why the same useful quality which is welcomed when it is the result of a person's natural endowment should be less valuable when it is the product of such circumstances as intelligent parents or a good home.

The value which most people attach to the institution of the family rests on the belief that, as a rule, parents can do more to prepare their children for a satisfactory life than anyone else. This means not only that the benefits which particular people derive from their family environment will be different but also that these benefits may operate cumulatively through several generations. What reason can there be for believing that a desirable quality in a person is less valuable to society if it has been the result of' family background than if it has not? There is, indeed, good reason to think that there are some socially valuable qualities which will be rarely acquired in a single generation but which will generally be formed only by the continuous efforts of two or three. This means simply that there are parts of the cultural heritage of a society that are more effectively transmitted through the family. Granted this, it would be unreasonable to deny that a society is likely to get a better elite if ascent is not limited to one generation, if individuals are not deliberately made to start from the same level, and if children are not deprived of the chance to benefit from the better education and material environment which their parents may be able to provide. To admit this is merely to recognize that belonging to a particular family is part of the individual personality, that society is made up as much of families as of individuals, and that the transmission of the heritage of civilization within the family is as important a tool in man's striving toward better things as is the heredity of beneficial physical attributes.

Many people who agree that the family is desirable as an instrument for the transmission of morals, tastes, and knowledge still question the desirability of the transmission of material property. Yet there can be little doubt that, in order that the former may be possible, some continuity of standards, of the external forms of life, is essential, and that this will be achieved only if it is possible to transmit not only immaterial but also material advantages. There is, of course, neither greater merit nor any greater injustice involved in some people being born to wealthy parents than there is in others being born to kind or intelligent parents. The fact is that it is no less of an advantage to the community if at least some children can start with the advantages which at any given time only wealthy homes can offer than if some children inherit great intelligence or are taught better morals at home.

We are not concerned here with the chief argument for private inheritance, namely, that it seems essential as a means to preserve the dispersal in the control of capital and as an inducement for its accumulation. Rather, our concern here is whether the fact that it confers unmerited benefits on some is a valid argument against the institution. It is unquestionably one of the institutional causes of inequality. In the present context we need not inquire whether liberty demands unlimited freedom of bequest. Our problem here is merely whether people ought to be free to pass on to children or others such material possessions as will cause substantial inequality.

Once we agree that it is desirable to harness the natural instincts of parents to equip the new generation as well as they can, there seems no sensible ground for limiting this to nonmaterial benefits. The family's function of passing on standards and traditions is closely tied up with the possibility of transmitting material goods. And it is difficult to see how it would serve the true interest of society to limit the gain in material conditions to one generation.

There is also another consideration which, though it may appear somewhat cynical, strongly suggests that if we wish to make the best use of the natural partiality of parents for their children, we ought not to preclude the transmission of property. It seems certain that among the many ways in which those who have gained power and influence might provide for their children, the bequest of a fortune is socially by far the cheapest. Without this outlet, these men would look for other ways of providing for their children, such as placing them in positions which might bring them the income and the prestige that a fortune would have done; and this would cause a waste of resources and an injustice much greater than is caused by the inheritance of property. Such is the case with all societies in which inheritance of property does not exist, including the Communist. Those who dislike the inequalities caused by inheritance should therefore recognize that, men being what they are, it is the least of evils, even from their point of view.

Though inheritance used to be the most widely criticized source of inequality, it is today probably no longer so. Egalitarian agitation now tends to concentrate on the unequal advantages due to differences in education. There is a growing tendency to express the desire to secure equality of conditions in the claim that the best education we have learned to provide for some should be made gratuitously available for all and that, if this is not possible, one should not be allowed to get a better education than the rest merely because one's parents are able to pay for it, but only those and all those who can pass a uniform test of ability should be admitted to the benefits of the limited resources of higher education.

The problem of educational policy raises too many issues to allow of their being discussed incidentally under the general heading of equality. . . . For the present we shall only point out that enforced equality in this field can hardly avoid preventing some from getting the education they otherwise might. Whatever we might do, there is no way of preventing those advantages which only some can have, and which it is desirable that some should have, from going to people who neither individually merit them nor will make as good a use of them as some other person might have done. Such a problem cannot be satisfactorily solved by the exclusive and coercive powers of the state.

It is instructive at this point to glance briefly at the change that the ideal of equality has undergone in this field in modern times. A hundred years ago, at the height of the classical liberal movement, the demand was generally expressed by the phrase *la carrière ouverte aux talents*. It was a demand that all man-made obstacles to the rise of some should be removed, that all privileges of individuals should be abolished, and that what the state contributed to the chance of improving one's conditions should be the same for all. That so long as people were different and grew up in different families this could not assure an equal start was fairly generally accepted. It was understood that the duty of government was not to ensure that everybody had the same prospect of reaching a given position but merely to make available to all on equal terms those facilities which in their nature depended on government action. That the results were bound to be different, not only because the individuals were different, but also because only a small part of the relevant circumstances depended on government action, was taken for granted.

This conception that all should be allowed to try has been largely replaced by the altogether different conception that all must be assured an equal start and the same prospects. This means little less than that the government, instead of providing the same circumstances for all, should aim at controlling all conditions relevant to a particular individual's prospects and so adjust them to his capacities as to assure him of the same prospects as everybody else. Such deliberate adaptation of opportunities to individual aims and capacities would, of course, be the opposite of freedom. Nor could it be justified as a means of making the best use of all available knowledge except on the assumption that government knows best how individual capacities can be used.

When we inquire into the justification of these demands, we find that they rest on the discontent that the success of some people often produces in those that are less successful, or, to put it bluntly, on envy. The modern tendency to gratify this passion and to disguise it in the respectable garment of social justice is developing into a serious threat to freedom. Recently an attempt was made to base these demands on the argument that it ought to be the aim of politics to remove all sources of discontent.[8] This would, of course, necessarily mean that it is the responsibility of government to see that nobody is healthier or possesses a happier temperament, a better-suited spouse or more prospering children, than anybody else. If really all unfulfilled desires have a claim on the community, individual responsibility is at an end. However human, envy is certainly not one of the sources of discontent that a free society can eliminate. It is probably one of the essential conditions for the preservation of such a society that we do not countenance envy, nor sanction its demands by camouflaging it as social justice, but treat it, in the words of John Stuart Mill, as "the most anti-social and evil of all passions."[9]

While most of the strictly egalitarian demands are based on nothing better than envy, we must recognize that much that on the surface appears as a demand for greater equality is in fact a demand for a juster distribution of the good things of this world and springs therefore from much more creditable motives. Most people will object not to the bare fact of inequality but to the fact that the differences in reward do not correspond to any recognizable differences in the merits of those who receive them. The answer commonly given to this is that a free society on the whole achieves this kind of justice.[10] This, however, is an indefensible contention if by justice is meant proportionality of reward to moral merit. Any attempt to found the case for freedom on this argument is very damaging to it, since it concedes that material rewards ought to be made to correspond to recognizable merit and then opposes the conclusion that most people will draw from this by an assertion which is untrue. The proper answer is that in a free system it is neither desirable nor practicable that material rewards should be made generally to correspond to what men recognize as merit and that it is an essential characteristic of a free society that an individual's position should not necessarily depend on the views that his fellows hold about the merit he has acquired.

This contention may appear at first so strange and even shocking that I will ask the reader to suspend judgment until I have further explained the distinction between value and merit.[11] The difficulty in making the point clear is due to the fact that the term *merit*, which is the only one available to describe what I mean, is also used in a wider and vaguer sense. It will be used here exclusively to describe the attributes of conduct that make it deserving of praise, that is, the moral character of the action and not the value of the achievement.[12]

As we have seen throughout our discussion, the value that the performance or capacity of a person has to his fellows has no necessary connection with its ascertainable merit in this sense. The inborn as well as the acquired gifts of a person clearly have a value to his fellows which does not depend on any credit due to him for possessing them. There is little a man can do to alter the fact that his special talents are very common or exceedingly rare. A good mind or a fine voice, a beautiful face or a skillful hand, and a ready wit or an attractive personality are in a large measure as independent of a person's efforts as the opportunities or the experiences he has had. In all these instances the value which a person's capacities or services have for us and for which he is recompensed has little relation to anything that we can call moral merit or deserts. Our problem is whether it is desirable that people should enjoy advantages in proportion to the benefits which their fellows derive from their activities or whether the distribution of these advantages should be based on other men's views of their merits.

Reward according to merit must in practice mean reward according to assessable merit, merit that other people can recognize and agree upon and not merit merely in the sight of some higher power. Assessable merit in this sense presupposes that we can ascertain that a man has done what some accepted rule of conduct demanded of him and that this has cost him some pain and effort. Whether this has been the case cannot be judged by the result: merit is not a matter of the objective outcome but of subjective effort. The attempt to achieve a valuable result may be highly meritorious but a complete failure, and full success may be entirely the result of accident and thus without merit. If we know that a man has done his best, we will often wish to see him rewarded irrespective of the result; and if we know that a most valuable achievement is almost entirely due to luck or favorable circumstances, we will give little credit to the author.

We may wish that we were able to draw this distinction in every instance. In fact, we can do so only rarely with any degree of assurance. It is possible only where we possess all the knowledge which was at the disposal of the acting person, including a knowledge of his skill and confidence, his state of mind and his feelings, his capacity for attention, his energy and persistence, etc. The possibility of a true judgment of merit thus depends on the presence of precisely those conditions whose general absence is the main argument for liberty. It is because we want people to use knowledge which we do not possess that we let them decide for themselves. But insofar as we want them to be free to use capacities and knowledge of facts which we do not have, we are not in a position to judge the merit of their achievements. To decide on merit presupposes that we can judge whether people have made such use of their opportunities as they ought to have made and how much effort of will or self-denial this has cost them; it presupposes also that we can distinguish between that part of their achievement which is due to circumstances within their control and that part which is not.

The incompatibility of reward according to merit with freedom to choose one's pursuit is most evident in those areas where the uncertainty of the outcome is particularly great and our individual estimates of the chances of various kinds of effort very different.[13] In those speculative efforts which we call "research" or "exploration," or in economic activities which we commonly describe as "speculation," we cannot expect to attract those best qualified for them unless we give the successful ones all the credit or gain, though many others may have striven as meritoriously. For the same reason that nobody can know beforehand who will be the successful ones, nobody can say who has earned greater merit. It would clearly not serve our purpose if we let all who have honestly striven share in the prize. Moreover, to do so would make it necessary that somebody have the right to decide who is to be allowed to strive for it. If in their pursuit of uncertain goals people are to use their own knowledge and capacities, they must be guided, not by what other people think they ought to do, but by the value others attach to the result at which they aim.

What is so obviously true about those undertakings which we commonly regard as risky is scarcely less true of any chosen object we decide to pursue. Any such decision is beset with uncertainty, and if the choice is to be as wise as it is humanly possible to make it, the alternative results anticipated must be labeled according to

their value. If the remuneration did not correspond to the value that
the product of a man's efforts has for his fellows, he would have no
basis for deciding whether the pursuit of a given object is worth the
effort and risk. He would necessarily have to be told what to do, and
some other person's estimate of what was the best use of his capacities would have to determine both his duties and his remuneration.*

The fact is, of course, that we do not wish people to earn a maximum of merit but to achieve a maximum of usefulness at a minimum
of pain and sacrifice and therefore a minimum of merit. Not only
would it be impossible for us to reward all merit justly, but it would
not even be desirable that people should aim chiefly at earning a
maximum of merit. Any attempt to induce them to do this would
necessarily result in people being rewarded differently for the same
service. And it is only the value of the result that we can judge with
any degree of confidence, not the different degrees of effort and care
that it has cost different people to achieve it.

The prizes that a free society offers for the result serve to tell
those who strive for them how much effort they are worth. However,
the same prizes will go to all those who produce the same result,
regardless of effort. What is true here of the remuneration for the
same services rendered by different people is even more true of the
relative remuneration for different services requiring different gifts
and capacities: they will have little relation to merit. The market will
generally offer for services of any kind the value they will have for
those who benefit from them; but it will rarely be known whether it
was necessary to offer so much in order to obtain these services, and
often, no doubt, the community could have had them for much less.
The pianist who was reported not long ago to have said that he would
perform even if he had to pay for the privilege probably described

---

* It is often maintained that justice requires that remuneration be proportional
to the unpleasantness of the job and that for this reason the street cleaner or the
sewage worker ought to be paid more than the doctor or office worker. This,
indeed, would seem to be the consequence of the principle of remuneration
according to merit (or "distributive justice"). In a market such a result would
come about only if all people were equally skillful in all jobs so that those who
could earn as much as others in the more pleasant occupations would have to
be paid more to undertake the distasteful ones. In the actual world those unpleasant jobs provide those whose usefulness in the more attractive jobs is small
an opportunity to earn more than they could elsewhere. That persons who have
little to offer their fellows should be able to earn an income similar to that of
the rest only at a much greater sacrifice is inevitable in any arrangement under
which the individual is allowed to choose his own sphere of usefulness.

the position of many who earn large incomes from activities which are also their chief pleasure.

Though most people regard as very natural the claim that nobody should be rewarded more than he deserves for his pain and effort, it is nevertheless based on a colossal presumption. It presumes that we are able to judge in every individual instance how well people use the different opportunities and talents given to them and how meritorious their achievements are in the light of all the circumstances which have made them possible. It presumes that some human beings are in a position to determine conclusively what a person is worth and are entitled to determine what he may achieve. It presumes, then, what the argument for liberty specifically rejects: that we can and do know all that guides a person's action.

A society in which the position of the individuals was made to correspond to human ideas of moral merit would therefore be the exact opposite of a free society. It would be a society in which people were rewarded for duty performed instead of for success, in which every move of every individual was guided by what other people thought he ought to do, and in which the individual was thus relieved of the responsibility and the risk of decision. But if nobody's knowledge is sufficient to guide all human action, there is also no human being who is competent to reward all efforts according to merit.

In our individual conduct we generally act on the assumption that it is the value of a person's performance and not his merit that determines our obligation to him. Whatever may be true in more intimate relations, in the ordinary business of life we do not feel that, because a man has rendered us a service at a great sacrifice, our debt to him is determined by this, so long as we could have had the same service provided with ease by somebody else. In our dealings with other men we feel that we are doing justice if we recompense value rendered with equal value, without inquiring what it might have cost the particular individual to supply us with these services. What determines our responsibility is the advantage we derive from what others offer us, not their merit in providing it. We also expect in our dealings with others to be remunerated not according to our subjective merit but according to what our services are worth to them. Indeed, so long as we think in terms of our relations to particular people, we are generally quite aware that the mark of the free man is to be dependent for his livelihood not on other people's views of his merit but solely on what he has to offer them. It is only when we think of our position or our income as determined by "society" as a whole that we demand reward according to merit.

Though moral value or merit is a species of value, not all value is moral value, and most of our judgments of value are not moral judgments. That this must be so in a free society is a point of cardinal importance; and the failure to distinguish between value and merit has been the source of serious confusion. We do not necessarily admire all activities whose product we value; and in most instances where we value what we get, we are in no position to assess the merit of those who have provided it for us. If a man's ability in a given field is more valuable after thirty years' work than it was earlier, this is independent of whether these thirty years were most profitable and enjoyable or whether they were a time of unceasing sacrifice and worry. If the pursuit of a hobby produces a special skill or an accidental invention turns out to be extremely useful to others, the fact that there is little merit in it does not make it any less valuable than if the result had been produced by painful effort.

This difference between value and merit is not peculiar to any one type of society—it would exist anywhere. We might, of course, attempt to make rewards correspond to merit instead of value, but we are not likely to succeed in this. In attempting it, we would destroy the incentives which enable people to decide for themselves what they should do. Moreover, it is more than doubtful whether even a fairly successful attempt to make rewards correspond to merit would produce a more attractive or even a tolerable social order. A society in which it was generally presumed that a high income was proof of merit and a low income of the lack of it, in which it was universally believed that position and remuneration corresponded to merit, in which there was no other road to success than the approval of one's conduct by the majority of one's fellows, would probably be much more unbearable to the unsuccessful ones than one in which it was frankly recognized that there was no necessary connection between merit and success.[14]

It would probably contribute more to human happiness if, instead of trying to make remuneration correspond to merit, we made clearer how uncertain is the connection between value and merit. We are probably all much too ready to ascribe personal merit where there is, in fact, only superior value. The possession by an individual or a group of a superior civilization or education certainly represents an important value and constitutes an asset for the community to which they belong; but it usually constitutes little merit. Popularity and esteem do not depend more on merit than does financial success. It is, in fact, largely because we are so used to assuming an often nonexistent merit wherever we find value that we balk when, in particular instances, the discrepancy is too large to be ignored.

There is every reason why we ought to endeavor to honor special merit where it has gone without adequate reward. But the problem of rewarding action of outstanding merit which we wish to be widely known as an example is different from that of the incentives on which the ordinary functioning of society rests. A free society produces institutions in which, for those who prefer it, a man's advancement depends on the judgment of some superior or of the majority of his fellows. Indeed, as organizations grow larger and more complex, the task of ascertaining the individual's contribution will become more difficult; and it will become increasingly necessary that, for many, merit in the eyes of the managers rather than the ascertainable value of the contribution should determine the rewards. So long as this does not produce a situation in which a single comprehensive scale of merit is imposed upon the whole society, so long as a multiplicity of organizations compete with one another in offering different prospects, this is not merely compatible with freedom but extends the range of choice open to the individual.

Justice, like liberty and coercion, is a concept which, for the sake of clarity, ought to be confined to the deliberate treatment of men by other men. It is an aspect of the intentional determination of those conditions of people's lives that are subject to such control. Insofar as we want the efforts of individuals to be guided by their own views about prospects and chances, the results of the individual's efforts are necessarily unpredictable, and the question as to whether the resulting distribution of incomes is just has no meaning.[15] Justice does require that those conditions of people's lives that are determined by government be provided equally for all. But equality of those conditions must lead to inequality of results. Neither the equal provision of particular public facilities nor the equal treatment of different partners in our voluntary dealings with one another will secure reward that is proportional to merit. Reward for merit is reward for obeying the wishes of others in what we do, not compensation for the benefits we have conferred upon them by doing what we thought best.

It is, in fact, one of the objections against attempts by government to fix income scales that the state must attempt to be just in all it does. Once the principle of reward according to merit is accepted as the just foundation for the distribution of incomes, justice would require that all who desire it should be rewarded according to that principle. Soon it would also be demanded that the same principle be applied to all and that incomes not in proportion to recognizable merit not be tolerated. Even an attempt merely to distinguish between those incomes or gains which are "earned" and those which are not will set up a principle which the state will have to try to apply but cannot in fact apply generally.[16] And every such attempt at deliberate control of some remunerations is bound to create further demands for new controls. The principle of distributive justice, once introduced, would not be fulfilled until the whole of society was organized in accordance with it. This would produce a kind of society which in all essential respects would be the opposite of a free society—a society in which authority decided what the individual was to do and how he was to do it.

In conclusion we must briefly look at another argument on which the demands for a more equal distribution are frequently based, though it is rarely explicitly stated. This is the contention that membership in a particular community or nation entitles the individual to a particular material standard that is determined by the general wealth of the group to which he belongs. This demand is in curious conflict with the desire to base distribution on personal merit. There is clearly no merit in being born into a particular community, and no argument of justice can be based on the accident of a particular individual's being born in one place rather than another. A relatively wealthy community in fact regularly confers advantages on its poorest members unknown to those born in poor communities. In a wealthy community the only justification its members can have for insisting on further advantages is that there is much private wealth that the government can confiscate and redistribute and that men who constantly see such wealth being enjoyed by others will have a stronger desire for it than those who know of it only abstractly, if at all.

There is no obvious reason why the joint efforts of the members of any group to ensure the maintenance of law and order and to organize the provision of certain services should give the members a claim to a particular share in the wealth of this group. Such claims would be especially difficult to defend where those who advanced them were unwilling to concede the same rights to those who did not belong to the same nation or community. The recognition of such claims on a national scale would in fact only create a new kind of collective (but not less exclusive) property right in the resources of the nation that could not be justified on the same grounds as individual property. Few people would be prepared to recognize the justice of these demands on a world scale. And the bare fact that within a given nation the majority had the actual power to enforce such demands, while in the world as a whole it did not yet have it, would hardly make them more just.

There are good reasons why we should endeavor to use whatever political organization we have at our disposal to make provision for the weak or infirm or for the victims of unforeseeable disaster. It may well be true that the most effective method of providing against certain risks common to all citizens of a state is to give every citizen protection against those risks. The level on which such provisions against common risks can be made will necessarily depend on the general wealth of the community.

It is an entirely different matter, however, to suggest that those who are poor, merely in the sense that there are those in the same community who are richer, are entitled to a share in the wealth of the latter or that being born into a group that has reached a particular level of civilization and comfort confers a title to a share in all its benefits. The fact that all citizens have an interest in the common provision of some services is not justification for anyone's claiming as a right a share in all the benefits. It may set a standard for what some ought to be willing to give, but not for what anyone can demand.

National groups will become more and more exclusive as the acceptance of this view that we have been contending against spreads. Rather than admit people to the advantages that living in their country offers, a nation will prefer to keep them out altogether; for, once admitted, they will soon claim as a right a particular share in its wealth. The conception that citizenship or even residence in a country confers a claim to a particular standard of living is becoming a serious source of international friction. And since the only justification for applying the principle within a given country is that its government has the power to enforce it, we must not be surprised if we find the same principle being applied by force on an international scale. Once the right of the majority to the benefits that minorities enjoy is recognized on a national scale, there is no reason why this should stop at the boundaries of the existing states.

NOTES

1. See, e.g., R. H. Tawney, *Equality* (London: Allen and Unwin, 1931), p. 47.
2. Roger J. Williams, *Free and Unequal: The Biological Basis of Individual Liberty* (Austin: University of Texas Press, 1953), pp. 23 and 70; cf. also J.B.S. Haldane, *The Inequality of Man* (London: Chatto and Windus, 1932); and P. B. Medawar, *The Uniqueness of the Individual* (London, 1957).
3. Williams, *Free and Equal*, p. 152.
4. See the description of this fashionable view in H.M. Kallen's article "Behaviorism," *Encyclopedia of the Social Sciences 1930–35*, II, 498: "At birth human infants, regardless of their heredity, are as equal as Fords."
5. Cf. Plato *Laws* 6. 757A: "To unequals equals become unequal."

6. Cf. F. H. Knight, *Freedom and Reform* (New York: Harper and Brothers, 1947), p. 151: "There is no visible reason why anyone is more or less entitled to the earnings of inherited personal capacities than to those of inherited property in any other form"; and the discussion in William Roepke, *Mass and Mitte* (Erlenbach and Zurich: E. Rentsch, 1950), pp. 65–75.

7. This is the position of R. H. Tawney as summarized by J. P. Plamenatz, "Equality of Opportunity," in *Aspects of Human Equality*, Lyman Bryson et al., eds. (New York, 1956), p. 100.

8. Charles Crosland, *The Future of Socialism* (London, 1956), p. 205.

9. John Stuart Mill, *On Liberty*, ed. R.B. McCallum (Oxford: Basil Blackwell, 1946), p. 70.

10. Cf. W. B. Gallie, "Liberal Morality and Socialist Morality," in *Philosophy, Politics, and Society*, ed. Peter Laslett (Oxford: Basil Blackwell, 1956), pp. 123–25. The author represents it as the essence of "liberal morality" that it claims that rewards are equal to merit in a free society. This was the position of some nineteenth-century liberals which often weakened their argument. A characteristic example is W. G. Sumner, who argued (*What Social Classes Owe to Each Other*, reprinted in *Freeman*, 6 [Los Angeles, n.d.], p. 141) that if all "have equal chances so far as chances are provided or limited by society," this will "produce inequal results—that is results which shall be proportioned to the merits of individuals." This is true only if "merit" is used in the sense in which we have used "value," without any moral connotations, but certainly not if it is meant to suggest proportionality to any endeavor to do the good or right thing, or to any subjective effort to conform to an ideal standard.

 But, as we shall presently see, Mr. Gallie is right that, in the Aristotelian terms he uses, liberalism aims at commutative justice and socialism at distributive justice. But, like most socialists, he does not see that distributive justice is irreconcilable with freedom in the choice of one's activities: it is the justice of a hierarchic organization, not of a free society.

11. Although I believe that this distinction between merit and value is the same as that which Aristotle and Thomas Aquinas had in mind when they distinguished "distributive justice" from "commutative justice," I prefer not to tie up the discussion with all the difficulties and confusions which in the course of time have become associated with these traditional concepts. That what we call here "reward according to merit" corresponds to the Aristotelian distributive justice seems clear. The difficult concept is that of "commutative justice," and to speak of justice in this sense seems always to cause a little confusion. Cf. Max Salomon, *Der Begriff der Gerechtigkeit bei Aristoteles* (Leiden: A.W. Sijthoff, 1937); and for a survey of the extensive literature Georgio del Vecchio, *Die Gerechtigkeit*, 2nd ed. (Basel: Verlag fur Recht und Gesellschaft, 1950).

12. The terminological difficulties arise from the fact that we use the word *merit* also in an objective sense and will speak of the "merit" of an idea, a book, or a picture, irrespective of the merit acquired by the person who has created them. Sometimes the word is also used to describe what we regard as the "true" value of some achievement as distinguished from its market value. Yet even a human achievement which has the greatest value or merit

in this sense is not necessarily proof of moral merit on the part of him to whom it is due. It seems that our use has the sanction of philosophical tradition. Cf., for instance, David Hume, *A Treatise of Human Nature*, ed. C. A. Selby-Bigge (Oxford: Clarendon Press, 1969). "The external performance has no merit. We must look within to find the moral quality. . . . The ultimate object of our praise and approbation is the motive, that produc'd them."

13. Cf. the important essay by Armen A. Alchian, "Uncertainty, Evolution, and Economic Theory," *Journal of Political Economy,* 58 (1950), esp. 213–14, sec. 2, headed "Success Is Based on Results, Not Motivation." It probably is also no accident that the American economist who has done most to advance our understanding of a free society, Frank H. Knight, began his professional career with a study of *Risk, Uncertainity, and Profit* (Boston: Houghton Mifflin, 1957). Cf. also Bertrand de Jouvenel, *Power* (London: Hutchinson, 1948), p. 298.

14. Cf. Crosland, *Future of Socialism*, p. 235: "Even if all the failures could be convinced that they had an equal chance, their discontent would still not be assuraged; indeed it might actually be intensified. When opportunites are known to be unequal, and the selection clearly biased towards wealth or lineage, people can comfort themselves for failure by saying that they never had a proper chance—the system was unfair, the scales too heavily weighted against them. But if the selection is obviously by merit, this source of comfort disappears, and failure induces a total sense of inferiority, with no excuse or consolation; and this, by a natural quirk of human nature, actually increases the envy and resentment at the success of others." Cf. also chap. 24, at n. 8. I have not yet seen Michael Young, *The Rise of the Meritocracy* (London: Penguin, 1958), which, judging from reviews, appears to bring out these problems very clearly.

15. See the interesting discussion in R. G. Collingwood, "Economics as a Philosophical Science," *Ethics* 36 (1926), pp. 162–185, who concludes (p. 174): "A just price, a just wage, a just rate of interest, is a contradiction in terms. The question what a person ought to get in return for his goods and labor is a question absolutely devoid of meaning. The only valid questions are what he *can* get in return for his goods or labor, and whether he ought to sell them at all."

16. It is, of course, possible to give the distinction between "earned" and "unearned" incomes, gains, or increments a fairly precise legal meaning, but it then rapidly ceases to correspond to the moral distinction which provides its justification. Any serious attempt to apply the moral distinction in practice soon meets the same insuperable difficulties as any attempt to assess subjective merit. How little these difficulties are generally understood by philosophers (except in rare instances, as that quoted in the preceding note) is well illustrated by a discussion in Susan Stebbing, *Thinking to Some Purpose* (London: Pelican Books, 1939), p. 184, in which, as an illustration of a distinction which is clear but not sharp, she chooses that between "legitimate" and "excess" profits and asserts: "The distinction is clear between 'excess profits' (or 'profiteering') and 'legitimate profits,' although it is not a sharp distinction."

JOHN RAWLS

Distributive Justice*

We may think of a human society as a more or less self-sufficient association regulated by a common conception of justice and aimed at advancing the good of its members. As a cooperative venture for mutual advantage, it is characterized by a conflict as well as an identity of interests. There is an identity of interests since social cooperation makes possible a better life for all than any would have if everyone were to try to live by his own efforts; yet at the same time men are not indifferent as to how the greater benefits produced by their joint labors are distributed, for in order to further their own aims each prefers a larger to a lesser share. A conception of justice is a set of principles for choosing between the social arrangements which determine this division and for underwriting a consensus as to the proper distributive shares.

Now at first sight the most rational conception of justice would seem to be utilitarian. For consider: each man in realizing his own good can certainly balance his own losses against his own gains. We can impose a sacrifice on ourselves now for the sake of a greater advantage later. A man quite properly acts, as long as others are not affected, to achieve his own greatest good, to advance his ends as far as possible. Now, why should not a society act on precisely the same principle? Why is not that which is rational in the case of one man right in the case of a group of men? Surely the simplest and most direct conception of the right, and so of justice, is that of maximizing the good. This assumes a prior understanding of what is good, but we can think of the good as already given by the interests of rational individuals. Thus just as the principle of individual choice is to achieve one's greatest good, to advance so far as possible one's own system of rational desires, so the principle of social choice is to realize the greatest good (similarly defined) summed over all the members of society. We arrive at the principle of utility in a natural way: by this principle a society is rightly ordered, and hence just,

* In this essay I try to work out some of the implications of the two principles of justice discussed in "Justice as Fairness" which first appeared in the *Philosophical Review* vol. 67, 1958, pp. 164–94.

Source: *Philosophy, Politics, and Society* (3rd series), ed. Peter Laslett and W.G. Runciman, (Oxford: Basil Blackwell, 1967). Reprinted with permission of the author.

when its institutions are arranged so as to realize the greatest sum of satisfactions.

The striking feature of the principle of utility is that it does not matter, except indirectly, how this sum of satisfactions is distributed among individuals, any more than it matters, except indirectly, how one man distributes his satisfactions over time. Since certain ways of distributing things affect the total sum of satisfactions, this fact must be taken into account in arranging social institutions; but according to this principle the explanation of common-sense precepts of justice and their seemingly stringent character is that they are those rules which experience shows must be strictly respected and departed from only under exceptional circumstances if the sum of advantages is to be maximized. The precepts of justice are derivative from the one end of attaining the greatest net balance of satisfactions. There is no reason in principle why the greater gains of some should not compensate for the lesser losses of others; or why the violation of the liberty of a few might not be made right by a greater good shared by many. It simply happens, at least under those conditions, that the greatest sum of advantages is not generally achieved in this way. From the standpoint of utility the strictness of common-sense notions of justice has a certain usefulness, but as a philosophical doctrine it is irrational.

If, then, we believe that as a matter of principle each member of society has an inviolability founded on justice which even the welfare of everyone else cannot override, and that a loss of freedom for some is not made right by a greater sum of satisfactions enjoyed by many, we shall have to look for another account of the principles of justice. The principle of utility is incapable of explaining the fact that in a just society the liberties of equal citizenship are taken for granted, and the rights secured by justice are not subject to political bargaining nor to the calculus of social interests. Now, the most natural alternative to the principle of utility is its traditional rival, the theory of the social contract. The aim of the contract doctrine is precisely to account for the strictness of justice by supposing that its principles arise from an agreement among free and independent persons in an original position of equality and hence reflect the integrity and equal sovereignty of the rational persons who are the contractees. Instead of supposing that a conception of right, and so a conception of justice, is simply an extension of the principle of choice for one man to society as a whole, the contract doctrine assumes that the rational individuals who belong to society must choose together, in one joint act, what is to count among them as just and unjust. They are to decide among themselves once and for all what is to be their conception of justice. This decision is thought of as being made in a suitably defined initial situation, one of the significant features of which is that no one knows his position in society, nor even his place in the distribution of natural talents and abilities. The principles of justice to which all are forever bound are chosen in the absence of this sort of specific information. A veil of ignorance prevents anyone from being advantaged or disadvantaged by the contingencies of social class and fortune; and hence the bargaining problems which arise in everyday life from the possession of this knowledge do not affect the choice of principles. On the contract doctrine, then, the theory of justice, and indeed ethics itself, is part of the general theory of rational choice, a fact perfectly clear in its Kantian formulation.

Once justice is thought of as arising from an original agreement of this kind, it is evident that the principle of utility is problematical. For why should rational individuals who have a system of ends they wish to advance agree to a violation of their liberty for the sake of a greater balance of satisfactions enjoyed by others? It seems more plausible to suppose that, when situated in an original position of equal right, they would insist upon institutions which returned compensating advantages for any sacrifices required. A rational man would not accept an institution merely because it maximized the sum of advantages irrespective of its effect on his own interests. It appears, then, that the principle of utility would be rejected as a principle of justice, although we shall not try to argue this important question here. Rather, our aim is to give a brief sketch of the conception of distributive shares implicit in the principles of justice which, it seems, would be chosen in the original position. The philosophical appeal of utilitariansim is that it seems to offer a single principle on the basis of which a consistent and complete conception of right can be developed. The problem is to work out a contractarian alternative in such a way that it has comparable if not all the same virtues.

In our discussion we shall make no attempt to derive the two principles of justice which we shall examine; that is, we shall not try to show that they would be chosen in the original position.[1] It must suffice that it is plausible that they would be, at least in preference to the standard forms of traditional theories. Instead we shall be mainly concerned with three questions: first, how to interpret these principles so that they define a consistent and complete conception of justice; second, whether it is possible to arrange the institutions of a constitutional democracy so that these principles are satisfied, at least approximately; and third, whether the conception of distributive shares which they define is compatible with common-sense notions of justice. The significance of these principles is that they allow for the strictness of the claims of justice; and if they can be understood so as to yield a consistent and complete conception, the contractarian alternative would seem all the more attractive.

The two principles of justice which we shall discuss may be formulated as follows: first, each person engaged in an institution or affected by it has an equal right to the most extensive liberty compatible with a like liberty for all; and second, inequalities as defined by the institutional structure or fostered by it are arbitrary unless it is reasonable to expect that they will work out to everyone's advantage and provided that the positions and offices to which they attach or from which they may be gained are open to all. These principles regulate the distributive aspects of institutions by controlling the assignment of rights and duties throughout the whole social structure, beginning with the adoption of a political constitution in accordance with which they are then to be applied to legislation. It is upon a correct choice of a basic structure of society, its fundamental system of rights and duties, that the justice of distributive shares depends.

The two principles of justice apply in the first instance to this basic structure, that is, to the main institutions of the social system and their arrangement, how they are combined together. Thus this structure includes the political constitution and the principal economic and social institutions which together define a person's liberties and rights and affect his life prospects, what he may expect to be and how well he may expect to fare. The intuitive idea here is that those born into the social system at different positions, say in different social classes, have varying life prospects determined, in part, by the system of political liberties and personal rights, and by the economic and social opportunities which are made available to these positions. In this way the basic structure of society favors certain men over others, and these are the basic inequalities, the ones which affect their whole life prospects. It is inequalities of this kind, presumably inevitable in any society, with which the two principles of justice are primarily designed to deal.

Now the second principle holds that an inequality is allowed only if there is reason to believe that the institution with the inequality, or permitting it, will work out for the advantage of every person engaged in it. In the case of the basic structure this means that all inequalities which affect life prospects, say the inequalities of income and wealth which exist between social classes, must be to the advantage of everyone. Since the principle applies to institutions, we interpret this to mean that inequalities must be to the advantage of the representative man for each relevant social position; they should improve each such man's expectation. Here we assume that it is possible to attach to each position an expectation, and that this expectation is a function of the whole institutional structure: it can be raised and lowered by reassigning rights and duties throughout the system. Thus the expectation of any position depends upon the expectations of the others, and these in turn depend upon the pattern of rights and duties established by the basic structure. But it is not clear what is meant by saying that inequalities must be to the advantage of every representative man, and hence our first question.

One possibility is to say that everyone is made better off in comparison with some historically relevant bench mark. An interpretation of this kind is suggested by Hume.[2] He sometimes says that the institutions of justice, that is, the rules regulating property and contracts, and so on, are to everyone's advantage, since each man can count himself the gainer on balance when he considers his permanent interests. Even though the application of the rules is sometimes to his disadvantage, and he loses in the particular case, each man gains in the long run by the steady administration of the whole system of justice. But all Hume seems to mean by this is that everyone is better off in comparison with the situation of men in the state of nature, understood either as some primitive condition or as the circumstances which would obtain at any time if the existing institutions of justice were to break down. While this sense of everyone's being made better off is perhaps clear enough, Hume's interpretation is surely unsatisfactory. For even if all men including slaves are made better off by a system of slavery than they would be in the state of nature, it is not true that slavery makes everyone (even a slave) better off, at least not in a sense which makes the arrangement just. The benefits and burdens of social cooperation are unjustly distributed even if everyone does gain in comparison with the state of nature; this historical or hypothetical bench mark is simply irrelevant to the question of justice. In fact, any past state of society other than a recent one seems irrelevant offhand, and this suggests that we should look for an interpretation independent of historical comparisons altogether. Our problem is to identify the correct hypothetical comparisons defined by currently feasible changes.

Now the well-known criterion of Pareto[3] offers a possibility along these lines once it is formulated so as to apply to institutions. Indeed, this is the most natural way of taking the second principle (or rather the first part of it, leaving aside the requirement about open positions). This criterion says that group welfare is at an optimum when it is impossible to make any one man better off without at the same time making at least one other man worse off. Applying this criterion to allocating a given bundle of goods among given individuals, a particular allocation yields an optimum if there is no redistribution which would improve one individual's position without worsening that of another. Thus a distribution is optimal when there is no further exchange which is to the advantage of both parties, or to the advantage of one and not to the disadvantage of the other. But there are many such distributions, since there are many ways of allocating commodities so that no further mutually beneficial exchange is possible. Hence the Pareto criterion, as important as it is, admittedly does not identify the best distribution, but rather a class of optimal, or efficient, distributions. Moreover, we cannot say that a given optimal distribution is better than any nonoptimal one; it is only superior to those which it dominates. The criterion is at best an incomplete principle for ordering distributions.

Pareto's idea can be applied to institutions. We assume, as remarked above, that it is possible to associate with each social position an expectation which depends upon the assignment of rights and duties in the basic structure. Given this assumption, we get a principle which says that the pattern of expectations (inequalities in life prospects) is optimal if and only if it is impossible to change the rules, to redefine the scheme of rights and duties, so as to raise the expectations of any representative man without at the same time lowering the expectations of some other representative man. Hence the basic structure satisfies this principle when it is impossible to change the assignment of fundamental rights and duties and to alter the availability of economic and social opportunities so as to make some representative man better off without making another worse off. Thus, in comparing different arrangements of the social system, we can say that one is better than another if in one arrangement all expectations are at least as high, and some higher, than in the other. The principle gives grounds for reform, for if there is an arrangement which is optimal in comparison with the existing state of things, then, other things equal, it is a better situation all around and should be adopted.

The satisfaction of this principle, then, defines a second sense in which the basic structure makes everyone better off; namely, that from the standpoint of its representative men in the relevant positions, there exists no change which would improve anyone's condition without worsening that of another. Now we shall assume that this principle would be chosen in the original position, for surely it is a desirable feature of a social system that it is optimal in this sense. In fact, we shall suppose that this principle defines the concept of efficiency for institutions, as can be seen from the fact that if the social system does not satisfy it, this implies that there is some change which can be made which will lead people to act more effectively so that the expectations of some at least can be raised. Perhaps an economic reform will lead to an increase in production with given resources and techniques, and with greater output someone's expectations are raised.

It is not difficult to see, however, that while this principle provides another sense for an institution's making everyone better off, it is an inadequate conception of justice. For one thing, there is the same incompleteness as before. There are presumably many arrangements of an institution and of the basic structure which are optimal in this sense. There may also be many arrangements which are optimal with respect to existing conditions, and so many reforms which would be improvements by this principle. If so, how is one to choose between them? It is impossible to say that the many optimal arrangements are equally just, and the choice between them a matter of indifference, since efficient institutions allow extremely wide variations in the pattern of distributive shares.

Thus it may be that under certain conditions serfdom cannot be significantly reformed without lowering the expectations of some representative man, say that of landowners, in which case serfdom is optimal. But equally it may happen under the same conditions that a system of free labor could not be changed without lowering the expectations of some representative man, say that of free laborers, so that this arrangement likewise is optimal. More generally, whenever a society is relevantly divided into a number of classes, it is possible, let's suppose, to maximize with respect to any one of its representative men at a time. These maxima give at least this many optimal positions, for none of them can be departed from to raise the expectations of any man without lowering those of another, namely, the man with respect to whom the maximum is defined. Hence each of these extremes is optimal. All this corresponds to the obvious fact that, in distributing particular goods to given individuals, those distributions are also optimal which give the whole stock to any one person; for once a single person has everything, there is no change which will not make him worse off.

We see, then, that social systems which we should judge very differently from the standpoint of justice may be optimal by this criterion. This conclusion is not surprising. There is no reason to think that, even when applied to social systems, justice and efficiency come to the same thing. These reflections only show what we knew all along, which is that we must find another way of interpreting the second principle, or rather the first part of it. For while the two principles taken together incorporate strong requirements of equal liberty and equality of opportunity, we cannot be sure that even these constraints are sufficient to make the social structure acceptable from the standpoint of justice. As they stand the two principles would appear to place the burden of ensuring justice entirely upon these prior constraints and to leave indeterminate the preferred distributive shares.

There is, however, a third interpretation which is immediately suggested by the previous remarks, and this is to choose some social position by reference to which the pattern of expectations as a whole is to be judged, and then to maximize with respect to the expectations of this representative man consistent with the demands of equal liberty and equality of opportunity. Now, the one obvious candidate is the representative man of those who are least favored by the system of institutional inequalities. Thus we arrive at the following idea: the basic structure of the social system affects the life prospects of typical individuals according to their initial places in society, say the various income classes into which they are born, or depending upon certain natural attributes, as when institutions make discriminations between men and women or allow certain advantages to be gained by those with greater natural abilities. The fundamental problem of distributive justice concerns the differences in life prospects which come about in this way. We interpret the second principle to hold that these differences are just if and only if the greater expectations of the more advantaged, when playing a part in the working of the whole social system, improve the expectations of the least advantaged. The basic structure is just throughout when the advantages of the more fortunate promote the well-being of the least fortunate, that is, when a decrease in their advantages would make the least fortunate even worse off than they are. The basic structure is perfectly just when the prospects of the least fortunate are as great as they can be.

In interpreting the second principle (or rather the first part of it which we may, for obvious reasons, refer to as the difference principle), we assume that the first principle requires a basic equal liberty for all, and that the resulting political system, when circumstances permit, is that of a constitutional democracy in some form. There must be liberty of the person and political equality as well as liberty of conscience and freedom of thought. There is one class of equal citizens which defines a common status for all. We also assume that there is equality of opportunity and a fair competition for the available positions on the basis of reasonable qualifications. Now, given this background, the differences to be justified are the various economic and social inequalities in the basic structure which must inevitably arise in such a scheme. These are the inequalities in the distribution of income and wealth and the distinctions in social prestige and status which attach to the various positions and classes. The difference principle says that these inequalities are just if and only if they are part of a larger system in which they work out to the advantage of the most unfortunate representative man. The just distributive shares determined by the basic structure are those specified by this constrained maximum principle.

Thus, consider the chief problem of distributive justice, that concerning the distribution of wealth as it affects the life prospects of those starting out in the various income groups. These income classes define the relevant representative men from which the social system is to be judged. Now, a son of a member of the entrepreneurial class (in a capitalist society) has a better prospect than that of the son of an unskilled laborer. This will be true, it seems, even when the social injustices which presently exist are removed and the two men are of equal talent and ability; the inequality cannot be done away with as long as something like the family is maintained. What, then, can justify this inequality in life prospects? According to the second principle it is justified only if it is to the advantage of the representative man who is worst off, in this case the representative unskilled laborer. The inequality is permissible because lowering it would, let's suppose, make the working man even worse off than he is. Presumably, given the principle of open offices (the second part of the second principle), the greater expectations allowed to entrepreneurs has the effect in the longer run of raising the life prospects of the laboring class. The inequality in expectation provides an incentive so that the economy is more efficient, industrial advance proceeds at a quicker pace, and so on, the end result of which is that greater material and other benefits are distributed throughout the system. Of course, all of this is familiar, and whether true or not in particular cases, it is the sort of thing which must be argued if the inequality in income and wealth is to be acceptable by the difference principle.

We should now verify that this interpretation of the second principle gives a natural sense in which everyone may be said to be made better off. Let us suppose that inequalities are chain connected: that is, if an inequality raises the expectations of the lowest position, it raises the expectations of all positions in between. For example, if the greater expectations of the representative entrepreneur raises that of the unskilled laborer, it also raises that of the semiskilled. Let us

further assume that inequalities are close-knit: that is, it is impossible
to raise (or lower) the expectation of any representative man without
raising (or lowering) the expectations of every other representative
man, and in particular, without affecting one way or the other that
of the least fortunate. There is no loose-jointedness, so to speak, in
the way in which expectations depend upon one another. Now, with
these assumptions, everyone does benefit from an inequality which
satisfies the difference principle, and the second principle as we have
formulated it reads correctly. For the representative man who is
better off in any pair-wise comparison gains by being allowed to have
his advantage, and the man who is worse off benefits from the contribution which all inequalities make to each position below. Of course,
chain connection and close-knitness may not obtain; but in this case
those who are better off should not have a veto over the advantages
available for the least advantaged. The stricter interpretation of the
difference principle should be followed, and all inequalities should
be arranged for the advantage of the most unfortunate even if some
inequalities are not to the advantage of those in middle positions.
Should these conditions fail, then, the second principle would have
to be stated in another way.

It may be observed that the difference principle represents, in
effect, an original agreement to share in the benefits of the distribution of natural talents and abilities, whatever this distribution
turns out to be, in order to alleviate as far as possible the arbitrary
handicaps resulting from our initial starting places in society. Those
who have been favored by nature, whoever they are, may gain from
their good fortune only on terms that improve the well-being of
those who have lost out. The naturally advantaged are not to gain
simply because they are more gifted, but only to cover the costs of
training and cultivating their endowments and for putting them to
use in a way which improves the position of the less fortunate. We
are led to the difference principle if we wish to arrange the basic
social structure so that no one gains (or loses) from his luck in the
natural lottery of talent and ability, or from his initial place in
society, without giving (or receiving) compensating advantages in return. (The parties in the original position are not said to be attracted
by this idea and so agree to it; rather, given the symmetries of their
situation, and particularly their lack of knowledge, and so on, they
will find it to their interest to agree to a principle which can be
understood in this way.) And we should note also that when the
difference principle is perfectly satisfied, the basic structure is
optimal by the efficiency principle. There is no way to make anyone
better off without making someone else worse off, namely, the least

fortunate representative man. Thus the two principles of justice define distributive shares in a way compatible with efficiency, at least as long as we move on this highly abstract level. If we want to say (as we do, although it cannot be argued here) that the demands of justice have an absolute weight with respect to efficiency, this claim may seem less paradoxical when it is kept in mind that perfectly just institutions are also efficient.

Our second question is whether it is possible to arrange the institutions of a constitutional democracy so that the two principles of justice are satisfied, at least approximately. We shall try to show that this can be done provided the government regulates a free economy in a certain way. More fully, if law and government act effectively to keep markets competitive, resources fully employed, property and wealth widely distributed over time, and to maintain the appropriate social minimum, then if there is equality of opportunity underwritten by education for all, the resulting distribution will be just. Of course, all of these arrangements and policies are familiar. The only novelty in the following remarks, if there is any novelty at all, is that this framework of institutions can be made to satisfy the difference principle. To argue this, we must sketch the relations of these institutions and how they work together.

First of all, we assume that the basic social structure is controlled by a just constitution which secures the various liberties of equal citizenship. Thus the legal order is administered in accordance with the principle of legality, and liberty of conscience and freedom of thought are taken for granted. The political process is conducted, so far as possible, as a just procedure for choosing between governments and for enacting just legislation. From the standpoint of distributive justice, it is also essential that there be equality of opportunity in several senses. Thus, we suppose that, in addition to maintaining the usual social overhead capital, government provides for equal educational opportunities for all either by subsidizing private schools or by operating a public school system. It also enforces and underwrites equality of opportunity in commercial ventures and in the free choice of occupation. This result is achieved by policing business behavior and by preventing the establishment of barriers and restriction to the desirable positions and markets. Lastly, there is a guarantee of a social minimum which the government meets by family allowances and special payments in times of unemployment, or by a negative income tax.

In maintaining this system of institutions the government may be thought of as divided into four branches. Each branch is represented by various agencies (or activities thereof) charged with preserving certain social and economic conditions. These branches do not necessarily overlap with the usual organization of government, but should be understood as purely conceptual. Thus the allocation branch is to keep the economy feasibly competitive, that is, to prevent the formation of unreasonable market power. Markets are competitive in this sense when they cannot be made more so consistent with the requirements of efficiency and the acceptance of the facts of consumer preferences and geography. The allocation branch is also charged with identifying and correcting, say by suitable taxes and subsidies wherever possible, the more obvious departures from efficiency caused by the failure of prices to measure accurately social benefits and costs. The stabilization branch strives to maintain reasonably full employment so that there is no waste through failure to use resources and the free choice of occupation and the deployment of finance are supported by strong effective demand. These two branches together are to preserve the efficiency of the market economy generally.

The social minimum is established through the operations of the transfer branch. Later on we shall consider at what level this minimum should be set, since this is a crucial matter; but for the moment, a few general remarks will suffice. The main idea is that the workings of the transfer branch take into account the precept of need and assign it an appropriate weight with respect to the other common-sense precepts of justice. A market economy ignores the claims of need altogether. Hence there is a division of labor between the parts of the social system as different institutions answer to different common-sense precepts. Competitive markets (properly supplemented by government operations) handle the problem of the efficient allocation of labor and resources and set a weight to the conventional precepts associated with wages and earnings (the precepts of each according to his work and experience, or responsibility and the hazards of the job, and so on), whereas the transfer branch guarantees a certain level of well-being and meets the claims of need. Thus it is obvious that the justice of distributive shares depends upon the whole social system and how it distributes total income, wages plus transfers. There is with reason strong objection to the competitive determination of total income, since this would leave out of account the claims of need and of a decent standard of life. From the standpoint of the original position it is clearly rational to insure oneself against these contingencies. But now, if the appropriate minimum is provided by transfers, it may be perfectly fair that the other part of total income is competitively determined. Moreover, this way of dealing with the claims of need is doubtless more efficient, at least from a theoretical point of view, than trying to regulate prices by minimum wage standards and so on. It is preferable to handle these claims by a separate branch which supports a social minimum. Henceforth, in considering whether the second principle of justice is satisfied, the answer turns on whether the total income of the least advantaged, that is, wages plus transfers, is such as to maximize their long-term expectations consistent with the demands of liberty.

Finally, the distribution branch is to preserve an approximately just distribution of income and wealth over time by affecting the background conditions of the market from period to period. Two aspects of this branch may be distinguished. First of all, it operates a system of inheritance and gift taxes. The aim of these levies is not to raise revenue, but gradually and continually to correct the distribution of wealth and to prevent the concentrations of power to the detriment of liberty and equality of opportunity. It is perfectly true, as some have said,[4] that unequal inheritance of wealth is no more inherently unjust than unequal inheritance of intelligence; as far as possible the inequalities founded on either should satisfy the difference principle. Thus, the inheritance of greater wealth is just as long as it is to the advantage of the worst off and consistent with liberty, including equality of opportunity. Now by the latter we do not mean, of course, the equality of expectations between classes, since differences in life prospects arising from the basic structure are inevitable, and it is precisely the aim of the second principle to say when these differences are just. Instead, equality of opportunity is a certain set of institutions which assures equally good education and chances of culture for all and which keeps open the competition for positions on the basis of qualities reasonably related to performance, and so on. It is these institutions which are put in jeopardy when inequalities and concentrations of wealth reach a certain limit; and the taxes imposed by the distribution branch are to prevent this limit from being exceeded. Naturally enough where this limit lies is a matter for political judgment guided by theory, practical experience, and plain hunch; on this question the theory of justice has nothing to say.

The second part of the distribution branch is a scheme of taxation for raising revenue to cover the costs of public goods, to make transfer payments, and the like. This scheme belongs to the distribution branch since the burden of taxation must be justly shared. Although we cannot examine the legal and economic complications involved, there are several points in favor of proportional expenditure taxes as part of an ideally just arrangement. For one thing, they are preferable to income taxes at the level of common-sense precepts of justice, since they impose a levy according to how much a man takes out of the common store of goods and not according to how much he contributes (assuming that income is fairly earned in return for productive efforts). On the other hand, proportional taxes treat everyone in a clearly defined uniform way (again assuming that income is fairly earned) and hence it is preferable to use progressive rates only when they are necessary to preserve the justice of the system as a whole, that is, to prevent large fortunes hazardous to liberty and equality of opportunity, and the like. If proportional expenditure taxes should also prove more efficient, say because they interfere less with incentives, or whatever, this would make the case for them decisive provided a feasible scheme could be worked out.[5] Yet these are questions of political judgment which are not our concern; and, in any case, a proportional expenditure tax is part of an idealized scheme which we are describing. It does not follow that even steeply progressive income taxes, given the injustice of existing systems, do not approve justice and efficiency all things considered. In practice we must usually choose between unjust arrangements and then it is a matter of finding the lesser injustice.

Whatever form the distribution branch assumes, the argument for it is to be based on justice: we must hold that once it is accepted the social system as a whole—the competitive economy surrounded by a just constitutional and legal framework—can be made to satisfy the principles of justice with the smallest loss in efficiency. The long-term expectations of the least advantaged are raised to the highest level consistent with the demands of equal liberty. In discussing the choice of a distribution scheme we have made no reference to the traditional criteria of taxation according to ability to pay or benefits received; nor have we mentioned any of the variants of the sacrifice principle. These standards are subordinate to the two principles of justice; once the problem is seen as that of designing a whole social system, they assume the status of secondary precepts with no more independent force than the precepts of common sense in regard to wages. To suppose otherwise is not to take a sufficiently comprehensive point of view. In setting up a just distribution branch these precepts may or may not have a place depending upon the demands of the two principles of justice when applied to the entire system.

Our problem now is whether the whole system of institutions which we have described, the competitive economy surrounded by the four branches of government, can be made to satisfy the two principles of justice. It seems intuitively plausible that this can be done, but we must try to make sure. We assume that the social system as a whole meets the demands of liberty; it secures the rights required by the first principle and the principle of open offices. Thus the question is whether, consistent with these liberties, there is any way of operating the four branches of government so as to bring the inequalities of the basic structure in line with the difference principle.

Now, quite clearly the thing to do is to set the social minimum at the appropriate level. So far we have said nothing about how high this minimum should be. Common sense might be content to say that the right level depends on the average wealth of the country, and that, other things equal, the minimum should be higher if this average is higher; or it might hold that the proper level depends on customary expectations. Both of these ideas are unsatisfactory. The first is not precise enough since it does not state how the minimum should depend on wealth and it overlooks other relevant considerations such as distribution; and the second provides no criterion for when customary expectations are themselves reasonable. Once the difference principle is accepted, however, it follows that the minimum should be set at the level which, taking wages into account, maximizes the expectations of the lowest income class. By adjusting the amount of transfers, and the benefits from public goods which improve their circumstances, it is possible to increase or decrease the total income of the least advantaged (wages plus transfers plus benefits from public goods). Controlling the sum of transfers and benefits, thereby raising or lowering the social minimum, gives sufficient leeway in the whole scheme to satisfy the difference principle.

Now, offhand it might appear that this arrangement requires a very high minimum. It is easy to imagine the greater wealth of those better off being scaled down until eventually all stand on nearly the same level. But this is a misconception. The relevant expectation of the least advantaged is their long-term expectation extending over all generations; and hence over any period of time the economy must put aside the appropriate amount of real-capital accumulation. Assuming for the moment that this amount is given, the social minimum is determined in the following way. Suppose, for simplicity, that transfer payments and the benefits from public goods are supported by expenditure (or income) taxes. Then raising the minimum entails raising the constant proportion at which consumption (or income) is taxed. Now presumably as this proportion is increased there comes a point beyond which one of two things happens: either the savings required cannot be made or the increased taxes interfere so much with the efficiency of the economy that the expectations of the lowest class for that period no longer improve but begin to decline. In either case the appropriate level for the minimum has been reached and no further increase should be made.

In order to make the whole system of institutions satisfy the two principles of justice, a just-savings principle is presupposed. Hence we must try to say something about this difficult question. Unfortunately there are no very precise limits on what the rate of saving should be; how the burden of real saving should be shared between generations seems to admit of no definite answer. It does not follow, however, that certain general bounds cannot be prescribed which are ethically significant. For example, it seems clear that the classical principle of utility, which requires us to maximize total well-being over all generations, results in much too high a rate of saving, at least for the earlier generations. On the contract doctrine the question is approached from the standpoint of the parties in the original position who do not know to which generation they belong, or what comes to the same things, they do not know the stage of economic advance of their society. The veil of ignorance is complete in this respect. Hence the parties ask themselves how much they would be willing to save at each stage on the assumption that other generations save at the same rates. That is, a person is to consider his willingness to save at every phase of development with the understanding that the rates he proposes will regulate the whole span of accumulation. Since no one knows to which generation he belongs, the problem is looked at from the standpoint of each. Now it is immediately obvious that all generations, except possibly the first, gain from a reasonable rate of accumulation being maintained. Once the saving process is begun, it is to the advantage of all later generations. Each generation passes on to the next a fair equivalent in real capital as defined by a just-savings principle, this equivalent being in return for what is received from previous generations and enabling the later ones to have a higher standard of life than would otherwise be possible. Only those in the first generation do not benefit, let's suppose; while they begin the whole process, they do not share in the fruits of their provision. At this initial stage, then, in order to obtain unanimity from the point of view of generations, we must assume that fathers, say, are willing to save for the sake of their sons, and hence that, in this case at least, one generation cares for its immediate descendants. With these suppositions, it seems that some just-savings principle would be agreed to.

Now a just-savings principle will presumably require a lower rate of saving in the earlier stages of development when a society is poor, and a greater rate as it becomes wealthier and more industralized. As their circumstances become easier men would find it reasonable to agree to save more since the real burden is less. Eventually, perhaps, there will come a point beyond which the rate of saving may decline or stop altogether, at least if we suppose that there is a state of affluence when a society may concentrate on other things and it is sufficient that improvements in productive techniques be introduced only to the extent covered by depreciation. Here we are referring to what a society must save as a matter of justice; if it wishes to save for various grand projects, this is another matter.

We should note a special feature of the reciprocity principle in the case of just savings. Normally this principle applies when there is an exchange of advantages, that is, when each party gives something to the other. But in the accumulation process no one gives to those from whom he has received. Each gives to subsequent generations and receives from his predecessors. The first generation obtains no benefits at all, whereas the last generations, those living when no further saving is required, gain the most and give the least. Now this may appear unjust; and contrary to the formulation of the difference principle, the worst off save for those better off. But although this relation is unusual, it does not give rise to any difficulty. It simply expresses the fact that generations are spread out in time and exchanges between them can take place in only one direction. Therefore, from the standpoint of the original position, if all are to gain, they must agree to receive from their predecessors and to pass along a fair equivalent to those who come after them. The criterion of justice is the principle which would be chosen in the original position; and since a just-savings principle would, let's suppose, be agreed to, the accumulation process is just. The savings principle may be reconciled with the difference principle by assuming that the representative man in any generation required to save belongs to the lowest income class. Of course, this saving is not done so much, if at all, by taking an active part in the investment process; rather it takes the form of approving of the economic arrangements which promote accumulation. The saving of those worse off is undertaken by accepting, as a matter of political judgment, those policies designed to improve the standard of life, thereby abstaining from the immediate advantages which are available to them. By supporting these arrangements and policies the appropriate savings can be made, and no representative man regardless of generation can complain of another for not doing his part.

Of the nature of the society at which the saving process aims we can give only the most general description. It is a society of persons with the greatest equal talent enjoying the benefits of the greatest equal liberty under economic conditions reached immediately after the highest average income per capita at which any saving at all is required. There is no longer a lowest income class in the traditional sense; such differences in wealth as exist are freely chosen and accepted as a price of doing things less in demand. All of this is, unfortunately, terribly vague. But, in any case, this general conception specifies a horizon of sorts at which the savings process aims so that the just-savings principle is not completely indeterminate. That is, we suppose that the intention is to reach a certain social state, and the problem of the proper rate of accumulation is how to share fairly in the burdens of achieving it. The contractarian idea is that if we look at this question from the perspective of those in the original position, then, even though the savings principle which results is inevitably imprecise, it does impose ethically significant bounds. What is of first importance is that the problem of just savings be approached in the right way; the initial conception of what we are to do determines everything else. Thus, from the standpoint of the original position, representatives of all generations, so to speak, must agree on how to distribute the hardships of building and preserving a just society. They all gain from adopting a savings principle, but also they have their own interest which they cannot sacrifice for another.

The sketch of the system of institutions satisfying the two principles of justice is now complete. For once the just rate of savings is determined, at least within broad limits, we have a criterion for setting the level of the social minimum. The sum of transfers should be that which maximizes the expectations of the lowest income class consistent with the appropriate saving being undertaken and the system of equal liberties maintained. This arrangement of institutions working over time results in a definite pattern of distributive shares, and each man receives a total income (wages plus transfers) to which he is entitled under the rules upon which his legitimate expectations are founded. Now an essential feature of this whole scheme is that it contains an element of pure procedural justice. That is, no attempt is made to specify the just distribution of particular goods and services to particular persons, as if there were only one way in which, independently of the choices of economic agents, these things should be shared. Rather, the idea is to design a scheme such that the resulting distribution, whatever it is, which is brought about by the efforts of those engaged in cooperation and elicited by their legitimate expectations, is just.

The notion of pure procedural justice may be explained by a comparison with perfect and imperfect procedural justice. Consider the simplest problem of fair division. A number of men are to divide a cake: assuming that a fair division is an equal one, which procedure will give this outcome? The obvious solution is to have the man who divides the cake take the last piece. He will divide it equally, since in this way he assures for himself as large a share as he can. Now in this case there is an independent criterion for which is the fair division. The problem is to devise a procedure, a set of rules for dividing the cake, which will yield this outcome. The problem of fair division exemplifies the features of perfect procedural justice. There is an independent criterion for which the outcome is just—and we can design a procedure guaranteed to lead to it.

The case of imperfect procedural justice is found in a criminal trial. The desired outcome is that the defendant should be declared guilty if and only if he has committed the offence as charged. The trial procedure is framed to search for and to establish this result, but we cannot design rules guaranteed to reach it. The theory of trial procedures examines which rules of evidence, and the like, are best calculated to advance this purpose. Different procedures may reasonably be expected in different circumstances to yield the right result, not always, but at least most of the time. Hence a trial is a case of imperfect procedural justice. Even though the law may be carefully followed, and the trial fairly and properly conducted, it may reach the wrong outcome. An innocent man may be found guilty, a guilty man may be set free. In such cases we speak of a miscarriage of justice: the injustice springs from no human fault but from a combination of circumstances which defeats the purpose of the rules.

The notion of pure procedural justice is illustrated by gambling. If a number of persons engage in a series of fair bets, the distribution of cash after the last bet is fair, or at least not unfair, whatever this distribution is. (We are assuming, of course, that fair bets are those which define a zero expectation, that the bets are made voluntarily, that no one cheats, and so on.) Any distribution summing to the initial stock of cash held by everyone could result from a series of fair bets; hence all of these distributions are, in this sense, equally fair. The distribution which results is fair simply because it is the outcome. Now when there is pure procedural justice, the procedure for determining the just result must actually be carried out; for in this case there is no independent criterion by reference to which an outcome can be known to be just. Obviously we cannot say that a particular state of affairs is just because it could have been reached by following a just procedure. This would permit far too much and lead to absurdly unjust consequences. In the case of gambling, for example, it would entail that any distribution whatever could be imposed. What makes the final outcome of the betting fair, or not unfair, is that it is the one which has arisen after a series of fair gambles.

In order, therefore, to establish just distributive shares a just

total system of institutions must be set up and impartially administered. Given a just constitution and the smooth working of the four
branches of government, and so on, there exists a procedure such
that the actual distribution of wealth, whatever it turns out to be,
is just. It will have come about as a consequence of a just system of
institutions satisfying the principles to which everyone would agree
and against which no one can complain. The situation is one of pure
procedural justice, since there is no independent criterion by which
the outcome can be judged. Nor can we say that a particular distribution of wealth is just because it is one which could have resulted
from just institutions although it has not, as this would be to allow
too much. Clearly there are many distributions which may be reached
by just institutions, and this is true whether we count patterns of
distributions among social classes or whether we count distributions
of particular goods and services among particular individuals. There
are indefinitely many outcomes and what makes one of these just is
that it has been achieved by actually carrying out a just scheme of
cooperation as it is publicly understood. It is the result which has
arisen when everyone receives that to which he is entitled given his
and others' actions guided by their legitimate expectations and their
obligations to one another. We can no more arrive at a just distribution of wealth except by working together within the framework
of a just system of institutions than we can win or lose fairly without
actually betting.

This account of distributive shares is simply an elaboration of the
familiar idea that economic rewards will be just once a perfectly
competitive price system is organized as a fair game. But in order to
do this we have to begin with the choice of a social system as a whole,
for the basic structure of the entire arrangement must be just. The
economy must be surrounded with the appropriate framework of
institutions, since even a perfectly efficient price system has no
tendency to determine just distributive shares when left to itself.
Not only must economic activity be regulated by a just constitution
and controlled by the four branches of government, but a just-saving
function must be adopted to estimate the provision to be made for
future generations. Thus, we cannot, in general, consider only piece-
wise reforms, for unless all of these fundamental questions are
properly handled, there is no assurance that the resulting distributive
shares will be just; while if the correct initial choices of institutions
are made, the matter of distributive justice may be left to take care
of itself. Within the framework of a just system men may be permitted to form associations and groupings as they please so long as they
respect the like liberty of others. With social ingenuity it should be

possible to invent many different kinds of economic and social activities appealing to a wide variety of tastes and talents; and as long as the justice of the basic structure of the whole is not affected, men may be allowed, in accordance with the principle of free association, to enter into and to take part in whatever activities they wish. The resulting distribution will be just whatever it happens to be. The system of institutions which we have described is, let's suppose, the basic structure of a well-ordered society. This system exhibits the content of the two principles of justice by showing how they may be perfectly satisfied; and it defines a social ideal by reference to which political judgment among second-bests, and the long-range direction of reform, may be guided.

We may conclude by considering the third question: whether this conception of distributive shares is compatible with common-sense notions of justice. In elaborating the contract doctrine we have been led to what seems to be a rather special, even eccentric, conception, the peculiarities of which center in the difference principle. Clear statements of it seem to be rare, and it differs rather widely from traditional utilitarian and intuitionist notions.[6] But this question is not an easy one to answer, for philosophical conceptions of justice, including the one we have just put forward, and our common-sense convictions, are not very precise. Moreover, a comparison is made difficult by our tendency in practice to adopt combinations of principles and precepts the consequences of which depend essentially upon how they are weighted; but the weighing may be undefined and allowed to vary with circumstances, and thus relies on the intuitive judgments which we are trying to systematize.

Consider the following conception of right: social justice depends positively on two things, on the equality of distribution (understood as equality in levels of well-being) and total welfare (understood as the sum of utilities taken over all individuals). On this view one social system is better than another without ambiguity if it is better on both counts, that is, if the expectations it defines are both less unequal and sum to a larger total. Another conception of right can be obtained by substituting the principle of a social minimum for the principle of equality; and thus an arrangement of institutions is preferable to another without ambiguity if the expectations sum to a larger total and it provides for a higher minimum. The idea here is to maximize the sum of expectations subject to the constraint that no one be allowed to fall below some recognized standard of life. In these conceptions the principles of equality and of a social minimum represent the demands of justice, and the principle of total welfare that of efficiency. The principle of utility assumes the role of the principle of efficiency, the force of which is limited by a principle of justice.

Now in practice combinations of principles of this kind are not without value. There is no question but that they identify plausible standards by reference to which policies may be appraised, and given the appropriate background of institutions, they may give correct conclusions. Consider the first conception: a person guided by it may frequently decide rightly. For example, he would be in favor of equality of opportunity, for it seems evident that having more equal chances for all both improves efficiency and decreases inequality. The real question arises, however, when an institution is approved by one principle but not by the other. In this case everything depends on how the principles are weighted, but how is this to be done? The combination of principles yields no answer to this question, and the judgment must be left to intuition. For every arrangement combining a particular total welfare with a particular degree of inequality one simply has to decide, without the guidance from principle, how much of an increase (or decrease) in total welfare, say, compensates for a given decrease (or increase) in equality.

Anyone using the two principles of justice, however, would also appear to be striking a balance between equality and total welfare. How do we know, then, that a person who claims to adopt a combination of principles does not, in fact, rely on the two principles of justice in weighting them, not consciously certainly, but in the sense that the weights he gives to equality and total welfare are those which he would give to them if he applied to two principles of justice? We need not say, of course, that those who in practice refer to a combination of principles, or whatever, rely on the contract doctrine, but only that until their conception of right is completely specified the question is still open. The leeway provided by the determination of weights leaves the matter unsettled.

Moreover, the same sort of situation arises with other practical standards. It is widely agreed, for example, that the distribution of income should depend upon the claims of entitlement, such as training and experience, responsibility and contribution, and so on, weighed against the claims of need and security. But how are these common-sense precepts to be balanced? Again, it is generally accepted that the ends of economic policy are competitive efficiency, full employment, an appropriate rate of growth, a decent social minimum, and a more equal distribution of income. In a modern democratic state these aims are to be advanced in ways consistent with equal liberty and equality of opportunity. There is no argument with these objectives; they would be recognized by anyone who accepted the two principles of justice. But different political views balance these ends differently, and how are we to choose between them? The fact is that we agree to little when we acknowledge precepts and ends of this kind; it must be recognized that a fairly detailed weighting is implicit in any complete conception of justice. Often we content ourselves with enumerating, sense precepts and objectives of policy, adding that on particular questions we must strike a balance between them having studied the relevant facts. While this is sound practical advice, it does not express a conception of justice. Whereas on the contract doctrine all combinations of principle, precepts, and objectives of policy are given a weight in maximizing the expectations of the lowest income class consistent with making the required saving and maintaining the system of equal liberty and equality of opportunity.

Thus despite the fact that the contract doctrine seems at first to be a somewhat special conception, particularly in its treatment of inequalities, it may still express the principles of justice which stand in the background and control the weights expressed in our everyday judgments. Whether this is indeed the case can be decided only by developing the consequences of the two principles in more detail and noting if any discrepancies turn up. Possibly there will be no conflicts; certainly we hope there are none with the fixed points of our considered judgments. The main question perhaps is whether one is prepared to accept the further definition of one's conception of right which the two principles represent. For, as we have seen, common sense presumably leaves the matter of weights undecided. The two principles may not so much oppose ordinary ideas as provide a relatively precise principle where common sense has little to say.

Finally, it is a political convention in a democratic society to appeal to the common good. No political party would admit to pressing for legislation to the disadvantage of any recognized social interest. But how, from a philosophical point of view, is this convention to be understood? Surely it is something more than the principle of efficiency (in its Paretian form) and we cannot assume that government always affects everyone's interests equally. Yet since we cannot maximize with respect to more than one point of view, it is natural, given the ethos of a democratic society, to single out that of the least advantaged and maximize their long-term prospects consistent with the liberties of equal citizenship. Moreover, it does seem that the policies which we most confidently think to be just do at least contribute positively to the well-being of this class, and hence that these policies are just throughout. Thus the difference principle is a reasonable extension of the political convention of a democracy once we face up to the necessity of choosing a complete conception of justice.

NOTES

1. This question is discussed very briefly in "Justice as Fairness," see pp. 138–41. The intuitive idea is as follows. Given the circumstances of the original position, it is rational for a man to choose as if he were designing a society in which his enemy is to assign him his place. This, in particular, given the complete lack of knowledge (which makes the choice one under uncertainty), the fact that the decision involves one's life prospects as a whole and is constrained by obligations to third parties (e.g., one's descendants) and duties to certain values (e.g., to religious truth), it is rational to be conservative and so to choose in accordance with an analogue of the maximin principle. Viewing the situation in this way, the interpretation given to the principles of justice . . . is perhaps natural enough. Moreover, it seems clear how the principle of utility can be interpreted: it is the analogue of the Laplacean principle for choice uncertainty. For a discussion of these choice criteria, see Robert Luce and Howard Raiffa, *Games and Decisions* (New York: Wiley, 1957), pp. 275-98.
2. For this observation I am indebted to Brian Barry.
3. Introduced by him in his *Manuel d'économie politique* (Paris: V. Giard et E. Briese, 1909) and long since a basic principle of welfare economics.
4. See for example F. von Hayek, *The Constitution of Liberty* [See "Equality, Value, and Merit," pp. 155-172 in this text].
5. See Nickolas Kaldor, *An Expenditure Tax* (London: Allen and Unwin, 1955).
6. The nearest statement known to me is by George Santayana. See the last part of ch. 4 in *Reason and Society*, vol. 2 (New York: Scribner's, 1906) on the aristocratic ideal. He says, for example, ". . . an aristocratic regimen can only be justified by radiating benefit and by proving that were less given to those above, less would be attained by those beneath them." But see also Christian Bay, *The Structure of Freedom* (Palo Alto: Stanford University Press, 1958), who adopts the principle of maximizing freedom, giving special attention to the freedom of the marginal, least-privileged man. Cf. pp. 59, 374f.

ROBERT NOZICK

Distributive Justice

THE ENTITLEMENT THEORY

The subject of justice in holdings consists of three major topics. The first is the *original acquisition of holdings*, the appropriation of un-held things. This includes the issues of how unheld things may come to be held, the process, or processes, by which unheld things may come to be held, the things that may come to be held by these pro-cesses, the extent of what comes to be held by a particular process, and so on. We shall refer to the complicated truth about this topic, which we shall not formulate here, as the principle of justice in acquisition. The second topic concerns the *transfer of holdings* from one person to another. By what processes may a person transfer holdings to another? How may a person acquire a holding from another who holds it? Under this topic come general descriptions of voluntary exchange, and gift and (on the other hand) fraud, as well as reference to particular conventional details fixed upon in a given society. The complicated truth about this subject (with place holders for conventional details) we shall call the principle of justice in transfer. (And we shall suppose it also includes principles gov-erning how a person may divest himself of a holding, passing it into an unheld state.)

If the world were wholly just, the following inductive definition would exhaustively cover the subject of justice in holdings.

- *a.* A person who acquires a holding in accordance with the princi-ple of justice in acquisition is entitled to that holding.
- *b.* A person who acquires a holding in accordance with the princi-ple of justice in transfer, from someone else entitled to the holding, is entitled to the holding.
- *c.* No one is entitled to a holding except by (repeated) applications of (a) and (b).

Source: *Anarchy, State, and Utopia* by Robert Nozick. Pp. 149-164, 167-182. Copyright © 1974 by Basic Books, Publishers, New York.

The complete principle of distributive justice would say simply that a distribution is just if everyone is entitled to the holdings they possess under the distribution.

A distribution is just if it arises from another just distribution by legitimate means. The legitimate means of moving from one distribution to another are specified by the principle of justice in transfer. The legitimate first "moves" are specified by the principle of justice in acquisition.* Whatever arises from a just situation by just steps is itself just. The means of change specified by the principle of justice in transfer preserve justice. As correct rules of inference are truth preserving, and any conclusion deduced via repeated application of such rules from only true premises is itself true, so the means of transition from one situation to another specified by the principle of justice in transfer are justice preserving, and any situation actually arising from repeated transitions in accordance with the principle from a just situation is itself just. The parallel between justice-preserving transformations and truth-preserving transformations illuminates where it fails as well as where it holds. That a conclusion could have been deduced by truth preserving means from premises that are true suffices to show its truth. That from a just situation a situation *could* have arisen via justice-preserving means does *not* suffice to show its justice. The fact that a thief's victims voluntarily *could* have presented him with gifts does not entitle the thief to his ill-gotten gains. Justice in holdings is historical; it depends upon what actually has happened. We shall return to this point later.

Not all actual situations are generated in accordance with the two principles of justice in holdings: the principle of justice in acquisition and the principle of justice in transfer. Some people steal from others, or defraud them, or enslave them, seizing their product and preventing them from living as they choose, or forcibly exclude others from competing in exchanges. None of these are permissible modes of transition from one situation to another. And some persons acquire holdings by means not sanctioned by the principle of justice in acquisition. The existence of past injustice (previous violations of the first two principles of justice in holdings) raises the third major topic under justice in holdings: the rectification of injustice in holdings. If past injustice has shaped present holdings in various ways,

---

* Applications of the principle of justice in acquisition may also occur as part of the move from one distribution to another. You may find an unheld thing now and appropriate it. Acquisitions also are to be understood as included when, to simplify, I speak only of transitions by transfers.

some identifiable and some not, what now, if anything, ought to be done to rectify these injustices? What obligations do the performers of injustice have toward those whose position is worse than it would have been had the injustice not been done? Or, than it would have been had compensation been paid promptly? How, if at all, do things change if the beneficiaries and those made worse off are not the direct parties in the act of injustice, but, for example, their descendants? Is an injustice done to someone whose holding was itself based upon an unrectified injustice? How far back must one go in wiping clean the historical slate of injustices? What may victims of injustice permissibly do in order to rectify the injustices being done to them, including the many injustices done by persons acting through their government? I do not know of a thorough or theoretically sophisticated treatment of such issues. Idealizing greatly, let us suppose theoretical investigation will produce a principle of rectification. This principle uses historical information about previous situations and injustices done in them (as defined by the first two principles of justice and rights against interference) and information about the actual course of events that flowed from these injustices until the present, and it yields a description (or descriptions) of holdings in the society. The principle of rectification presumably will make use of its best estimate of subjunctive information about what would have occurred (or a probability distribution over what might have occurred, using the expected value) if the injustice had not taken place. If the actual description of holdings turns out not to be one of the descriptions yielded by the principle, then one of the descriptions yielded must be realized.*

The general outlines of the theory of justice in holdings are that the holdings of a person are just if he is entitled to them by the principles of justice in acquisition and transfer, or by the principle of rectification of injustice (as specified by the first two principles). If each person's holdings are just, then the total set (distribution) of holdings is just. To turn these general outlines into a specific theory we would have to specify the details of each of the three principles

---

* If the principle of rectification of violations of the first two principles yields more than one description of holdings, then some choice must be made as to which of these is to be realized. Perhaps the sort of considerations about distributive justice and equality that I argue against play a legitimate role in *this* subsidiary choice. Similarly, there may be room for such considerations in deciding which otherwise-arbitrary features a statute will embody, when such features are unavoidable because other considerations do not specify a precise line; yet a line must be drawn.

of justice in holdings: the principle of acquisition of holdings, the principle of transfer of holdings, and the principle of rectification of violations of the first two principles. I shall not attempt that task here. (Locke's principle of justice in acquisition is discussed below.)

HISTORICAL PRINCIPLES AND END-RESULT PRINCIPLES

The general outlines of the entitlement theory illuminate the nature and defects of other conceptions of distributive justice. The entitlement theory of justice in distribution is *historical*; whether a distribution is just depends upon how it came about. In contrast, *current-time-slice principles* of justice hold that the justice of a distribution is determined by how things are distributed (who has what) as judged by some *structural* principle(s) of just distribution. A utilitarian who judges between any two distributions by seeing which has the greater sum of utility and, if the sums tie, applies some fixed equality criterion to choose the more equal distribution, would hold a current-time-slice principle of justice. As would someone who had a fixed schedule of trade-offs between the sum of happiness and equality. According to a current-time-slice principle, all that needs to be looked at, in judging the justice of a distribution, is who ends up with what; in comparing any two distributions one need look only at the matrix presenting the distributions. No further information need be fed into a principle of justice. It is a consequence of such principles of justice that any two structurally identical distributions are equally just. (Two distributions are structurally identical if they present the same profile, but perhaps have different persons occupying the particular slots. My having ten and your having five, and my having five and your having ten are structurally identical distributions.) Welfare economics is the theory of current-time-slice principles of justice. The subject is conceived as operating on matrices representing only current information about distribution. This, as well as some of the usual conditions (for example, the choice of distribution is invariant under relabeling of columns), guarantees that welfare economics will be a current-time-slice theory, with all of its inadequacies.

Most persons do not accept current-time-slice principles as constituting the whole story about distributive shares. They think it relevant in assessing the justice of a situation to consider not only the distribution it embodies, but also how that distribution came about. If some persons are in prison for murder or war crimes, we do not say that to assess the justice of the distribution in the society we must look only at what this person has, and that person has, and that person has . . . at the current time. We think it relevant to ask whether someone did something so that he *deserved* to be punished, deserved to have a lower share. Most will agree to the relevance of further information with regard to punishments and penalties. Consider also desired things. One traditional socialist view is that workers are entitled to the product and full fruits of their labor; they have earned it; a distribution is unjust if it does not give the workers what they are entitled to. Such entitlements are based upon some past history. No socialist holding this view would find it comforting to be told that because the actual distribution A happens to coincide structurally with the one he desires D, A therefore is no less just than D; it differs only in that the "parasitic" owners of capital receive under A what the workers are entitled to under D, and the workers receive under A what the owners are entitled to under D, namely very little. This socialist rightly, in my view, holds onto the notions of earning, producing, entitlement, desert, and so forth, and he rejects current-time-slice principles that look only to the structure of the resulting set of holdings. (The set of holdings resulting from what? Isn't it implausible that how holdings are produced and come to exist has no effect at all on who should hold what?) His mistake lies in this view of what entitlements arise out of what sorts of productive processes.

We construe the position we discuss too narrowly by speaking of *current*-time-slice principles. Nothing is changed if structural principles operate upon a time sequence of current-time-slice profiles and, for example, give someone more now to counterbalance the less he has had earlier. A utilitarian or an egalitarian or any mixture of the two over time will inherit the difficulties of his more myopic comrades. He is not helped by the fact that *some* of the information others consider relevant in assessing a distribution is reflected, unrecoverably, in past matrices. Henceforth, we shall refer to such unhistorical principles of distributive justice, including the current-time-slice principles, as *end-result principles* or *end-state principles*.

In contrast to end-result principles of justice, *historical principles* of justice hold that past circumstances or actions of people can create differential entitlements or differential deserts to things. An injustice can be worked by moving from one distribution to another structurally identical one, for the second, in profile the same, may violate people's entitlements or deserts; it may not fit the actual history.

PATTERNING

The entitlement principles of justice in holdings that we have sketched
are historical principles of justice. To better understand their precise
character, we shall distinguish them from another subclass of the
historical principles. Consider, as an example, the principle of distribution according to moral merit. This principle requires that total
distributive shares vary directly with moral merit; no person should
have a greater share than anyone whose moral merit is greater. (If
moral merit could be not merely ordered but measured on an interval
or ratio scale, stronger principles could be formulated.) Or consider
the principle that results by substituting "usefulness to society" for
"moral merit" in the previous principle. Or instead of "distribute
according to moral merit," or "distribute according to usefulness to
society," we might consider "distribute according to the weighted
sum of moral merit, usefulness to society, and need," with the
weights of the different dimensions equal. Let us call a principle of
distribution *patterned* if it specifies that a distribution is to vary
along with some natural dimension, weighted sum of natural dimensions, or lexicographic ordering of natural dimensions. And let us say
a distribution is patterned if it accords with some patterned principle.
(I speak of natural dimensions, admittedly without a general criterion for them, because for any set of holdings some artificial dimensions can be gimmicked up to vary along with the distribution of the
set.) The principle of distribution in accordance with moral merit is a
patterned historical principle, which specifies a patterned distribution. "Distribute according to I.Q." is a patterned principle that
looks to information not contained in distributional matrices. It is
not historical, however, in that it does not look to any past actions
creating differential entitlements to evaluate a distribution; it requires
only distributional matrices whose columns are labeled by I.Q. scores.
The distribution in a society, however, may be composed of such
simple patterned distributions, without itself being simply patterned.
Different sectors may operate different patterns, or some combination of patterns may operate in different proportions across a society.
A distribution composed in this manner, from a small number of
patterned distributions, we also shall term *patterned*. And we extend
the use of *pattern* to include the overall designs put forth by combinations of end-state principles.

Almost every suggested principle of distributive justice is patterned: to each according to his moral merit, or needs, or marginal
product, or how hard he tries, or the weighted sum of the foregoing,
and so on. The principle of entitlement we have sketched is *not*

patterned.* There is no one natural dimension or weighted sum or combination of a small number of natural dimensions that yields the distributions generated in accordance with the principle of entitlement. The set of holdings that results when some persons receive their marginal products, others win at gambling, others receive a share of their mate's income, others receive gifts from foundations, others receive interest on loans, others receive gifts from admirers, others receive returns on investment, others make for themselves much of what they have, others find things, and so on, will not be patterned. Heavy strands of patterns will run through it; significant portions of the variance in holdings will be accounted for by pattern variables. If most people most of the time choose to transfer some of their entitlements to others only in exchange for something from them, then a large part of what many people hold will vary with what they held that others wanted. More details are provided by the theory of marginal productivity. But gifts to relatives, charitable donations, bequests to children, and the like, are not best conceived, in the first instance, in this manner. Ignoring the strands of pattern, let us suppose for the moment that a distribution actually arrived at by the operation of the principle of entitlement is random with respect to any pattern. Though the resulting set of holdings will be unpatterned, it will not be incomprehensible, for it can be seen as arising from the operation of a small number of principles. These principles specify how an initial distribution may arise (the principle of acquisition of holdings) and how distributions may be transformed into others (the principle of transfer of holdings). The process whereby the set of holdings is generated will be intelligible, though the set of holdings itself that results from this process will be unpatterned.

---

* One might try to squeeze a patterned conception of distributive justice into the framework of the entitlement conception, by formulating a gimmicky obligatory "principle of transfer" that would lead to the pattern. For example, the principle that if one has more than the mean income one must transfer everything one holds above the mean to persons below the mean so as to bring them up to (but not over) the mean. We can formulate a criterion for a "principle of transfer" to rule out such obligatory transfers, or we can say that no correct principle of transfer, no principle of transfer in a free society, will be like this. The former is probably the better course, though the latter also is true.

Alternatively, one might think to make the entitlement conception instantiate a pattern, by using matrix entries that express the relative strength of a person's entitlements as measured by some real-valued function. But even if the limitation to natural dimensions failed to exclude this function, the resulting edifice would *not* capture our system of entitlements to *particular* things.

The writings of F. A. Hayek focus less than is usually done upon what patterning distributive justice requires. Hayek argues that we cannot know enough about each person's situation to distribute to each according to his moral merit (but would justice demand we do so if we did have this knowledge?); and he goes on to say, "our objection is against all attempts to impress upon society a deliberately chosen pattern of distribution, whether it be an order of equality or of inequality."[1] However, Hayek concludes that in a free society there will be distribution in accordance with value rather than moral merit; that is, in accordance with the perceived value of a person's actions and services to others. Despite his rejection of a patterned conception of distributive justice, Hayek himself suggests a pattern he thinks justifiable: distribution in accordance with the perceived benefits given to others, leaving room for the complaint that a free society does not realize exactly this pattern. Stating this patterned strand of a free capitalist society more precisely, we get "To each according to how much he benefits others who have the resources for benefiting those who benefit them." This will seem arbitrary unless some acceptable initial set of holdings is specified, or unless it is held that the operation of the system over time washes out any significant effects from the initial set of holdings. As an example of the latter, if almost anyone would have bought a car from Henry Ford, the supposition that it was an arbitrary matter who held the money then (and so bought) would not place Henry Ford's earnings under a cloud. In any event, *his* coming to hold it is not arbitrary. Distribution according to benefits to others *is* a major patterned strand in a free capitalist society, as Hayek correctly points out, but it is only a strand and does not constitute the whole pattern of a system of entitlements (namely, inheritance, gifts for arbitrary reasons, charity, and so on) or a standard that one should insist a society fit. Will people tolerate for long a system yielding distributions that they believe are unpatterned? No doubt people will not long accept a distribution they believe is *unjust*. People want their society to be and to look just. But must the look of justice reside in a resulting pattern rather than in the underlying generating principles? We are in no position to conclude that the inhabitants of a society embodying an entitlement conception of justice in holdings will find it unacceptable. Still, it must be granted that were people's reasons for transferring some of their holdings to others always irrational or arbitrary, we would find this disturbing. (Suppose people always determined what holdings they would transfer, and to whom, by using a random device.) We feel more comfortable upholding the justice of an entitlement system if most of the transfers under it are done for reasons. This does not mean necessarily that all deserve what holdings they receive. It means only that there is a purpose or point to someone's transferring a holding to one person rather than to another; that usually we can see what the transferrer thinks he's gaining, what cause he thinks he's serving, what goals he thinks he's helping to achieve, and so forth. Since in a capitalist society people often transfer holdings to others in accordance with how much they perceive these others benefiting them, the fabric constituted by the individual transactions and transfers is largely reasonable and intelligible.* (Gifts to loved ones, bequests to children, charity to the needy also are nonarbitrary components of the fabric.) In stressing the large strand of distribution in accordance with benefit to others, Hayek shows the point of many transfers, and so shows that the system of transfer of entitlements is not just spinning its gear aimlessly. The system of entitlements is defensible when constituted by the individual aims of individual transactions. No overarching aim is needed, no distributional pattern is required.

To think that the task of a theory of distributive justice is to fill in the blank in "to each according to his _____" is to be predisposed to search for a pattern; and the separate treatment of "from each according to his _____" treats production and distribution as two separate and independent issues. On an entitlement view these are *not* two separate questions. Whoever makes something, having bought or contracted for all other held resources used in the process (transferring some of his holdings for these cooperating factors), is entitled to it. The situation is *not* one of something's getting made, and there being an open question of who is to get it. Things come into the world already attached to people having entitlements over them. From the point of view of the historical-entitlement conception of justice in holdings, those who start afresh to complete "to each according to his _____" treat objects as if they appeared from nowhere, out of nothing. A complete theory of justice might

---

* We certainly benefit because great economic incentives operate to get others to spend much time and energy to figure out how to serve us by providing things we will want to pay for. It is not mere paradox mongering to wonder whether capitalism should be criticized for most rewarding and hence encouraging, not individualists like Thoreau who go about their own lives, but people who are occupied with serving others and winning them as customers. But to defend capitalism one need not think businessmen are the finest human types. (I do not mean to join here the general maligning of businessmen, either.) Those who think the finest should acquire the most can try to convince their fellows to transfer resources in accordance with *that* principle.

cover this limit case as well; perhaps here is a use for the usual conceptions of distributive justice.

So entrenched are maxims of the usual form that perhaps we should present the entitlement conception as a competitor. Ignoring acquisition and rectification, we might say:

> From each according to what he chooses to do, to each according to what he makes for himself (perhaps with the contracted aid of others) and what others choose to do for him and choose to give him of what they've been given previously (under this maxim) and haven't yet expended or transferred.

This, the discerning reader will have noticed, has its defects as a slogan. So as a summary and great simplification (and not as a maxim with any independent meaning) we have:

> From each as they choose, to each as they are chosen.

HOW LIBERTY UPSETS PATTERNS

It is not clear how those holding alternative conceptions of distributive justice can reject the entitlement conception of justice in holdings. For suppose a distribution favored by one of these non-entitlement conceptions is realized. Let us suppose it is your favorite one and let us call this distribution D_1; perhaps everyone has an equal share, perhaps shares vary in accordance with some dimension you treasure. Now suppose that Wilt Chamberlain is greatly in demand by basketball teams, being a great gate attraction. (Also suppose contracts run only for a year, with players being free agents.) He signs the following sort of contract with a team: In each home game, twenty-five cents from the price of each ticket of admission goes to him. (We ignore the question of whether he is "gouging" the owners, letting them look out for themselves.) The season starts, and people cheerfully attend his team's games; they buy their tickets, each time dropping a separate twenty-five cents of their admission price into a special box with Chamberlain's name on it. They are excited about seeing him play; it is worth the total admission price to them. Let us suppose that in one season one million persons attend his home games, and Wilt Chamberlain winds up with $250,000, a much larger sum than the average income and larger even than anyone else has. Is he entitled to this income? Is this new distribution D_2, unjust? If so, why? There is *no* question about whether each of the people was entitled to the control over the resources they held in D_1; because that was the distribution (your favorite) that (for the purposes of argument) we assumed was acceptable. Each of these persons *chose* to give twenty-five cents of their money to Chamberlain. They could have spent it on going to the movies, or on candy bars, or on copies of *Dissent* magazine, or of *Monthly Review*. But they all, at least one million of them, converged on giving it to Wilt Chamberlain in exchange for watching him play basketball. If D_1 was a just distribution, and people voluntarily moved from it to D_2, transferring parts of their shares they were given under D_1 (what was it for if not to do something with?), isn't D_2 also just? If the people were entitled to dispose of the resources to which they were entitled (under D_1), didn't this include their being entitled to give it to, or exchange it with, Wilt Chamberlain? Can anyone else complain on grounds of justice? Each other person already has his legitimate share under D_1. Under D_1, there is nothing that anyone has that anyone else has a claim of justice against. After someone transfers something to Wilt Chamberlain, third parties *still* have their legitimate shares; *their* shares are not changed. By what process could such a transfer among two persons give rise to a legitimate claim of distributive justice on a portion of what was transferred, by a third party who had no claim of justice on any holding of the others *before* the transfer?* To cut off objections irrelevant here, we might imagine the exchanges occurring in a socialist society, after hours. After playing whatever basketball he does in his daily work, or doing whatever other daily work he does, Wilt Chamberlain decides to put in *overtime* to earn additional money. (First his work quota is set; he works time over

---

* Might not a transfer have instrumental effects on a third party, changing his feasible options? (But what if the two parties to the transfer independently had used their holdings in this fashion?) I discuss this question below, but note here that this question concedes the point for distributions of ultimate intrinsic non-instrumental goods (pure utility experiences, so to speak) that are transferable. It also might be objected that the transfer might make a third party more envious because it worsens his position relative to someone else. I find it incomprehensible how this can be thought to involve a claim of justice.

Here and elsewhere in this chapter, a theory which incorporates elements of pure procedural justice might find what I say acceptable, *if* kept in its proper place; that is, if background institutions exist to ensure the satisfaction of certain conditions on distributive shares. But if these institutions are not themselves the sum or invisible-hand result of people's voluntary (nonaggressive) actions, the constraints they impose require justification. At no point does *our* argument assume any background institutions more extensive than those of the minimal night-watchman state, a state limited to protecting persons against murder, assault, theft, fraud, and so forth.

that.) Or imagine it is a skilled juggler people like to see, who puts on shows after hours.

Why might someone work overtime in a society in which it is assumed their needs are satisfied? Perhaps because they care about things other than needs. I like to write in books that I read, and to have easy access to books for browsing at odd hours. It would be very pleasant and convenient to have the resources of Widener Library in my back yard. No society, I assume, will provide such resources close to each person who would like them as part of his regular allotment (under D_1). Thus, persons either must do without some extra things that they want, or be allowed to do something extra to get some of these things. On what basis could the inequalities that would eventuate be forbidden? Notice also that small factories would spring up in a socialist society, unless forbidden. I melt down some of my personal possessions (under D_1) and build a machine out of the material. I offer you, and others, a philosophy lecture once a week in exchange for your cranking the handle on my machine, whose products I exchange for yet other things, and so on. (The raw materials used by the machine are given to me by others who possess them under D_1, in exchange for hearing lectures.) Each person might participate to gain things over and above their allotment under D_1. Some persons even might want to leave their job in socialist industry and work full-time in this private sector. . . . Here I wish merely to note how private property even in means of production would occur in a socialist society that did not forbid people to use as they wished some of the resources they are given under the socialist distribution D_1. The socialist society would have to forbid capitalist acts between consenting adults.

The general point illustrated by the Wilt Chamberlain example and the example of the entrepreneur in a socialist society is that no end-state principle or distributional patterned principle of justice can be continuously realized without continuous interference with people's lives. Any favored pattern would be transformed into one unfavored by the principle, by people choosing to act in various ways; for example, by people exchanging goods and services with other people, or giving things to other people, things the transferrers are entitled to under the favored distributional pattern. To maintain a pattern one must either continually interfere to stop people from transferring resources as they wish to, or continually (or periodically) interfere to take from some persons resources that others for some reason chose to transfer to them. (But if some time limit is to be set on how long people may keep resources others voluntarily transfer to them, why let them keep these resources for *any* period of time? Why not have immediate confiscation?) It might be objected that all persons voluntarily will choose to refrain from actions which would upset the pattern. This presupposes unrealistically (1) that all will most want to maintain the pattern (are those who don't to be "reeducated" or forced to undergo "self-criticism"?); (2) that each can gather enough information about his own actions and the ongoing activities of others to discover which of his actions will upset the pattern; and (3) that diverse and far-flung persons can coordinate their actions to dovetail into the pattern. Compare the manner in which the market is neutral among persons' desires, as it reflects and transmits widely scattered information via prices, and coordinates persons' activities.

It puts things perhaps a bit too strongly to say that every patterned (or end-state) principle is liable to be thwarted by the voluntary actions of the individual parties transferring some of their shares they receive under the principle. For perhaps some *very* weak patterns are not so thwarted.* Any distributional pattern with any egalitarian component is overturnable by the voluntary actions of individual persons over time; as is every patterned condition with sufficient content so as actually to have been proposed as presenting the central core of distributive justice. Still, given the possibility that some weak conditions or patterns may not be unstable in this way, it would be better to formulate an explicit description of the kind of interesting and contentful patterns under discussion, and to prove a theorem about their instability. Since the weaker the patterning, the more likely it is that the entitlement system itself satisfies it, a plausible conjecture is that any patterning either is unstable or is satisfied by the entitlement system.

---

* Is the patterned principle stable that requires merely that a distribution be Pareto-optimal? One person might give another a gift or bequest that the second could exchange with a third to their mutual benefit. Before the second makes this exchange, there is not Pareto-optimality. Is a stable pattern presented by a principle choosing that among the pareto-optimal positions that satisfies some further condition C? It may seem that there cannot be a counterexample, for won't any voluntary exchange made away from a situation show that the first situation wasn't Pareto-optimal? (Ignore the implausibility of this last claim for the case of bequests.) But principles are to be satisfied over time, during which new possibilities arise. A distribution that at one time satisfies the criterion of Pareto-optimality might not do so when some new possibilities arise (Wilt Chamberlain grows up and starts playing basketball); and though people's activities will tend to move then to a new Pareto-optimal position, *this* new one need not satisfy the contentful condition C. Continual interference will be needed to insure the continual satisfaction of C. (The theoretical possibility of a pattern's being maintained by some invisible-hand process that brings it back to an equilibrium that fits the pattern when deviations occur should be investigated.)

REDISTRIBUTION AND PROPERTY RIGHTS

Apparently, patterned principles allow people to choose to expend upon themselves, but not upon others, those resources they are entitled to (or rather, receive) under some favored distributional pattern D_1. For if each of several persons chooses to expend some of his D_1 resources upon one other person, then that other person will receive more than his D_1 share, disturbing the favored distributional pattern. Maintaining a distributional pattern is individualism with a vengeance! Patterned distributional principles do not give people what entitlement principles do, only better distributed. For they do not give the right to choose what to do with what one has; they do not give the right to choose to pursue an end involving (intrinsically, or as a means) the enhancement of another's position. To such views, families are disturbing; for within a family occur transfers that upset the favored distributional pattern. Either families themselves become units to which distribution takes place, the column occupiers (on what rationale?), or loving behavior is forbidden. We should note in passing the ambivalent position of radicals toward the family. Its loving relationships are seen as a model to be emulated and extended across the whole society, at the same time that it is denounced as a suffocating institution to be broken and condemned as a focus of parochial concerns that interfere with achieving radical goals. Need we say that it is not appropriate to enforce across the wider society the relationships of love and care appropriate within a family, relationships which are voluntarily undertaken?* Incidentally, love is an interesting instance of another relationship that is historical, in that (like justice) it depends upon what actually occurred. An adult may come to love another because of the other's characteristics; but it is the other person, and not the characteristics, that is loved. The love is not transferable to someone else with the same characteristics, even to one who "scores" higher for these characteristics. And

---

* One indication of the stringency of Rawls's difference principle is its inappropriateness as a governing principle even within a family of individuals who love one another. Should a family devote its resources to maximizing the position of its least-well-off and least-talented child, holding back the other children or using resources for their education and development only if they will follow a policy through their lifetimes of maximizing the position of their least-fortunate sibling? Surely not. How then can this even be considered as the appropriate policy for enforcement in the wider society? (I discuss below what I think would be Rawls's reply: that some principles apply at the macro level which do not apply to microsituations.)

the love endures through changes of the characteristics that gave rise to it. One loves the particular person one actually encountered. Why love is historical, attaching to persons in this way and not to characteristics, is an interesting and puzzling question.

Proponents of patterned principles of distributive justice focus upon criteria for determining who is to receive holdings; they consider the reasons for which someone should have something, and also the total picture of holdings. Whether or not it is better to give than to receive, proponents of patterned principles ignore giving altogether. In considering the distribution of goods, income, and so forth, their theories are theories of recipient justice; they completely ignore any right a person might have to give something to someone. Even in exchanges where each party is simultaneously giver and recipient, patterned principles of justice focus only upon the recipient role and its supposed rights. Thus discussions tend to focus on whether people (should) have a right to inherit, rather than on whether people (should) have a right to bequeath or on whether persons who have a right to hold also have a right to choose that others hold in their place. I lack a good explanation of why the usual theories of distributive justice are so recipient oriented; ignoring givers and transferrers and their rights is of a piece with ignoring producers and their entitlements. But why is it *all* ignored?

Patterned principles of distributive justice necessitate *re*distributive activities. The likelihood is small that any actual freely arrived at set of holdings fits a given pattern; and the likelihood is nil that it will continue to fit the pattern as people exchange and give. From the point of view of an entitlement theory, redistribution is a serious matter indeed, involving, as it does, the violation of people's rights. (An exception is those takings that fall under the principle of the rectification of injustices.) From other points of view, also, it is serious.

Taxation of earnings from labor is on a par with forced labor.* Some persons find this claim obviously true: taking the earnings of n hours' labor is like taking n hours from the person; it is like forcing the person to work n hours for another's purpose. Others find the

---

* I am unsure as to whether the arguments I present below show that such taxation merely *is* forced labor; so that "is on a par with" means "is one kind of." Or alternatively, whether the arguments emphasize the great similarities between such taxation and forced labor, to show it is plausible and illuminating to view such taxation in the light of forced labor. This latter approach would remind one of how John Wisdom conceives of the claims of metaphysicians.

claim absurd. But even these, *if* they object to forced labor, would oppose forcing unemployed hippies to work for the benefit of the needy.[2] And they would also object to forcing each person to work five extra hours each week for the benefit of the needy. But a system that takes five hours' wages in taxes does not seem to them like one that forces someone to work five hours, since it offers the person forced a wider range of choice in activities than does taxation in kind with the particular labor specified. (But we can imagine a gradation of systems of forced labor, from one that specifies a particular activity, to one that gives a choice among two activities, to . . . ; and so on up.) Furthermore, people envisage a system with something like a proportional tax on everything above the amount necessary for basic needs. Some think this does not force someone to work extra hours, since there is no fixed number of extra hours he is forced to work, and since he can avoid the tax entirely by earning only enough to cover his basic needs. This is a very uncharacteristic view of forcing for those who *also* think people are forced to do something *whenever* the alternatives they face are considerably worse. However, *neither* view is correct. The fact that others intentionally intervene, in violation of a side constraint against aggression, to threaten force to limit the alternatives, in this case to paying taxes or (presumably the worse alternative) bare subsistence, makes the taxation system one of forced labor and distinguishes it from other cases of limited choices which are not forcings.

The man who chooses to work longer to gain an income more than sufficient for his basic needs prefers some extra goods or services to the leisure and activities he could perform during the possible non-working hours; whereas the man who chooses not to work the extra time prefers the leisure activities to the extra goods or services he could acquire by working more. Given this, if it would be illegitimate for a tax system to seize some of a man's leisure (forced labor) for the purpose of serving the needy, how can it be legitimate for a tax system to seize some of a man's goods for that purpose? Why should we treat the man whose happiness requires certain material goods or services differently from the man whose preferences and desires make such goods unnecessary for his happiness? Why should the man who prefers seeing a movie (and who has to earn money for a ticket) be open to the required call to aid the needy, while the person who prefers looking at a sunset (and hence need earn no extra money) is not? Indeed, isn't it surprising that redistributionists choose to ignore the man whose pleasures are so easily attainable without extra labor, while adding yet another burden to the poor unfortunate who must work for his pleasures? If anything, one would have expected the reverse. Why is the person with the nonmaterial or nonconsumption desire allowed to proceed unimpeded to his most favored feasible alternative, whereas the man whose pleasures or desires involve material things and who must work for extra money (thereby serving whomever considers his activities valuable enough to pay him) is constrained in what he can realize? Perhaps there is no difference in principle. And perhaps some think the answer concerns merely administrative convenience. (These questions and issues will not disturb those who think that forced labor to serve the needy or to realize some favored end-state pattern is acceptable.) In a fuller discussion we would have (and want) to extend our argument to include interest, entrepreneurial profits, and so on. Those who doubt that this extension can be carried through, and who draw the line here at taxation of income from labor, will have to state rather complicated patterned *historical* principles of distributive justice, since end-state principles would not distinguish *sources* of income in any way. It is enough for now to get away from end-state principles and to make clear how various patterned principles are dependent upon particular views about the sources or the illegitimacy or the lesser legitimacy of profits, interest, and so on; which particular views may well be mistaken.

What sort of right over others does a legally institutionalized end-state pattern give one? The central core of the notion of a property right in X, relative to which other parts of the notion are to be explained, is the right to determine what shall be done with X; the right to choose which of the constrained set of options concerning X shall be realized or attempted. The contraints are set by other principles or laws operating in the society; in our theory, by the Lockean rights people possess (under the minimal state). My property rights in my knife allow me to leave it where I will, but not in your chest. I may choose which of the acceptable options involving the knife is to be realized. This notion of property helps us to understand why earlier theorists spoke of people as having property in themselves and their labor. They viewed each person as having a right to decide what would become of himself and what he would do, and as having a right to reap the benefits of what he did.

This right of selecting the alternative to be realized from the constrained set of alternatives may be held by an *individual* or by a *group* with some procedure for reaching a joint decision; or the right may be passed back and forth, so that one year I decide what's to become of X, and the next year you do (with the alternative of destruction, perhaps, being excluded). Or, during the same time period, some types of decisions about X may be made by me, and others by you. And so on. We lack an adequate, fruitful, analytical apparatus for classifying the *types* of constraints on the set of options among which choices are to be made, and the *types* of ways decision powers can be held, divided, and amalgamated. A *theory* of property would, among other things, contain such a classification of constraints and decision modes, and from a small number of principles would follow a host of interesting statements about the *consequences* and effects of certain combinations of constraints and modes of decision.

When end-result principles of distributive justice are built into the legal structure of a society, they (as do most patterned principles) give each citizen an enforceable claim to some portion of the total social product; that is, to some portion of the sum total of the individually and jointly made products. This total product is produced by individuals laboring, using means of production others have saved to bring into existence, by people organizing production or creating means to produce new things or things in a new way. It is on this batch of individual activities that patterned distributional principles give each individual an enforceable claim. Each person has a claim to the activities and the products of other persons, independently of whether the other persons enter into particular relationships that give rise to these claims, and independently of whether they voluntarily take these claims upon themselves, in charity or in exchange for something.

Whether it is done through taxation on wages or on wages over a certain amount, or through seizure of profits, or through there being a big *social pot* so that it's not clear what's coming from where and what's going where, patterned principles of distributive justice involve appropriating the actions of other persons. Seizing the results of someone's labor is equivalent to seizing hours from him and directing him to carry on various activities. If people force you to do certain work, or unrewarded work, for a certain period of time, they decide what you are to do and what purposes your work is to serve apart from your decisions. This process whereby they take this decision from you makes them a *part owner* of you; it gives them a property right in you. Just as having such partial control and power of decision, by right, over an animal or inanimate object would be to have a property right in it.

End-state and most patterned principles of distributive justice institute (partial) ownership by others of people and their actions and labor. These principles involve a shift from the classical liberals' notion of self-ownership to a notion of (partial) property rights in *other* people.

Considerations such as these confront end-state and other patterned conceptions of justice with the question of whether the actions necessary to achieve the selected pattern don't themselves violate moral side constraints. Any view holding that there are moral side constraints on actions, that not all moral considerations can be built into end states that are to be achieved . . . must face the possibility that some of its goals are not achievable by any morally permissible available means. An entitlement theorist will face such conflicts in a society that deviates from the principles of justice for the generation of holdings, if and only if the only actions available to realize the principles themselves violate some moral constraint. Since deviation from the first two principles of justice (in acquisition and transfer) will involve other persons' direct and aggressive intervention to violate rights, and since moral constraints will not exclude defensive or retributive action in such cases, the entitlement theorist's problem rarely will be pressing. And whatever difficulties he has in applying the principle of rectification to persons who did not themselves violate the first two principles are difficulties in balancing the conflicting considerations so as correctly to formulate the complex principle of rectification itself; he will not violate moral side constraints by applying the principle. Proponents of patterned conceptions of justice, however, often will face head-on clashes (and poignant ones if they cherish each party to the clash) between moral side constraints on how individuals may be treated and their patterned conception of justice that presents an end state or other pattern that *must* be realized.

May a person emigrate from a nation that has institutionalized some end-state or patterned distributional principle? For some principles (for example, Hayek's) emigration presents no theoretical problem. But for others it is a tricky matter. Consider a nation having a compulsory scheme of minimal social provision to aid the neediest (or one organized so as to maximize the position of the worst-off group); no one may opt out of participating in it. (None may say, "Don't compel me to contribute to others and don't provide for me via this compulsory mechanism if I am in need.") Everyone above a certain level is forced to contribute to aid the needy. But if emigration from the country were allowed, anyone could choose to move to another country that did not have compulsory social provision but otherwise was (as much as possible) identical. In such a case, the person's *only* motive for leaving would be to avoid participating in the compulsory scheme of social provision. And if he does leave, the needy in his initial country will receive no (compelled) help from him. What rationale yields the result that the person be permitted to emigrate, yet forbidden to stay and opt out of the compulsory scheme of social provision? If providing for the needy is of overriding importance, this does militate against allowing internal opting out; but it also speaks against allowing external emigration. (Would it also support, to some extent, the kidnapping of persons living in a place without compulsory social provision, who could be forced to make a contribution to the needy in your community?) Perhaps the crucial component of the position that allows emigration solely to avoid certain arrangements, while not allowing anyone internally to opt out of them, is a concern for fraternal feelings within the country. "We don't want anyone here who doesn't contribute, who doesn't care enough about the others to contribute." That concern, in this case, would have to be tied to the view that forced aiding tends to produce fraternal feelings between the aided and the aider (or perhaps merely to the view that the knowledge that someone or other voluntarily is not aiding produces unfraternal feelings).

LOCKE'S THEORY OF ACQUISITION

Before we turn to consider other theories of justice in detail, we must introduce an additional bit of complexity into the structure of the entitlement theory. This is best approached by considering Locke's attempt to specify a principle of justice in acquisition. Locke views property rights in an unowned object as originating through someone's mixing his labor with it. This gives rise to many questions. What are the boundaries of what labor is mixed with? If a private astronaut clears a place on Mars, has he mixed his labor with (so that he comes to own) the whole planet, the whole uninhabited universe, or just a particular plot? Which plot does an act bring under ownership? The minimal (possibly disconnected) area such that an act decreases entropy in that area, and not elsewhere? Can virgin land (for the purposes of ecological investigation by high-flying airplane) come under ownership by a Lockean process? Building a fence around a territory presumably would make one the owner of only the fence (and the land immediately underneath it).

Why does mixing one's labor with something make one the owner of it? Perhaps because one owns one's labor, and so one comes to own a previously unowned thing that becomes permeated with what one owns. Ownership seeps over into the rest. But why isn't mixing what I own with what I don't own a way of losing what I own rather than a way of gaining what I don't? If I own a can of tomato juice and spill it in the sea so that its molecules (made radioactive, so I can check this) mingle evenly throughout the sea, do I thereby come to own the sea, or have I foolishly dissipated my tomato juice? Perhaps the idea, instead, is that laboring on something improves it and makes it more valuable; and anyone is entitled to own a thing whose value he has created. (Reinforcing this, perhaps, is the view that laboring is unpleasant. If some people made things effortlessly, as the cartoon characters in *The Yellow Submarine* trail flowers in their wake, would they have lesser claim to their own products whose making didn't *cost* them anything?) Ignore the fact that laboring on something may make it less valuable (spraying pink-enamel paint on a piece of driftwood that you have found). Why should one's entitlement extend to the whole object rather than just to the *added value* one's labor has produced? (Such reference to value might also serve to delimit the extent of ownership; for example, substitute "increases the value of" for "decreases entropy in" in the above entropy criterion.) No workable or coherent value-added property scheme has yet been devised, and any such scheme presumably would fall to objections (similar to those) that fell the theory of Henry George.

It will be implausible to view improving an object as giving full ownership to it, if the stock of unowned objects that might be improved is limited. For an object's coming under one person's ownership changes the situation of all others. Whereas previously they were at liberty (in Hohfeld's sense) to use the object, they now no longer are. This change in the situation of others (by removing their liberty to act on a previously unowned object) need not worsen their situation. If I appropriate a grain of sand from Coney Island, no one else may now do as they will with *that* grain of sand. But there are plenty of other grains of sand left for them to do the same with. Or if not grains of sand, then other things. Alternatively, the things I do with the grain of sand I appropriate might improve the position of others, counterbalancing their loss of the liberty to use that grain. The crucial point is whether appropriation of an unowned object worsens the situation of others.

Locke's proviso that there be "enough and as good left in common for others" (sect. 27) is meant to ensure that the situation of others is not worsened. (If this proviso is met is there any motivation for his further condition of nonwaste?) It is often said that this proviso once held but now no longer does. But there appears to be an argument for the conclusion that if the proviso no longer holds, then it cannot ever have held so as to yield permanent and inheritable property rights. Consider the first person Z for whom there is not enough and as good left to appropriate. The last person Y to appropriate left Z without his previous liberty to act on an object, and so worsened Z's situation. So Y's appropriation is not allowed under Locke's proviso. Therefore the next to last person X to appropriate left Y in a worse position, for X's act ended permissible appropriation. Therefore X's appropriation wasn't permissible. But then the appropriator two from last, W, ended permissible appropriation and so, since it worsened X's position, W's appropriation wasn't permissible. And so on back to the first person A to appropriate a permanent property right.

This argument, however, proceeds too quickly. Someone may be made worse off by another's appropriation in two ways: first, by losing the opportunity to improve his situation by a particular appropriation or any one; and second, by no longer being able to use freely (without appropriation) what he previously could. A *stringent* requirement that another not be made worse off by an appropriation would exclude the first way if nothing else counterbalances the diminution in opportunity, as well as the second. A *weaker* requirement would exclude the second way, though not the first. With the weaker requirement, we cannot zip back so quickly from Z to A, as in the above argument; for though person Z can no longer *appropriate*, there may remain some for him to *use* as before. In this case Y's appropriation would not violate the weaker Lockean condition. (With less remaining that people are at liberty to use, users might face more inconvenience, crowding, and so on; in that way the situation of others might be worsened, unless appropriation stopped far short of such a point.) It is arguable that no one legitimately can complain if the weaker provision is satisfied. However, since this is less clear than in the case of the more stringent proviso, Locke may have intended this stringent proviso by "enough and as good" remaining, and perhaps he meant the nonwaste condition to delay the end point from which the argument zips back.

Is the situation of persons who are unable to appropriate (there being no more accessible and useful unowned objects) worsened by a system allowing appropriation and permanent property? Here enter the various familiar social considerations favoring private property: it increases the social product by putting means of production in the hands of those who can use them most efficiently (profitably); experimentation is encouraged, because with separate persons controlling resources, there is no one person or small group whom someone with a new idea must convince to try it out; private property enables people to decide on the pattern and types of risks they wish to bear, leading to specialized types of risk bearing; private property protects future persons by leading some to hold back resources from current consumption for future markets; it provides alternate sources of employment for unpopular persons who don't have to convince any one person or small group to hire them; and so on. These considerations enter a Lockean theory to support the claim that appropriation of private property satisfies the intent behind the "enough and as good left over" proviso, *not* as a utilitarian justification of property. They enter to rebut the claim that because the proviso is violated no natural right to private property can arise by a Lockean process. The difficulty in working such an argument to show that the proviso is satisfied is in fixing the appropriate base line for comparison. Lockean appropriation makes people no worse off than they would be *how*? This question of fixing the base line needs more detailed investigation than we are able to give it here. It would be desirable to have an estimate of the general economic importance of original appropriation in order to see how much leeway there is for differing theories of appropriation and of the location of the base line. Perhaps this importance can be measured by the percentage of all income that is based upon untransformed raw materials and given resources (rather than upon human actions), mainly rental income representing the unimproved value of land, and the price of raw material *in situ*, and by the percentage of current wealth which represents such income in the past.[3]

We should note that it is not only persons favoring *private* property who need a theory of how property rights legitimately originate. Those believing in collective property, for example those believing that a group of persons living in an area jointly own the territory, or its mineral resources, also must provide a theory of how such property rights arise; they must show why the persons living there have rights to determine what is done with the land and resources there that persons living elsewhere don't have (with regard to the same land and resources).

THE PROVISO

Whether or not Locke's particular theory of appropriation can be spelled out so as to handle various difficulties, I assume that any adequate theory of justice in acquisition will contain a proviso similar to the weaker of the ones we have attributed to Locke. A process normally giving rise to a permanent bequeathable property right in a previously unowned thing will not do so if the position of others no longer at liberty to use the thing is thereby worsened. It is important to specify *this* particular mode of worsening the situation of others, for the proviso does not encompass other modes. It does not include the worsening due to more limited opportunities to appropriate (the first way above, corresponding to the more stringent condition), and it does not include how I "worsen" a seller's position if I appropriate materials to make some of what he is selling, and then enter into competition with him. Someone whose appropriation otherwise would violate the proviso still may appropriate provided he compensates the others so that their situation is not thereby worsened; unless he does compensate these others, his appropriation will violate the proviso of the principle of justice in acquisition and will be an illegitimate one.[4] A theory of appropriation incorporating this Lockean proviso will handle correctly the cases (objections to the theory lacking the proviso) where someone appropriates the total supply of something necessary for life.[5]

A theory which includes this proviso in its principle of justice in acquisition must also contain a more complex principle of justice in transfer. Some reflection of the proviso about appropriation constrains later actions. If my appropriating all of a certain substance violates the Lockean proviso, then so does my appropriating some and purchasing all the rest from others who obtained it without otherwise violating the Lockean proviso. If the proviso excludes someone's appropriating all the drinkable water in the world, it also excludes his purchasing it all. (More weakly, and messily, it may exclude his charging certain prices for some of his supply.) This proviso (almost?) never will come into effect; the more someone acquires of a scarce substance which others want, the higher the price of the rest will go, and the more difficult it will become for him to acquire it all. But still, we can imagine, at least, that something like this occurs: someone makes simultaneous secret bids to the separate owners of a substance, each of whom sells assuming he can easily purchase more from the other owners; or some natural catastrophe destroys all of the supply of something except that in one person's possession. The total supply could not be permissibly appropriated by one person at the beginning. His later acquisition of it all does not show that the original appropriation violated the proviso (even by a reverse argument similar to the one above that tried to zip back from Z to A). Rather, it is the combination of the original appropriation *plus* all the later transfers and actions that violates the Lockean proviso.

Each owner's title to his holding includes the historical shadow of the Lockean proviso on appropriation. This excludes his transferring it into an agglomeration that does violate the Lockean proviso and excludes his using it in a way, in coordination with others or independently of them, so as to violate the proviso by making the situation of others worse than their base line situation. Once it is known that someone's ownership runs afoul of the Lockean proviso, there are stringent limits on what he may do with (what it is difficult any longer unreservedly to call) "his property." Thus a person may not appropriate the only water hole in a desert and charge what he will. Nor may he charge what he will if he possesses one, and unfortunately it happens that all the water holes in the desert dry up, except for his. This unfortunate circumstance, admittedly no fault of his, brings into operation the Lockean proviso and limits his property rights.[6] Similarly, an owner's property right in the only island in an area does not allow him to order a castaway from a shipwreck off his island as a trespasser, for this would violate the Lockean proviso.

Notice that the theory does not say that owners do have these rights, but that the rights are overridden to avoid some catastrophe. (Overridden rights do not disappear; they leave a trace of a sort absent in the cases under discussion.) There is no such external (and ad hoc?) overriding. Considerations internal to the theory of property itself, to its theory of acquisition and appropriation, provide the means for handling such cases. The results, however, may be coextensive with some condition about catastrophe, since the base line for comparison is so low as compared to the productiveness of a society with private appropriation that the question of the Lockean proviso being violated arises only in the case of catastrophe (or a desert-island situation).

The fact that someone owns the total supply of something necessary for others to stay alive does *not* entail that his (or anyone's) appropriation of anything left some people (immediately or later) in a situation worse than the base line one. A medical researcher who synthesizes a new substance that effectively treats a certain disease and who refuses to sell except on his terms does not worsen the situation of others by depriving them of whatever he has appropriated. The others easily can possess the same materials he appropriated; the researcher's appropriation or purchase of chemicals didn't make those chemicals scarce in a way so as to violate the Lockean proviso. Nor would someone else's purchasing the total supply of the synthesized substance from the medical researcher. The fact that the medical researcher uses easily available chemicals to synthesize the drug no more violates the Lockean proviso than does the fact that the only surgeon able to perform a particular operation eats easily obtainable food in order to stay alive and to have the energy to work. This shows that the Lockean proviso is not an "end-state principle"; it focuses on a particular way that appropriative actions affect others, and not on the structure of the situation that results.

Intermediate between someone who takes all of the public supply and someone who makes the total supply out of easily obtainable substances is someone who appropriates the total supply of something in a way that does not deprive the others of it. For example, someone finds a new substance in an out-of-the-way place. He discovers that it effectively treats a certain disease and appropriates the total supply. He does not worsen the situation of others; if he did not stumble upon the substance no one else would have, and the others would remain without it. However, as time passes, the likelihood increases that others would have come across the substance; upon this fact might be based a limit to his property right in the substance so that others are not below their base-line position; for example, its bequest might be limited. The theme of someone worsening another's situation by depriving him of something he otherwise would possess may also illuminate the example of patents. An inventor's patent does not deprive others of an object which would not exist if not for the inventor. Yet patents would have this effect on others who independently invent the object. Therefore, these independent inventors, upon whom the burden of proving independent discovery may rest, should not be excluded from utilizing their own invention as they wish (including selling it to others). Furthermore, a known inventor drastically lessens the chances of actual independent invention. For persons who know of an invention usually will not try to reinvent it, and the notion of independent discovery here would be murky at best. Yet we may assume that in the absence of the original invention, sometime later someone else would have come up with it. This suggests placing a time limit on patents, as a rough rule of thumb to approximate how long it would have taken, in the absence of knowledge of the invention, for independent discovery.

I believe that the free operation of a market system will not actually run afoul of the Lockean proviso. (Recall that crucial to . . . how a protective agency becomes dominant and a de facto monopoly is the fact that it wields force in situations of conflict, and is not merely in competition with other agencies. A similar tale cannot be told about other businesses.) If this is correct, the proviso will not play a very important role in the activities of protective agencies and will not provide a significant opportunity for future state action. Indeed, were it not for the effects of previous *illegitimate* state action, people would not think the possibility of the proviso's being violated as of more interest than any other logical possibility. (Here I make an empirical historical claim; as does someone who disagrees with this.) This completes our indication of the complication in the entitlement theory introduced by the Lockean proviso.

NOTES

1. F. A. von Hayek, "Equality, Value, and Merit" [see this text, p. 155].
2. Nothing hangs on the fact that here and elsewhere I speak loosely of *needs*, since I go on, each time, to reject the criterion of justice which includes it. If, however, something did depend upon the notion, one would want to examine it more carefully. For a skeptical view, see Kenneth Minogue, *The Liberal Mind* (New York: Random House, 1963) pp. 103-112.
3. I have not seen a precise estimate. David Friedman, *The Machinery of Freedom* (New York: Harper & Row, 1973), pp. xiv and xv, discusses this issue and suggests 5 percent of U.S. national income as an upper limit for the first two factors mentioned. However he does not attempt to estimate the percentage of current wealth which is based upon such income in the past. (The vague notion of "based upon" merely indicates a topic needing investigation.)
4. Fourier held that since the process of civilization had deprived the members of society of certain liberties (to gather, pasture, engage in the chase), a socially guaranteed minimum provision for persons was justified as compensation for the loss (Alexander Gray, *The Socialist Tradition* [New York: Harper & Row, 1968], p. 188). But this puts the point too strongly. This compensation would be due those persons, if any, for whom the process of civilization was a *net loss*, for whom the benefits of civilization did not counterbalance being deprived of these particular liberties.
5. For example, Rashdall's case of someone who comes upon the only water in the desert several miles ahead of others who also will come to it and appropriates it all. Hastings Rashdall, "The Philosophical Theory of Property," in *Property, Its Duties and Rights* (London: Macmillan, 1915), pp. 35-68.

    We should note Ayn Rand's theory of property rights ("Man's Rights," *The Virtue of Selfishness* [New York: New American Library, 1964], p. 94), wherein these follow from the right to life, since people need physical things to live. But a right to life is not a right to whatever one needs to live; other people may have rights over these other things (see Chapter three of this book). At most, a right to life would be a right to have or strive for whatever one needs to live, provided that having it does not violate anyone else's rights. With regard to material things, the question is whether having it does violate any right of others. (Would appropriation of all unowned things do so? Would appropriating the water hole in Rashdall's example?) Since special considerations (such as the Lockean proviso) may enter with regard to material property, one *first* needs a theory of property rights one can apply any supposed right to life (as amended above). Therefore the right to life cannot provide the foundation for a theory of property rights.
6. The situation would be different if his water hole didn't dry up, due to special precautions he took to prevent this. Compare our discussion of the case in the text with Hayek, *The Constitution of Liberty*, p. 136; and also with Ronald Hamowy, "Hayek's Concept of Freedom: A critique," *New Individualists Review*, vol. 1, April 1961, pp. 28-31.

5.

Advertising—Generating Wants

Everyone in our society is exposed to a constant bombardment of advertising from dawn to dusk and from birth to death. This exposure is not passively and unconsciously suffered as some have contended, for there are very few who are not aware of it and who do not consider it with a good deal of skepticism and cynicism. For years comedians have known that satirizing inane advertisements is a good way to get easy laughs. Who could possibly be taken in by a bald-headed man who jumps through the kitchen window and claims to have a super-duper oven cleaner that will take the drudgery out of housework? How could anyone be so naive as to believe that a famous football player has any insight into whether a certain brand of panty hose is well made? These advertisements are laughable, but amid the peals of merriment, there is the sobering thought that the companies spending their money on these advertisements do not consider them as their contribution to the amount of laughter and fun in the world. People can laugh at advertisements, but they are a serious matter to those who are paying for them.

The purpose of advertising is to increase sales. There would be no point in spending the billions of dollars that are used for advertising unless there was reason to believe that the money will be well spent and that, as a result, companies will become more profitable. Apparently, this belief is justified. An advertising campaign does not necessarily mean that a company will make more money, and there are some examples of advertising gone sour, of which the Ford Company's Edsel is probably the most famous. But there are enough cases in which an increase in expenditure on advertising has led to an increase in revenue to leave little doubt whether advertising is effective. So, while many might think that it would take really gullible types to believe that a certain kind of toothpaste will enhance a person's love life, this kind of advertising sells toothpaste. Furthermore, upon inspection, one might very well find that the toothpaste in the bathroom is just the brand being touted by that ridiculous advertisement.

Advertising not only is effective, it also performs an important role in the economic system. It stimulates people to desire new things, and this is often necessary for the many companies that want to ensure their future success by showing continually increasing profits. If a company does not have increasing profits, it will probably find that investors are no longer interested in it, and the company may well develop financial trouble. If a company is producing product X, and if X is desired by a great number of people, there will come a time when everybody has an X. At this point the company's profits will go down, or at least, will not increase. The company must then turn its attention to a new product, say Y, and hope that Y will be as successful as X. But the company will not just hope that Y will be successful; it will try to make sure that it will be, and in order to do this, advertising is required. Advertising is supposed to spread the word about the new product and present it in a way that will make it desirable. If demonstrating an increasing growth of profits were not the way of attracting investors, there would be no need to develop new products, and, consequently, no real purpose for advertising. To no longer require companies to make their profits grow would be, as was shown in the section on profits, a drastic change in the system. As long as the emphasis in our system is on profit, there will be a need for advertising.

So far it has been pointed out that advertising is a source of amusement, that it is often effective, and that it has an important function in the economic system. None of these points leads necessarily to any conclusion about whether advertising is good or bad. The ethical discussion of advertising has centered around two main issues—both of which are raised in the article by Burton Leiser. These issues are whether advertising is essentially a form of deception, and whether advertising generates desires that would not have been formed without its influence.

These two issues, to be sure, are not completely distinct, but in order to see exactly what they are, it will be useful to discuss them separately. The issue of deception has certain variations that derive from the different ways one person can deceive another. The most obvious case of deception is the outright lie. One person tells another that something is true when he knows it is false. Jones tells Smith that he stayed home by himself when actually Jones went out with Smith's wife. This kind of outright lie has its counterpart in the world of advertising, as there have been cases in which companies have made claims for their products that they knew to be false. Although this kind of thing happens, it is defended by no one, and it is universally considered to be immoral. This does not mean it will not continue to happen; but when the perpetrators get caught, they usually say that they were unaware that what they were saying was false. They do not claim that they had a right to lie.

From the ethical standpoint the outright lie is not the source of much controversy. More intriguing and complicated is the case of a false implication. In this case a deceiver knows the truth and what he says literally is the truth; however, what is said implies something that the deceiver knows to be false. Consider the following example: A, a well-known rich man, has gone for a swim in a lake. When he is far from shore, he suddenly gets a cramp. As he is going down for the third time, he spots B in a boat nearby and he calls to him, "Help me! I am drowning. If you save my life, I will give you every penny I own." B is not a good swimmer himself, but out of a sense of being helpful, and also because he recognizes the drowning man as the wealthy A, he decides to risk his life in order to save A. He jumps into the water, and with great effort he saves A's life. A is grateful and he says to B, "You saved my life and I will keep my word. Here are the fourteen pennies I own. I have no others."

In this example B would clearly think that A had taken advantage of him. But what A promised to do, he did. Whether one thinks that A's actions were wrong depends on the answers one gives to two questions. The first question is whether a person is not only obligated to do what he says but also to do what he implies. If a person does not say precisely that he will do something, but he implies that he will, is there an obligation to do what was implied? Similarly, if a person says something that is true, but he knows it implies something that is false, is the person then a liar? The second question concerns whether the person hearing the statement—in the example, B—is responsible for analyzing the implications of the statement and then finding out whether the speaker intends to keep his word on all of them. Was it really B's responsibility before he rescued A to ask him to clarify his statement? If B does have this responsibility and he does not fulfill it, then are there grounds for saying that A's action was not wrong?

This is a more complicated kind of case than the outright lie, and the examples of advertising that fit into this category are correspondingly more difficult to judge from the ethical point of view. If a company puts the word *new* on the package of an established laundry detergent, there is the implication that the detergent has been improved. But suppose only the packaging has changed. The container and the detergent inside have been given a new color, but no improvement has been made in the effectiveness of the detergent itself. Is the company guilty of a lie if the marketers who designed the package realized that the word *new* implied things that were not really true? Or rather, is the company blameless because it is the customer's responsibility to investigate in order to find out whether the implications are true? This is an intricate issue; there are numerous subtle variations in different situations that can lead to different ethical judgments.

Finally, there is one other kind of example that presents even more difficulties for judging whether advertising is guilty of deception. Consider the common case in which an advertisement mentions all the positive qualities of a product but says nothing about its negative aspects. No advertisement would ever say that its client's automobiles have a very poor repair record. No ad would mention the fact that the refrigerator it praises uses much more energy than the competitive models. No ad would boast that the cereal it touts has been judged to be lower in nutritional value than any other cereal. These negative aspects, even if known, are not to be talked about, as it is one of the first principles of any kind of salesmanship that only the good points should be mentioned.

Is it right to only mention a product's good points? Those who say that this sort of advertising is wrong argue for their view by trying to assimilate this kind of example to the previous one about false implications. What this side says is that mentioning only the good points is deception because this advertising implies that the good points are all there are and that there is nothing bad that can be said. If the bad points are known by the advertiser, this kind of deception is immoral no matter how widespread it is.

The side that does not believe that this kind of advertising is wrong tries to distinguish it from the case of the false implication. This side would argue that advertisements that mention only the good points are not implying that there are no bad points. To support this view that no such implications are being made, an analysis of the whole concept of implication is sometimes offered. When a person says something, whether he is implying something else depends on the context. For example, if someone were to have guests over for dinner and say that the dessert was going to be special brownies, no implication about the ingredients of the brownies is necessarily being made. However, if the host says that the special brownies are going to be served and accompanies this statement with winks, giggles, and pokes to the guests' ribs, a clear implication is being made. If after dessert the guests ask what was special about the brownies, and the host replies that they were made with whole-wheat flour and raw sugar, the guests would probably think they had been tricked.

The point of this example is that whether an implication is really being made depends on certain features of the situation in which a statement is uttered. The same statement in one context can have an implication; whereas, in a different situation, no implication is being made at all. Furthermore, another important feature that determines whether an implication really is achieved is the sensitivity of the hearer to certain features of the context. If the guests at the dinner party are naive, unworldly types, they might have no idea what the host is getting at when he goes through his giggles, winks, and pokes. And if they are puzzled by his behavior, no implication is achieved and they will not be deceived (or disappointed) when they find out about the whole-wheat flour and the raw sugar.

The problem is to decide whether advertisements that mention only good points are implying that there are no bad points. Those on the side that says that no such implication is being made would point to certain features of the context to support their view. The most relevant feature is that in the context in which most advertisements are made, the audience is aware that only the good points will be mentioned. It would be difficult to find a person in contemporary America who is so unsophisticated that he believes a product's negative aspects exist only if an advertisement mentions them. Everybody knows, it is argued, that no salesman will tell you what is wrong with his product, and if one wants to find out about the negative aspects, one has to talk to the competitors in the field or do some personal investigation. If everybody does have this kind of information, then no implication is being made about the lack of negative aspects, and advertisements that mention only good points are not deceptive.

The more one examines the issue of deceptive advertising, the more it becomes clear that the crux of the problem is determining when an implication is successfully achieved. Philosophers of language have investigated this problem in recent years, but, as of yet, none of them has thought to apply the results of this research to advertising. The article by Leiser raises the issue of deceptive advertising, and the various arguments on each side, but it does not consider the problem of deception in great detail or use the work on the subject of implication that has been developed in philosophy.

The second major ethical issue connected with advertising concerns the problem of generating wants. This problem has been examined in greater detail than has the question of whether advertising is essentially deceptive. The issue of generating wants is raised in the article by Leiser, and it is specifically and carefully discussed in the following three articles by Galbraith, Hayek, and Braybrooke. This topic is also mentioned in articles in the previous sections, particularly those by Knight, Acton, and Rawls. The reason the question of generating wants is of such widespread concern is that it is intimately involved with one of the ways that the other aspects of the business system are defended.

One frequent strategy of defense of the American business system emphasizes that it gives people what they want. Even it if is true, it is argued, that the pursuit of profit makes people greedy, that competition has negative effects on people's characters, and that the system is unjust, the system is still justified from the ethical point of view when one realizes the great benefits that it provides. The previous sections have demonstrated that the criticisms centering on profits, competition, and justice are controversial in themselves, but the view that is now being considered admits that the criticisms might well be true. It is willing to admit this because it is claimed that even if these negative aspects are true, they are far outweighed by the positive benefits that the system provides by giving people what they want. The system satisfies desires, and anything that can accomplish that is clearly good. This is the kind of defense that can be found in Acton's discussion of profit and in Hayek's article on justice. In both of these cases the two writers more or less admit that the critics' charges are true. But they reply, "So what? Look at the abundance. Consider all those people who are getting the things they want. Think about the great numbers who take luxuries for granted that in the past only a minute fraction of the population could enjoy. When one considers these factors, the critics' charges can be seen to be trivial."

It is difficult to argue with the claim about abundance, especially if one compares our society with most of the others that currently exist or that existed in the past. The choices that people can make today of what to wear, eat, furnish their dwellings with, or entertain themselves by, have never been available to anybody else in history. But what about the claim that it is good to satisfy people's desires? This is a more controversial assertion and it is harder to assess. The problem in this case is not so much that some would say that it is good for people to be frustrated. The difficulty is due to the problem of weighing the good—the satisfaction of desires—against the supposed costs—the negative aspects of profits, competition, and injustice. These problems were already examined, however, in previous sections.

A more relevant criticism for this section of Acton and Hayek's argument admits that the system does provide an abundance of goods that satisfy people's desires. Despite this, the new criticism argues that the system cannot be defended for the very reason that it itself produces the desires that it then goes on to satisfy. The effect of this new criticism is to undercut the argument of the defenders, for it says that the claim that the American economic system satisfies wants better than any other system can be seen to be a crude simplification of a highly complex reality. The American business system, with its great emphasis on advertising, is very efficient in getting people to want more things. After people have been made to want something, it is true that they will feel frustration if they do not get it. But it is not clear that they would not have been just as well off never having had the desires in the first place. Thus, the argument runs, all talk about how efficiently the system satisfies wants is simply a distortion and a gloss of some very disturbing facts.

The basis of this new criticism is that advertising has the power to generate desires in people, but exactly how does it do this? How can anybody cause someone else to want something? The example of hypnotism might provide an answer to this question. Consider a hypnotist who tells a subject that upon awakening and hearing the word *elephant*, the subject will develop a powerful and overwhelming desire for strawberry ice cream. This is an obvious case of a want being generated for the subject, and not by him; but this example does not really seem to apply to advertising, especially now that subliminal advertising is illegal (and it is to be hoped, not used). One can think of other examples in which someone uses some unusual means similar to hypnosis (such as drugs or shock treatment) in order to get a subject to develop a particular desire, but none of these is very helpful in illuminating the way advertising is supposed to work.

A more fitting example is provided by the way that parents shape the desires of their children. There is no doubt that at least some of the desires that ten-year-old children display are the result of the influence of their parents. Many children who have a desire for neatness would find sloppiness less distressing had they been raised by different parents. Parents get their children to develop a desire for neatness by being ubiquitous features of the environment and by constantly repeating and demonstrating that neatness is important. The small child may resist this shaping of his wants, but it will be difficult. The parents are so dominating and repetitious, and the child has so little access to alternative environments, that after a few years the neat parents will have a neat child.

In a similar way, advertising is supposed to be a strong influence in making people desire certain things. Advertising is also a ubiquitous part of our environment. It constantly repeats certain slogans and names. It presents overwhelming images of great power that stick in one's mind, and very few can find an alternative environment in which advertising is absent. Thus, advertising forms desires in the same way that parents generate desires in their small children.

This is one model of the way that advertising works, but those who hold the view that advertising generates desires often have a different picture in mind. This second view is based on the model of an ignorant hearer and a knowledgeable speaker. The speaker tells the hearer about some object that the hearer had not been aware of, and the object is made to seem very desirable. Before he met the speaker, the hearer did not want the object because he did not know about it. But after hearing what the speaker says, the hearer develops a desire that he never had before. In a similar way, advertising generates desires; for it describes objects to an audience that did not know about them, and it makes these objects seem very appealing. After hearing or seeing an advertisement, one finds oneself desiring this new object.

It should be noted that this second model is quite different from the first. While it could be said that the parents developed a desire for neatness from scratch, the same cannot be said in this latter case. The second model assumes that the hearer already has certain general desires, for the way that the new object is made appealing is by trying to show that it would satisfy an already existing general desire. For example, one might have a strong desire to appear attractive and seductive to members of the opposite sex, but one might not have been aware of one particular way to satisfy that desire—having very white and shiny teeth. The general desire to appear attractive is not generated by advertising, but what advertising does do is make one think that having shiny white teeth is a particular way to satisfy this general desire.

While all the writers of the following articles agree that advertising works in ways that are similar to one of these two models, they reach very different conclusions about whether advertising is good or bad. One reason they do reach different conclusions is because of the differences between the two models and between the way each one represents the generation of desires. Hayek, who defends advertising, seems to believe that the knowledgeable speaker-ignorant hearer would be the more accurate way to view advertising's powers. The views of Leiser, Galbraith, and Braybrooke lean more to the parent-child model of advertising.

The differing views concerning how advertising works are one factor that accounts for the different ethical evaluations of advertising. Hayek finds nothing reprehensible about someone who is knowledgeable informing someone who is ignorant. This, he argues, is the very process that occurs in the development of aesthetic sensibilities and even of civilization itself. New and more refined desires must be generated in the barbarian in order to turn him into a person of culture. Hayek not only finds the process of advertising to be morally legitimate, but he also believes that the desires that are the result of the process are of significant value.

The opposition in this issue makes two major critical points. The first is again based on what they take to be the way that advertising works, the parent-child model. The critics believe that this method of creating desires is degrading, for it treats people as though they were passive, manipulable children. Feed in the proper stimuli in the forms of slogans, ditties, and images, and out will come new desires. But to treat people in this manner is to view them as being creatures with no will of their own, and it is a widely accepted belief that other people's autonomy should not be tampered with in this way. Advertising's method of generating desires, it is charged, violates this fundamental principle of ethics.

A second point of the criticism of advertising is not explicitly stated by the critics, but one can discern it beneath the surface of their arguments. This point is that advertising causes people to become insatiable, and this accusation can be illustrated by an image that seems to be in the minds of many of the critics. Think of a native in a South Seas island lounging on the beach. The sky is blue, there is an aroma of flowers in the air, and fish are jumping and playing in the water. When the native feels a desire for exercise, he goes swimming, and when he is hungry, he goes to a nearby tree to pick a banana. This would seem to be the kind of life that would be most highly prized by those people who judge things by amounts of pleasure and satisfaction.

But now suppose the native receives a television as a gift, and he begins to watch programs from the United States. Of course, if he watches the programs, he is also going to be exposed to the commercials; and after seeing a number of them, the native finds that he has new desires that he cannot satisfy if he continues to stay at the beach all day. He wants to have a motorboat, and he would like to buy a stereo phonograph, and he has the desire to stop wearing a necklace of flowers and start wearing after-shave lotion. In order to satisfy these wants the native realizes he must get a job; so he leaves the beach and becomes a drill-press operator at a nearby factory. He now gets paid every two weeks, and he begins to save in order to get the money to buy those things he has developed a desire for. After a few years of work he buys what he wants, but since he has kept his television set, he finds that he has more new desires and that he must continue to work in order to satisfy them. Is the native any better off now than he was before he had all of these new desires? Is he happier having to work in order to get what he wants than he would have been if he had just remained on the beach? The answer to these questions may not be clear, but one cannot simply say he is better off because he can now satisfy more desires than he could have previously. Satisfying a greater number of desires does not make one happier if the number of new desires that are demanding satisfaction keeps growing. One will be no better off trying to bail water out of a sinking boat, even if one works harder and harder bailing ever more water out, if the leak through which the water is coming in keeps getting bigger and bigger. The key to gaining satisfaction in that case is not to put more effort into getting the water out. The key is to plug the leak.

The critics thus argue that advertising turns us into insatiable creatures that lust after trivial novelties, while the defenders claim that it makes people more refined and civilized. Part of the disagreement is due to differing views about how advertising works. Another factor is a disagreement about the values of the desires that are generated. These issues, like the others in this area, are a complex mixture of conceptual, factual, and ethical problems, and a solution acceptable to all is not yet at hand.

BURTON LEISER

A Final Word on Advertising

Advertising has an important and constructive role to play in the life of the nation. It is not true that all advertising men are unscrupulous or that all businessmen are concerned only with selling, no matter what the cost to their customers. Nor is it true that advertisements are necessarily misleading or fraudulent.

David Ogilvy, one of the most successful advertising executives in the United States, is the creator of such successful advertising images as Schweppes's Commander Whitehead and Hathaway Shirt's man with the eye patch.* In his discussion of techniques for building a successful advertising campaign, he says:

> *Give the Facts.* Very few advertisements contain enough factual information to sell the product. There is a ludicrous tradition among copywriters that consumers aren't interested in facts. Nothing could be farther from the truth. Study the copy in the Sears, Roebuck catalogues; it sells a billion dollars' worth of merchandise every year by giving *facts*. In my Rolls-Royce advertisements I gave nothing but facts. No adjectives, no "gracious living."
>
> The consumer isn't a moron; she is your wife. You insult her intelligence if you assume that a mere slogan and a few vapid adjectives will persuade her to buy anything. She wants all the information you can give her.[1]

And he adds the following bit of advice that bears directly on our subject:

> You wouldn't tell lies to your own wife. Don't tell them to mine. Do as you would be done by.
>
> If you tell lies about a product, you will be found out—either by the Government, which will prosecute you, or by the consumer, who will punish you by not buying your product a second time.
>
> Good products can be sold by *honest* advertising. If you don't think the product is good, you have no business to be advertising it. If you tell lies, or weasel, you do your client a disservice, you increase your load of guilt, and you fan the flames of public resentment against the whole business of advertising.[2]

Source: Reprinted with permission of Macmillan Publishing Co. from *Liberty, Justice and Morals* by Burton M. Leiser. Copyright © 1973 by Burton M. Leiser.

* The firm is Ogilvy, Benson and Mather.

In short, Ogilvy believes that aside from any ethical reasons that might be advanced for factual, informative, and truthful advertising, it is in the best interests of both the advertising man and his client—from a purely practical point of view—to adhere to these principles, for they keep the attorney general and the FTC away from the door, and in the long run, they are more successful in the marketplace. He claims that the "combative-persuasive" type of advertising that so many people have condemned for its lack of taste is not nearly as profitable as informative advertising.

He argues also that advertising is a force for sustaining standards of quality and service. The advertisement contains a promise that must be fulfilled if the customer is to be satisfied. The public will eventually turn against any advertiser who fails to keep the promises he has made in his public pronouncements. Ogilvy tells of firms that have warned their employees to maintain the standards of service that have been described in their advertising, and of others that have warned that they would move their accounts to other agencies if their commercials were ever cited by government agencies for dishonesty. The fear of exposure by government agencies and consumer groups in the public press, and the adverse publicity that would result, is enough to deter some firms from engaging in deceptive advertising.

As for the charge that advertisers create needs or desires for things that people might well do without, this is what Ogilvy has to say:

> Does advertising make people want to buy products they don't need? If you don't think people need deodorants, you are at liberty to criticize advertising for having persuaded 87 percent of American women and 66 percent of American men to use them. If you don't think people need beer, you are right to criticize advertising for having persuaded 58 percent of the adult population to drink it. If you disapprove of social mobility, creature comforts, and foreign travel, you are right to blame advertising for encouraging such wickedness. If you dislike affluent society, you are right to blame advertising for inciting the masses to pursue it.
>
> If you are this kind of Puritan, I cannot reason with you. I can only call you a psychic masochist. Like Archbishop Leighton, I pray, "Deliver me, O Lord, from the errors of wise men, yea, and of good men."
>
> Dear old John Burns, the father of the Labor movement in England, used to say that the tragedy of the working class was the poverty of their desires. I make no apology for inciting the working class to desire less Spartan lives.[3]

There is certainly some truth in what Ogilvy says, but at some points he and I must part company. First, he gives the advertisers more credit than may be their due when he asserts that they have persuaded 58 percent of the adult population to drink beer. It is not at all unlikely that some people would be drinking beer even if it were never advertised. The drinking of beer far antedates the modern advertising industry, and may be traced to causes other than the efforts of copywriters. Secondly, the desires for social mobility, creature comforts, and foreign travel are all exploited by advertisers to sell their products, but advertisers did not invent them or create them. The critics of advertising do not believe that social mobility, creature comforts, and foreign travel are wicked, and to say that they do is to evade the issue. The issue is not the advertiser's *encouragement* of these desires, but his *exploitation* of them. Thirdly, unlike beer, social mobility, and foreign travel, there was never a demand for deodorants until the advertisers created it. They did so, not to create a better society, but to make money. Those who object to the exploitation of normal human desires by persons and corporations intent on making money at a great cost to their customers and by utilizing methods that conceal or distort the facts are not psychic masochists (whatever that may be), nor are they puritans. They are people who are outraged by what they consider to be the unconscionable methods utilized by some businesses to increase their profits at the expense of people who can often ill afford to be exploited.

Some two thousand years ago there was a debate between the scholars of two great academies as to whether it was proper to praise the beauty of an ugly bride. According to one faction, the principle that one should refrain from uttering any falsehood required that the honest man refrain from praising the ugly bride. The other group, however, insisted that principles of kindness should prevail and that even if one had to lie, one was obliged to add to the newlywed's happiness rather than to detract from it. They went on to say that in a matter of far less moment to a man than his marriage, the principle of kindness should take precedence, so that if a person had made a bad bargain at the market, one should not rub it in by telling him so.[4] If they were here to participate in a discussion on the issue presently under consideration, it is not hard to imagine that they might say:

> Thousands of men and women are too poor to afford foreign travel, or large and flashy automobiles, or Hathaway shirts, or expensive liquors, or costly cosmetics. What useful purpose is served by dangling these luxuries before their eyes? To some, perhaps, the enticing display of such luxuries may serve as an incentive, spurring them on to greater achievement so that they too may enjoy what their more affluent neighbors take for granted. But to many, and perhaps to most, the display may arouse feelings of frustration, anger, and hurt. "Why," they may ask, "are we unable to have all of these things, when so many others do? Why can we not give our children what those ads show

other people giving their children? Why can we not share the happiness that is depicted here?" Before a man is married, it might be appropriate to point out some of his fiancée's faults; but at the wedding, when it's obviously too late, it's unkind to dwell on them. For those who cannot afford the luxuries— and they are luxuries, whatever Ogilvy may say—offered in advertisements that are often directed *specifically at them*, it is cruel to hurt them by offering them what they cannot buy, or to seduce them with false promises of happiness or prestige or success into neglecting their primary obligations in order to seek the fantasy world portrayed in advertisements.

Everyone wants a beautiful bride, I suppose, and it may be good that the working classes no longer desire to live Spartan lives, if they ever did. But some men learn to live very happily with women whose proportions are not even close to those that are currently considered to be the standard of beauty, and it is wrong to jeopardize their happiness by constantly reminding them of that fact; and it would be infinitely worse to parade well-proportioned beauties before them and to urge them to switch. No one is married to a life of poverty. But some people, unable to escape from such a life themselves, have made the adjustment and have found that it is possible to be happy and respectable even on a severely limited income. Is it right to parade the latest fashions in "good living" before their eyes at every opportunity, urging them to buy them *"Now, while our limited supply lasts"*? Men who have been seduced into discontentment over their wives have been known to commit murder. So have some who have been seduced into dissatisfaction with their style of life. Some of the latter may be partially attributable to advertising.

This is not to say that all advertising is bad; but even when the message is not distorted, those who use the mass media to disseminate it should do so with some sense of social and public responsibility. It is far worse, though, when the message is distorted. And even David Ogilvy, for all his insistence on honesty in advertising, admits that he is "continually guilty of *suppressio veri* [the suppression of the truth]. Surely it is asking too much to expect the advertiser to describe the shortcomings of his product? One must be forgiven for putting one's best foot forward."[5] So the consumer is *not* to be told all the relevant information; he is *not* to be given all the facts that would be of assistance in making a reasonable decision about a given purchase. In particular, he will *not* be told about the weaknesses of a product, about its shock hazards, for example, if it is an electrical appliance; about the danger it poses to the consumer's health if it is a cleaning fluid; about the danger it poses to his life if it is an automobile at turnpike speeds; or, if one carries the doctrine to its final conclusion, about the possibly harmful side effects of a new drug that is advertised to the medical profession. Telling the truth combined with "*suppressio veri*" is *not* telling the truth. It is *not* asking too much of the advertiser to reveal such facts when they are known to him, and he should *not* be forgiven for "putting his best foot forward" at his customer's expense. Ogilvy admits, too, that he sometimes tells the truth about the products he advertises in such a way that it seems to the reader that his product is different, in those respects, from similar products, whereas Ogilvy knows that all other products of the same kind possess the same features. All aspirin is the same, for example, whether it is stamped *Bayer* and sells for $1.95 per hundred or whether it is an unadvertised brand of U.S.P. aspirin that sells for thirty-five cents per hundred. But the advertiser will try to convince you that what is true of Bayer aspirin is not true of the other product. This is unfair to the consumer, whether he is rich or poor; but it is particularly unfair to the poor consumer, who could use the money he spends paying for Bayer's advertising in other ways.

Advertising has an important role to fill in our society. It is not likely to disappear. But it is not always carried on in the most ethical manner. Its supporters tend to exaggerate the benefits that have flowed from it, and they are not at all shy about boasting about its effectiveness in their trade meetings and in their efforts to win new business. But they often shrug off any suggestion that their efforts may have harmful effects upon some segments of society by denying that they are all *that* effective. They cannot have it both ways. If advertising is as effective as its practitioners claim it to be, then it possesses enormous potential for harm as well as for good. Because many, though not all, advertisers are concerned primarily about selling their products and only secondarily, if at all, about telling the truth, it is reasonable to suggest that some government regulation be exercised over this industry; and in particular, that advertisers—both producers and agencies—be held liable for harm or damage that results to consumers from misleading or false claims in advertisements, and that they be required to make good any financial loss that consumers may suffer as a result of reliance upon any misleading advertisement, whether the advertisement was "fraudulent" in the criminal sense or not. If laws were passed, both on the federal level and at the state or provincial level, making agencies and producers responsible for restitution of damages suffered by customers who relied upon their "messages," there would be a great incentive for those concerned to confine their claims to those that could be substantiated and to resort to fewer misleading gimmicks. Though such legislation would not eliminate all abuses, it would go a long way toward assuring the public that the advertising messages to which it was exposed respected the truth.

NOTES

1. David Ogilvy, *Confessions of an Advertising Man* (New York: Atheneum, 1963), pp. 95 f.
2. Ibid., p. 99.
3. Ibid., p. 159.
4. Babylonian Talmud, *Ketuvot*, p. 17a. The academies were those that went under the names of Shammai and Hillel, respectively. The "debate" was not comparable to the kind of oratory contest that might be staged by college debating teams. It was a serious discussion on matters of legal and moral principle.
5. Ogilvy, *Confessions*, pp. 158 f.

JOHN KENNETH GALBRAITH

The Dependence Effect

The notion that wants do not become less urgent the more amply the individual is supplied is broadly repugnant to common sense. It is something to be believed only by those who wish to believe. Yet the conventional wisdom must be tackled on its own terrain. Intertemporal comparisons of an individual's state of mind do rest on technically vulnerable ground. Who can say for sure that the deprivation which afflicts him with hunger is more painful than the deprivation which afflicts him with envy of his neighbor's new car? In the time that has passed since he was poor, his soul may have become subject to a new and deeper searing. And where a society is concerned, comparisons between marginal satisfactions when it is

Source: *The Affluent Society*, Third Edition, Revised by John Kenneth Galbraith. Copyright © 1958, 1969, 1976 by John Kenneth Galbraith. Reprinted by permission of Houghton Mifflin Co.

poor and those when it is affluent will involve not only the same individual at different times but different individuals at different times. The scholar who wishes to believe that with increasing affluence there is no reduction in the urgency of desires and goods is not without points for debate. However plausible the case against him, it cannot be proven. In the defense of the conventional wisdom, this amounts almost to invulnerability.

However, there is a flaw in the case. If the individual's wants are to be urgent, they must be original with himself. They cannot be urgent if they must be contrived for him. And above all, they must not be contrived by the process of production by which they are satisfied. For this means that the whole case for the urgency of production, based on the urgency of wants, falls to the ground. One cannot defend production as satisfying wants if that production creates the wants.

Were it so that a man on arising each morning was assailed by demons which instilled in him a passion sometimes for silk shirts, sometimes for kitchenware, sometimes for chamber pots, and sometimes for orange squash, there would be every reason to applaud the effort to find the goods, however odd, that quenched this flame. But should it be that his passion was the result of his first having cultivated the demons, and should it also be that his effort to allay it stirred the demons to ever greater and greater effort, there would be question as to how rational was his solution. Unless restrained by conventional attitudes, he might wonder if the solution lay with more goods or fewer demons.

So it is that if production creates the wants it seeks to satisfy, or if the wants emerge *pari passu* with the production, then the urgency of the wants can no longer be used to defend the urgency of the production. Production only fills a void that it has itself created.

The point is so central that it must be pressed. Consumer wants can have bizarre, frivolous, or even immoral origins, and an admirable case can still be made for a society that seeks to satisfy them. But the case cannot stand if it is the process of satisfying wants that creates the wants. For then the individual who urges the importance of production to satisfy these wants is precisely in the position of the onlooker who applauds the efforts of the squirrel to keep abreast of the wheel that is propelled by his own efforts.

That wants are, in fact, the fruit of production will now be denied by few serious scholars. And a considerable number of economists, though not always in full knowledge of the implications, have conceded the point. . . . Keynes noted that needs of "the second class," i.e., those that are the result of efforts to keep abreast or ahead of one's fellow being, "may indeed be insatiable; for the higher the general level, the higher still are they."[1] And emulation has always played a considerable role in the views of other economists of want creation. One man's consumption becomes his neighbor's wish. This already means that the process by which wants are satisfied is also the process by which wants are created. The more wants that are satisfied, the more new ones are born.

However, the argument has been carried farther. A leading modern theorist of consumer behavior, Professor Duesenberry, has stated explicitly that "ours is a society in which one of the principal social goals is a higher standard of living. . . . [This] has great significance for the theory of consumption . . . the desire to get superior goods takes on a life of its own. It provides a drive to higher expenditure which may even be stronger than that arising out of the needs which are supposed to be satisfied by that expenditure."[2] The implications of this view are impressive. The notion of independently established need now sinks into the background. Because the society sets great store by ability to produce a high living standard, it evaluates people by the products they possess. The urge to consume is fathered by the value system which emphasizes the ability of the society to produce. The more that is produced, the more that must be owned in order to maintain the appropriate prestige. The latter is an important point, for, without going as far as Duesenberry in reducing goods to the role of symbols of prestige in the affluent society, it is plain that his argument fully implies that the production of goods creates the wants that the goods are presumed to satisfy.[3]

The even more direct link between production and wants is provided by the institutions of modern advertising and salesmanship. These cannot be reconciled with the notion of independently determined desires, for their central function is to create desires—to bring into being wants that previously did not exist.* This is accomplished by the producer of the goods or at his behest. A broad empirical

---

* Advertising is not a simple phenomenon. It is also important in competitive strategy and want creation is, ordinarily, a complementary result of efforts to shift the demand curve of the individual firm at the expense of others or (less importantly, I think) to change its shape by increasing the degree of product differentiation. Some of the failure of economists to identify advertising with want creation may be attributed to the undue attention that its use in purely competitive strategy has attracted. It should be noted, however, that the competitive manipulation of consumer desire is only possible, at least on any appreciable scale, when such need is not strongly felt.

relationship exists between what is spent on production of consumer goods and what is spent in synthesizing the desires for that production. A new consumer product must be introduced with a suitable advertising campaign to arouse an interest in it. The path for an expansion of output must be paved by a suitable expansion in the advertising budget. Outlays for the manufacturing of a product are not more important in the strategy of modern business enterprise than outlays for the manufacturing of demand for the product. None of this is novel. All would be regarded as elementary by the most retarded student in the nation's most primitive school of business administration. The cost of this want formation is formidable. In 1974, total advertising expenditure— though, as noted, not all of it may be assigned to the synthesis of wants—amounted to approximately \$25 billion. The increase in previous years was by about a billion dollars a year. Obviously, such outlays must be integrated with the theory of consumer demand. They are too big to be ignored.

But such integration means recognizing that wants are dependent on production. It accords to the producer the function both of making the goods and of making the desires for them. It recognizes that production, not only passively through emulation, but actively through advertising and related activities, creates the wants it seeks to satisfy.

The businessman and the lay reader will be puzzled over the emphasis which I give to a seemingly obvious point. The point is indeed obvious. But it is one which, to a singular degree, economists have resisted. They have sensed, as the layman does not, the damage to established ideas which lurks in these relationships. As a result, incredibly, they have closed their eyes (and ears) to the most obtrusive of all economic phenomena, namely, modern want creation.

This is not to say that the evidence affirming the dependence of wants on advertising has been entirely ignored. It is one reason why advertising has so long been regarded with such uneasiness by economists. Here is something which cannot be accommodated easily to existing theory. More pervious scholars have speculated on the urgency of desires which are so obviously the fruit of such expensively contrived campaigns for popular attention. Is a new breakfast cereal or detergent so much wanted if so much must be spent to compel in the consumer the sense of want? But there has been little tendency to go on to examine the implications of this for the theory of consumer demand and even less for the importance of production and productive efficiency. These have remained sacrosanct. More often, the uneasiness has been manifested in a general disapproval of advertising and advertising men, leading to the occasional suggestion that they shouldn't exist. Such suggestions have usually been ill received in the advertising business.

And so the notion of independently determined wants still survives. In the face of all the forces of modern salesmanship, it still rules, almost undefiled, in the textbooks. And it still remains the economist's mission—and on few matters is the pedagogy so firm— to seek unquestioningly the means for filling these wants. This being so, production remains of prime urgency. We have here, perhaps, the ultimate triumph of the conventional wisdom in its resistance to the evidence of the eyes. To equal it, one must imagine a humanitarian who was long ago persuaded of the grievous shortage of hospital facilities in the town. He continues to importune the passersby for money for more beds and refuses to notice that the town doctor is deftly knocking over pedestrians with his car to keep up the occupancy.

And in unraveling the complex, we should always be careful not to overlook the obvious. The fact that wants can be synthesized by advertising, catalyzed by salesmanship, and shaped by the discreet manipulations of the persuaders shows that they are not very urgent. A man who is hungry need never be told of his need for food. If he is inspired by his appetite, he is immune to the influence of Messrs, Batten, Barton, Durstine & Osborn. The latter are effective only with those who are so far removed from physical want they they do not already know what they want. In this state alone, men are open to persuasion.

The general conclusion of these pages is of such importance for this essay that it had perhaps best be put with some formality. As a society becomes increasingly affluent, wants are increasingly created by the process by which they are satisfied. This may operate passively. Increases in consumption, the counterpart of increases in production, act by suggestion or emulation to create wants. Expectation rises with attainment. Or producers may proceed actively to create wants through advertising and salesmanship. Wants thus come to depend on output. In technical terms, it can no longer be assumed that welfare is greater at an all-around higher level of production than at a lower one. It may be the same. The higher level of production has, merely, a higher level of want creation necessitating a higher level of want satisfaction. There will be frequent occasion to refer to the way wants depend on the process by which they are satisfied. It will be convenient to call it the *dependence effect*.

We may now contemplate briefly the conclusions to which this analysis has brought us.

Plainly, the theory of consumer demand is a peculiarly treacherous friend of the present goals of economics. At first glance, it seems to defend the continuing urgency of production and our preoccupation with it as a goal. The economist does not enter into the dubious moral arguments about the importance or virtue of the wants to be satisfied. He doesn't pretend to compare mental states of the same or different people at different times and to suggest that one is less urgent than another. The desire is there. That for him is sufficient. He sets about in a workmanlike way to satisfy desire, and accordingly, he sets the proper store by the production that does. Like woman's, his work is never done.

But this rationalization, handsomely though it seems to serve, turns destructively on those who advance it once it is conceded that wants are themselves both passively and deliberately the fruits of the process by which they are satisfied. Then the production of goods satisfies the wants that the consumption of these goods creates or that the producers of goods synthesize. Production induces more wants and the need for more production. So far, in a major tour de force, the implications have been ignored. But this obviously is a perilous solution. It cannot long survive discussion.

Among the many models of the good society, no one has urged the squirrel wheel. Moreover, as we shall see presently, the wheel is not one that revolves with perfect smoothness. Aside from its dubious cultural charm, there are serious structural weaknesses which may one day embarrass us. For the moment, however, it is sufficient to reflect on the difficult terrain which we are traversing. Previously, we saw how deeply we were committed to production for reasons of economic security. Not the goods but the employment provided by their production was the thing by which we set ultimate store. Now we find our concern for goods further undermined. It does not arise in spontaneous consumer need. Rather, the dependence effect means that it grows out of the process of production itself. If production is to increase, the wants must be effectively contrived. In the absence of the contrivance, the increase would not occur. This is not true of all goods, but that it is true of a substantial part is sufficient. It means that since the demand for this part would not exist, were it not contrived, its utility or urgency, ex contrivance, is zero. If we regard this production as marginal, we may say that the marginal utility of present aggregate output, ex advertising and salesmanship, is zero. Clearly the attitudes and values which make production the central achievement of our society have some exceptionally twisted roots.

Perhaps the thing most evident of all is how new and varied become the problems we must ponder when we break the nexus with the work of Ricardo and face the economics of affluence of the world in which we live. It is easy to see why the conventional wisdom resists so stoutly such change. It is far, far better and much safer to have a firm anchor in nonsense than to put out on the troubled seas of thought.

NOTES

1. J. M. Keynes, "Economic Possibilities for Our Grandchildren," *Essays in Persuasion* (London: Macmillan, 1931), p. 365.
2. James S. Duesenberry, *Income, Saving, and the Theory of Consumer Behavior* (Cambridge, Mass.: Harvard University Press, 1949), p. 28.
3. A more recent and definitive study of consumer demand has added even more support. Professors Houthakker and Taylor, in a statistical study of the determinants of demand, found that for most products price and income, the accepted determinants, were less important than past consumption of the product. This "psychological stock," as they called it, concedes the weakness of traditional theory; current demand cannot be explained without recourse to past consumption. Such demand nurtures the need for its own increase. H. S. Houthakker and L. D. Taylor, *Consumer Demand in the United States,* 2nd ed., enl. (Cambridge, Mass.: Harvard University Press, 1970).

F. A. VON HAYEK

The Non Sequitur of the "Dependence Effect"

For well over a hundred years the critics of the free-enterprise system have resorted to the argument that if production were only organized rationally, there would be no economic problem. Rather than face the problem which scarcity creates, socialist reformers have tended

Source: *Southern Economic Journal,* Vol. 27, April, 1961. Reprinted with permission of the editor.

to deny that scarcity existed. Ever since the Saint-Simonians their contention has been that the problem of production has been solved and only the problem of distribution remains. However absurd this contention must appear to us with respect to the time when it was first advanced, it still has some persuasive power when repeated with reference to the present.

The latest form of this old contention is expounded in *The Affluent Society* by Professor J. K. Galbraith. He attempts to demonstrate that in our affluent society the important private needs are already satisfied and the urgent need is therefore no longer a further expansion of the output of commodities but an increase in those services which are supplied (and presumably can be supplied only) by government. Though this book has been extensively discussed since its publication in 1958, its central thesis still requires some further examination.

I believe the author would agree that his argument turns upon the "dependence effect" [which is] explained in [the article which precedes this one]. The argument starts from the assertion that a great part of the wants which are still unsatisfied in modern society are not wants which would be experienced spontaneously by the individual if left to himself, but are wants which are created by the process by which they are satisfied. It is then represented as self-evident that for this reason such wants cannot be urgent or important. This crucial conclusion appears to be a complete non sequitur and it would seem that with it the whole argument of the book collapses.

The first part of the argument is of course perfectly true: we would not desire any of the amenities of civilization—or even of the most primitive culture—if we did not live in a society in which others provide them. The innate wants are probably confined to food, shelter, and sex. All the rest we learn to desire because we see others enjoying various things. To say that a desire is not important because it is not innate is to say that the whole cultural achievement of man is not important.

The cultural origin of practically all the needs of civilized life must of course not be confused with the fact that there are some desires which aim, not at a satisfaction derived directly from the use of an object, but only from the status which its consumption is expected to confer. In a passage which Professor Galbraith quotes, Lord Keynes seems to treat the latter sort of Veblenesque conspicuous consumption as the only alternative "to those needs which are absolute in the sense that we feel them whatever the situation of our fellow human beings may be."[1] If the latter phrase is interpreted to exclude all the needs for goods which are felt only because these goods are known to be produced, these two Keynesian classes describe of course only extreme types of wants, but disregard the overwhelming majority of goods on which civilized life rests. Very few needs indeed are "absolute" in the sense that they are independent of social environment or of the example of others, and that their satisfaction is an indispensable condition for the preservation of the individual or of the species. Most needs which make us act are needs for things which only civilization teaches us exist at all, and these things are wanted by us because they produce feelings or emotions which we would not know if it were not for our cultural inheritance. Are not in this sense probably all our aesthetic feelings "acquired tastes"?

How complete a non sequitur Professor Galbraith's conclusion represents is seen most clearly if we apply the argument to any product of the arts, be it music, painting, or literature. If the fact that people would not feel the need for something if it were not produced did prove that such products were of small value, all those products of human endeavor would be of small value. Professor Galbraith's argument could be easily employed, without any change of the essential terms, to demonstrate the worthlessness of literature or any other form of art. Surely an individual's want for literature is not original with himself in the sense that he would experience it if literature were not produced. Does this then mean that the production of literature cannot be defended as satisfying a want because it is only the production which provokes the demand? In this, as in the case of all cultural needs, it is unquestionably, in Professor Galbraith's words, "the process of satisfying the wants that creates the wants." There have never been "independently determined desires for" literature before literature has been produced and books certainly do not serve the "simple mode of enjoyment which requires no previous conditioning of the consumer." Clearly my taste for the novels of Jane Austen or Anthony Trollope or C. P. Snow is not "original with myself." But is it not rather absurd to conclude from this that it is less important than, say, the need for education? Public education indeed seems to regard it as one of its tasks to instill a taste for literature in the young and even employs producers of literature for that purpose. Is this want creation by the producer reprehensible? Or does the fact that some of the pupils may possess a taste for poetry only because of the efforts of their teachers prove that since "it does not arise in spontaneous consumer need and the demand would not exist were it not contrived, its utility or urgency, ex contrivance, is zero"?

The appearance that the conclusions follow from the admitted facts is made possible by an obscurity of the wording of the argument with respect to which it is difficult to know whether the author is

himself the victim of a confusion or whether he skillfully uses ambig-
uous terms to make the conclusion appear plausible. The obscurity
concerns the implied assertion that the wants of consumers are determined by the producers. Professor Galbraith avoids in this connection any terms as crude and definite as *determine*. The expressions he
employs, such as that wants are "dependent on" or the "fruits of"
production, or that "production creates the wants" do, of course,
suggest determination but avoid saying so in plain terms. After what
has already been said it is of course obvious that the knowledge of
what is being produced is one of the many factors on which depends
what people will want. It would scarcely be an exaggeration to say
that contemporary man, in all fields where he has not yet formed
firm habits, tends to find out what he wants by looking at what his
neighbors do and at various displays of goods (physical or in cata-
logues or advertisements) and then choosing what he likes best.

In this sense the tastes of man, as is also true of his opinions and
beliefs and indeed much of his personality, are shaped in a great
measure by his cultural environment. But though in some contexts
it would perhaps be legitimate to express this by a phrase like "production creates the wants," the circumstances mentioned would
clearly not justify the contention that particular producers can deliberately determine the wants of particular consumers. The efforts of
all producers will certainly be directed toward that end; but how far
any individual producer will succeed will depend not only on what
he does but also on what others do and on a great many other influences operating upon the consumer. The joint but uncoordinated
efforts of the producers merely create one element of the environment by which the wants of the consumers are shaped. It is because
each individual producer thinks that the consumers can be persuaded
to like his products that he endeavors to influence them. But though
this effort is part of the influences which shape consumers' tastes, no
producer can in any real sense "determine" them. This, however, is
clearly implied in such statements as that wants are "both passively
and deliberately the fruits of the process by which they are satisfied."
If the producer could in fact deliberately determine what the consumers will want, Professor Galbraith's conclusions would have some
validity. But though this is skillfully suggested, it is nowhere near
made credible, and could hardly be made credible because it is not
true. Though the range of choice open to the consumers is the joint
result of, among other things, the efforts of all producers who vie
with each other in making their respective products appear more
attractive than those of their competitors, every particular consumer
still has the choice between all those different offers.

A fuller examination of this process would, of course, have to consider how, after the efforts of some producers have actually swayed some consumers, it becomes the example of the various consumers thus persuaded which will influence the remaining consumers. This can be mentioned here only to emphasize that even if each consumer were exposed to pressure of only one producer, the harmful effects which are apprehended from this would soon be offset by the much more powerful example of his fellows. It is of course fashionable to treat this influence of the example of others (or, what comes to the same thing, the learning from the experience made by others) as if it all amounted to an attempt at keeping up with the Joneses and for that reason was to be regarded as detrimental. It seems to me not only that the importance of this factor is usually greatly exaggerated but also that it is not really relevant to Professor Galbraith's main thesis. But it might be worthwhile briefly to ask what, assuming that some expenditure were actually determined solely by a desire of keeping up with the Jonses, that would really prove?

At least in Europe we used to be familiar with a type of person who often denied himself even enough food in order to maintain an appearance of respectibility or gentility in dress and style of life. We may regard this as a misguided effort, but surely it would not prove that the income of such persons was larger than they knew how to use wisely. That the appearance of success or wealth may to some people seem more important than other needs does in no way prove that the needs they sacrifice to the former are unimportant. In the same way, even though people are often persuaded to spend unwisely, this surely is no evidence that they do not still have important unsatisfied needs.

Professor Galbraith's attempt to give an apparent scientific proof for the contention that the need for the production of more commodities has greatly decreased seems to me to have broken down completely. With it goes the claim to have produced a valid argument which justifies the use of coercion to make people employ their income for those purposes of which he approves. It is not to be denied that there is some originality in this latest version of the old socialist argument. For over a hundred years we have been exhorted to embrace socialism because it would give us more goods. Since it has so lamentably failed to achieve this where it has been tried, we are now urged to adopt it because more goods after all are not important. The aim is still to progressively increase the share of the resources whose use is determined by political authority and coercion of any dissenting minority. It is not surprising, therefore, that Professor Galbraith's thesis has been most enthusiastically received by the intellectuals of the British Labour Party where his influence bids fair to displace that of the late Lord Keynes. It is more curious that in this country it is not recognized as an outright socialist argument and often seems to appeal to people on the opposite end of the political spectrum. But this is probably only another instance of the familiar fact that on these matters the extremes frequently meet.

NOTES

1. John M. Keyes, "Economic Possibilities, your Grandchildren" in *Essays in Persuasion* (London: Macmillan, 1931), pp. 365–66.

DAVID BRAYBROOKE

Skepticism of Wants, and Certain Subversive Effects of Corporations on American Values

The observations found in the paper that Professor Kaysen contributed to the Mason volume on *The Corporation in Modern Society*[1] remain topical. I am inclined to agree very nearly completely with what he said then. I am also persuaded by the suggestions of waste that he joined in raising against the annual model changes of the automobile corporations[2]—though I am more skeptical about the changes being what the consumers wanted, even at the time. Unsportingly exploiting the automobile giants as conveniently familiar examples, though already much-vexed ones, I shall fling some further darts at them.

I propose to amplify Professor Kaysen's point about the "irresponsibility of business power."[3] I shall touch upon the effects, which

Source: Reprinted from *Human Values and Economic Policy* edited by Sidney Hook. Copyright © 1967 by New York University, by permission of New York University Press.

Kaysen likewise mentioned, of business power on the tone of the mass media[4] and on the tastes and styles of American life.[5] I shall also, like Kaysen, call attention to the discretion that corporation managements exercise regarding innovation in products.[6]

Professor Friedman, relying like Adam Smith on market controls to check the predatory tendencies of business, has scornfully repudiated the claims of businessmen and their public-relations experts that corporations have lately taken on public responsibilities in broad social spheres.[7] Who authorized them to do that? Let them stick to their trade, while we see to it that their trade continues to be competitive. Kaysen has been equally doubtful: "It is not sufficient for the business leaders to announce that they are thinking hard and wrestling earnestly with their wide responsibilities, if, in fact, the power of unreviewed and unchecked decision remains with them, and they remain a small, self-selecting group."[8] Like Friedman, he has been inclined to ask for more vigorous antitrust policy, regardless of business protestations about their self-imposed responsibilities.[9]

The charge of irresponsibility does not therefore necessarily entrain an exhortation to corporation management to take larger views and assume wider responsibilities. What is being charged is not neglect of responsibilities duly assigned—they have not been assigned in advance, and Taylor has indicated, among other things, that the law as it stands makes assigning them post hoc, in the way of remedy, problematic.[10] What is being charged is the creation of untoward effects in fields where there are insufficient external controls, whether these are controls established by new legal assignments of responsibility or other sorts of controls (such as more vigorous competition). The point about irresponsibility is thus, in fact, not really a charge at all, but an index designating a problem. The charges against corporation leaders are, properly speaking, that some of them, some of the time, pretend no problem exists, and that (by this and other means) they obstruct efforts to deal with the problem.

I wish to focus my comments on one particular—familiar and deplorably effective—device used by corporation management, their public-relations experts, and other apologists to keep up the pretense that no problem exists. This is the device of saying, "We only give the public what it wants." In the manner of ordinary language philosophy, I want to examine this statement very literally and deliberately. This examination, though it will begin with what may seem to be petty details, will fairly quickly bring us to matters of deep concern about economic judgments. It will also, by the way, justify at least in part the provocative suggestion contained in my title. Corporations do subvert American values, very extensively, in important ways, though I do not mean to suggest that everything any corporation does amounts to such subversion, or that all corporations do so all of the time. Corporations also, no doubt, do much good; but since they spend night and day singing their own praises, the praises need not be repeated here.

At first sight, the statement, made on behalf of the corporations, "We only give the public what it wants," may be taken for an excuse. But I think no one—especially not those putting the statement forward—would want to hold that it is an excuse when they take a second look at it. For to be an excuse, the statement would have to be relevant in a certain way to the actions or policies being excused. It is a necessary condition of its being relevant in this way that there be something objectionable about those actions or policies—else why do they need an excuse? I think spokesmen for the corporations would be unwilling to grant that (barring occasional imperfections) there is something objectionable about what they produce and sell. But suppose it is insisted that there is. Then the statement, "We only give the public what it wants," would fulfill one condition of being an excuse; but it would immediately fail others. For by its very meaning, the statement could not be accepted as an excuse; we in fact clearly rule it out as a way of excusing people from supplying objectionable commodities. It is no excuse for the drug peddler to say that his customers wanted the drugs; for the mail-order antitank merchant to say that he only gave the safe-crackers what they wanted; for the manufacturer of defective automobiles to say that the public wanted them. One does not excuse oneself from contributing to evil by saying that other people wanted the contribution.

If it is not an excuse, the statement, "We only give the public what it wants," may still be regarded as a device for escaping blame, now not as a device for diminishing it or transferring it to someone else, but as one for preventing questions about blame or praise from arising.[11] I think it does this by, on this interpretation, presupposing that the transactions at issue fall within the free moral competence of the customers to choose what they want; and by implying that the goods that the customers receive are those that they have, within this competence, expressed themselves as wanting.

So interpreted, the statement is a very effective one. It calls into play not only our generalized feelings in favor of personal liberty and against interfering with other people's choices, even trivial ones, but also the refined scruples of economists about respecting other people's preferences, and the theory of market optima in which these scruples are assumed. It is no drawback to the effectiveness of the statement, furthermore, that so interpreted it seems to be substantially true. Most things bought in the United States are chosen within the free moral competence of the customers to choose; and the customers do receive what within that competence they express themselves as wanting.

Moreover, are not the customers who express these wants the ultimate authorities on what those wants are? If a person, N, says, given a choice of x, y, or z, "I want z," it follows that he does want z (in the sense of "want" that corresponds to the philosophical term "desire") provided that, knowing the language, he speaks sincerely and provided that the name or description represented by "z" accurately designates what N intends it to designate. Philosophers have thought that these provisos suffice to guarantee the truth of certain first-person statements; indeed, they have thought that the first proviso, about speaking sincerely, knowing the language, suffices,[12] and they have called such statements "logically incorrigible." This "I am in pain" is regarded as logically incorrigible; and "I want," taken as expressing an inner experience or feeling, may be thought to be on somewhat the same footing.[13]

There may seem to be nothing more to be said. Very likely, the spokesmen for the corporations would gratefully join us in believing that there is nothing more to be said; our ideas (and their ideas) about personal liberty and consumer sovereignty, as well perhaps as some awareness of the philosophical point just made, cooperate in silencing us. But we all know lots more to say, of which we need only be reminded. N's statement, "I want z," made under the provisos mentioned, and given a suitable time coordinate, will properly be recorded as true, and the record will stand; but this doesn't mean that his statement is very happily called "incorrigible." By its very use of the concept of want, it invites criticism; and it is corrigible, as first-person statements about pain and (in suitable circumstances) about seeing afterimages are not. It is corrigible by being superseded, as N revises his view of what he wants. Without implying that he did not want z at the time, N will now, on revision, say that he was *mistaken* in wanting it. Thus "I want z" assimilates to "I believe p" rather than to "I am in pain."[14]

The dimensions of criticism that might lead to revisions of want statements support six reasons for thinking that the claim made by the corporations, "We only give the public want it wants," is in respect to one or another of its implications much less than fully warranted. I shall now canvass these reasons.

In the first place, the evidence about consumers getting what they want may be indeterminate; the evidence to decide crucial questions of economic policy all too often is. The automobile companies have said that car buyers did not want safety, when safety features were offered them. But, I wonder, how conclusive was their evidence on this point? Does it rule out what in the eyes of the consumers themselves would have been misjudgments of what they wanted? Was the information about safety as widely distributed, and as effectively communicated, as other information about the cars being offered? If N did not know of the presence of all three alternatives, x, y, and z, or did not know of certain properties of these alternatives, or failed to apply certain principles to which he himself subscribes, but whose relevance then escaped him, N's statement, "I want z," is ripe for revision. Now, this consideration would be effective even if all consumers had been unanimous in expressing themselves as wanting cars other than those with the safety features; but it is of interest to inquire whether there was not in fact a sizable proportion of consumers who did then want the cars with the safety features, perhaps a proportion large enough to cover the costs of producing such cars, if the consumers making it up had been reached with information and offers. One might note, furthermore, that there are other ways in which the evidence about consumers not wanting safety features may be defective. How did the cars with these new features compare with other cars on other points? Was there agreement between companies and the public on what features of cars are most important for safety?

Rather than branch out, however, into such general skeptical considerations, healthy as they are, let us return to the particular subject of wants. The second reason for distrusting the statement by the corporations, "We only give the public what it wants," is that the corporations have had a good deal to do with instilling these wants in the public; they have done enough, one would think, to destroy any implication depending on those wants being spontaneously the consumers' own. The automobile companies have shaped the public's ideas about safety, and hence the wants related to safety: negatively, by suppressing information about the dangers of the cars that they produce; and positively, by extolling speed, and selling cars on the basis of power. Half a century of dilation on speed, power, and thrills has fostered and intensified wants that now seem questionable to many; and those who have the wants, without now questioning them, might be brought to revise them by perceiving the interested part that the automobile companies have played in instilling them.[15] When N discovers that he was more under someone else's influence than he thought, he has a good reason for reconsidering his statement, "I want z."

The automobile companies and the advertising that they have paid for have operated to subvert the American value of safety. A third reason for refusing to agree to all the implications of the statement, "We only give the public what it wants," consists in the extent to which this subversion has been carried through the whole field of American values. The subversion affects not only safety—which we profess to cherish, and mean to, but which the automobile companies connive with us in undermining—but all sorts of other values, in many insidious ways. American business spends a great deal of time and energy confusing the public about values, and thus deliberately produces the sort of misjudgment about x, y, and z that will lead N to revise his expression when he detects his mistake. I shall mention just two further illustrations. There is, specifically, the systematic abuse of sexual interests, so that people have their wants for automobiles and all sorts of other things seriously mixed up with their sexual desires. The automobile companies (though certainly not these alone) have strenuously assisted in mixing us up about sex, making it more urgent, but also more diffuse, and commonly misdirected. More generally, I might mention the besetting clamor about goods and gadgets, which all the corporations join in generating. How often do members of the public get a chance to think quietly in a sustained way about what they might want out of life? Do they ever have time to reflect that perhaps they want too many things already and could well do without wanting still more?[16]

In the fourth place, the claim "We only give the public what it wants" is suspect because the corporations not only assist in confusing the public about what it might want; they also obstruct institutional remedies for the lack of information that leads N and his fellow consumers into misjudgments about wants. A simple-minded man might ask, if the corporations were devoted to the public interest (as they so continually and profusely profess), would they not press for greatly enlarged facilities, public or private, but at any rate disinterested (and known to be so), for consumers' research? For public standards of quality? For trade fairs giving prizes for honest workmanship? Perhaps the corporations have objections to the relevance and thoroughness of the particular tests used by going consumers' research organizations; but such objections do not explain why the corporations resist disinterested tests of any kind, by any institutions with the capacity to do more thorough research than consumers can do for themselves. How shameful to find, besides the automobile companies dragging their feet about safety standards, the tire companies doing the same thing; the grocers and packagers objecting to truth in packaging; the credit firms protesting against truth in lending. If corporations wonder why they do not attract idealistic young men fresh from college, they need only consider the impression that such conduct makes on people outside the corporations.

One must remark, fifth, carrying forward an observation of Professor Kaysen's, that corporations often have a considerable amount of discretion respecting innovation,[17] and hence respecting the variety of products that they offer the public. In the automobile industry, with its high concentration and high barriers to entry, the variety of products is especially subject to arbitrary limitation on the producers' side. But from the fact that given a choice between x, y, and z, N expresses himself as wanting z, nothing can be inferred about his wants for u, v, w, goods that were not offered him. Many consumers might prefer very different cars—if they are never produced, so that consumers never have a chance to see them or to try them out, how can it be known that they are not wanted? It is true, one could say of *any* industry that there might be some other products that the industry is not now offering the public, but that the public would prefer to anything that is being offered. But I do not believe the fact that this could always be said makes it sometimes entirely trivial to say it. Saying it is not trivial as a reminder of the limitations on what can be inferred about wants from the wants expressed the face of some limited set of alternatives. In the case of the automobiles offered the public, moreover, it is not nature, or even the market, that determines what shall figure in the set of alternatives. The very corporations that affect to be doing no more than responding to the wants of the public determine what range of wants shall be expressed. Furthermore, the alternative products that have not been introduced can be significantly specified—for example, the various backward-seating safety cars.

The sixth and last reason that I shall mention for distrusting the statement by the corporations, "We only give the public what it wants," lies in the existence, or possible existence, of wants that consumers may have but can satisfy only by concerted action, not in the market. Historic cases in point are legislation for safety in factories or legislation against child labor (in which consumers have been joined by conscientious producers, unable to risk independent self-restraint). I do not think that the allowances economists make for third-party costs or neighborhood effects suffice for wants respecting concerted action. For such wants may range even beyond the examples just given, to wants regarding the overall structure and development of the economy. One might well think, because of the resources that it uses up, and the pressures that it creates, ranging from conspicuous consumption to the destruction of urban amenities, the automobile industry is much too large for the country to keep going, much less continue expanding. Rising to another sort of choice, between r, s, and t, N may express himself as wanting an alternative that would either entail not choosing z or preclude choosing between x, y, and z at all. So many people might, confronted with such a choice, want to have the automobile industry reduced in size; but such a choice could hardly be effective unless it were not a market choice, but a political one, offering the possibility of concerted action.

My six reasons are (I think) so obvious, once stated, and so compelling, that it might well be asked, How could any of them be overlooked? Now, if they are overlooked in some connections, they are of course frequently mentioned in others, though not perhaps all at once. All of them, I am sure, have often been mentioned by economists. Indeed, what is correct in the way that I have stated the reasons may depend on the teaching of economists; the mistakes are my own contribution. Yet I believe, for all the familiarity with which economists will greet the six reasons, one of the effects of economic teaching has been to divert attention from them, and so to open the way for general unthinking acquiescence in the corporations' contention, "We only give the public what it wants." The trouble is that the core of economic teaching is the fascinating idea of the free, self-regulating market—which I join Professors Arrow and Boulding and Friedman in admiring as one of the most beautiful thoughts ever to occur to man. The six reasons are all distressing qualifications to the application of the market idea. I conjecture that economists are happier refining the idea by expressing it in elegant models than entangling themselves with the qualifications that must be entered to it. Moreover, the qualifications that economists do elaborate are mainly qualifications on the supply side of the market—monopoly in its various degrees. Finally, economists have backed steadily away from the criticism of wants, first, by renouncing Benthamite utility, which was both intersubjective and normative; next by discarding the notion of subjective satisfaction—the pleasure, however perverse, that the consumer might realize from the goods that he bought; and lately, I gather, by abandoning in favor of "revealed preference" even subjective expectations of satisfaction.

These tendencies on the part of economists, combined with the incautious simplifications of their students, lead to the statement, "We only give the public what it wants," frequently, I think, being taken at face value. Dare I suggest that sometimes even economists let it slip by without protesting? The wants at issue are identified with the wants *assumed* by the economist as expressed within his models, defining the demand side of the market. But one of the most important observations to make about wants actually observed is that they are not to be taken for granted; they require examination and invite criticism. What people want is even in their own eyes always contingent on the circumstances in which their expressions of wants have been called for.[18]

NOTES

1. Carl Kaysen, "The Corporation: How Much Power? What Scope?" in *The Corporation in Modern Society*, ed., Edward S. Mason, (Cambridge, Mass.: Harvard University Press, 1959).
2. F. M. Fisher, Z. Griliches, and C. Kaysen, "The Costs of Automobile Changes since 1949," abstract in *Papers and Proceedings of the 74th Annual Meeting of the American Economic Association, American Economic Review* 52 (May 1962): 259-61; article with same title, *Journal of Political Economy* 70 (October 1962): 433-51.
3. Kaysen, pp. 102-03.
4. Ibid., p. 100.
5. Ibid., p. 101.
6. Ibid., p. 93.
7. Milton Friedman, *Capitalism and Freedom* (Chicago: University of Chicago Press, 1962), pp. 133 ff.
8. Kaysen, p. 104.
9. Ibid., p. 103.
10. John F. A. Taylor, "Is the corporation above the law?" *Harvard Business Review* 43 (March-April 1965): especially pp. 127-28.
11. In its main lines the treatment of excuses adumbrated in paragraphs 6 and 7 seems to accord with the main lines on which J. L. Austin approached the subject in his "A Plea for Excuses," *Philosophical Papers* (Oxford: Clarendon Press, 1961), pp. 123-52. Though not consciously anticipated, the accord may well reflect reading the article some time ago and attending Austin's seminar on excuses even earlier.
12. Against such views, see the remarks of Austin, in the second section (i.e., pp. 161-69) of his "Other Minds," *Proceedings of the Aristotelian Society, Supplementary Volume 20* (1946): 148-87.
13. Cf. the interesting discussion, with which I agree only in part, by F. E. Sparshott, *Enquiry into Goodness* (Toronto: University of Toronto Press, 1958), pp. 139-41.

14. In the articles on automobile-model changes (cited above), Kaysen and his coauthors suggest, on the one hand, that consumers did not fully understand how much they were paying for annual model changes, estimated by the authors to cost as much as $5 billion a year. They say, on the other hand, that since new cars without the more significant changes continued to be available in the period under study, while consumers turned to buying models with the changes, "it is difficult not to conclude that car owners thought the costs worth incurring at the time" (abstract). The subject seems to me to be much more complex than the subject of safety features, and I do not want to get entangled with it; but I might point out, in the light of my own argument, that accepting wants as being accurately expressed at some given time does not make them incorrigible even in the view of the people expressing them. They may in fact be drastically corrigible, and deserve a very skeptical reception. Compare the concession of my eight paragraph—in which I concur with Kaysen and his coauthors—with the six countervailing reasons of later paragraphs—which give the concession some much-needed skeptical ventilation.

15. "Je dirai qu'il y a aussi mauvaise foi si je choisis de déclarer que certaines valeurs existent avant moi; je suis en contradiction avec moi-meme si, a la fois, je les veux et déclare qu'elles s'imposent à moi." Jean-Paul Sartre, *L'Existentialisme est un humanisme* (Paris: Les Editions Nagel, 1946), p. 81.

16. Cf. remarks by Sir Geoffrey Vickers on "the metabolic criterion"—that a high rate of exchange with the environment is good *per se*—and "the criterion of material expansion"—that it is good for this rate to increase without limit, both of which he ascribes to Western culture, especially in North America. *The Undirected Society* (Toronto: University of Toronto Press, 1959), pp. 73–75.

17. Kaysen, p. 93.

18. This study was written while I enjoyed a research appointment in the department of philosophy, University of Pittsburgh, to work on the values-study project supported by the Carnegie Corporation of New York and IBM. My aims in the study will perhaps be fully appreciated only if I publicly recall that the comment was prepared for delivery a few weeks after the *New York Times Magazine* had published an attack on contemporary American philosophy for discussing trivial questions of language rather than offering religious inspiration (or some robust substitute for inspiration). I set out to demonstrate that minute questions about language may quickly lead to important questions of social policy, and that answers to the one may crucially affect answers to the other.